Personal Development and Clinic

Personal Development and Clinical Psychology

Edited by Jan Hughes and Sheila Youngson

The British Psychological Society

BPS Blackwell

This edition first published 2009 by the British Psychological Society and Blackwell Publishing Ltd
© 2009 Jan Hughes and Sheila Youngson

BPS Blackwell is an imprint of Blackwell Publishing, which was acquired by John Wiley & Sons in February 2007. Blackwell's publishing program has been merged with Wiley's global Scientific, Technical, and Medical business to form Wiley-Blackwell.

Registered Office
John Wiley & Sons Ltd, The Atrium, Southern Gate, Chichester, West Sussex, PO19 8SQ, UK
Editorial Offices
350 Main Street, Malden, MA 02148-5020, USA
9600 Garsington Road, Oxford, OX4 2DQ, UK
The Atrium, Southern Gate, Chichester, West Sussex, PO19 8SQ, UK

For details of our global editorial offices, for customer services, and for information about how to apply for permission to reuse the copyright material in this book please see our website at www.wiley.com/wiley-blackwell.

The right of Jan Hughes and Sheila Youngson to be identified as the authors of the editorial material in this work has been asserted in accordance with the Copyright, Designs and Patents Act 1988.

Library of Congress Cataloging-in-Publication Data

Hughes, Jan N., 1949–
    Personal development and clinical psychology / Jan Hughes and Sheila Youngson.
      p. ; cm.
    Includes bibliographical references and index.
    ISBN 978-1-4051-5866-4 (pbk. : alk. paper) 1. Clinical psychologists. 2. Clinical psychology. 3. Maturation (Psychology) I. Youngson, Sheila. II. Title.
    [DNLM: 1. Psychology, Clinical–methods. 2. Personnel Management–methods. 3. Psychology, Industrial–methods. WM 105 H893p 2009]
    RC467.H768 2009
    616.89–dc22
                                                                                2008028049

A catalogue record for this book is available from the British Library.

Set in 10.5 on 13 pt Minion by SNP Best-set Typesetter Ltd., Hong Kong
Printed in Singapore by Markono Print Media Pte Ltd

The British Psychological Society's free Research Digest e-mail service rounds up the latest research and relates it to your syllabus in a user-friendly way. To subscribe go to www.researchdigest.org.uk or send a blank e-mail to subscribe-rd@lists.bps.org.uk .

1 2009

Contents

Notes on Contributors

Kevin Baker

Kevin Baker originally worked as an academic at some universities in the Midlands teaching psychology at undergraduate and master's levels as well as carrying out various bits of research. He decided to retrain as a clinical psychologist partly because of the challenge this held for him and partly because he wanted to be able to carry out research that would be more applied than academic. He now works in the National High Secure Deaf Service at Rampton Hospital in Nottinghamshire and is involved in research to adapt assessments and interventions for use with deaf adults.

Garry Brownbridge

Garry Brownbridge, consultant clinical psychologist and group analyst, currently works at The Retreat, York, with the Specialist Psychosis and Recovery and the Specialist Older Peoples' Services. He is also Senior Clinical Tutor and Honorary Senior Lecturer on the University of Leeds' Doctoral Training Programme in Clinical Psychology. He has previously worked in university research posts and NHS clinical posts. He gained a PhD in Psychology at the University of Sheffield in 1987 and completed MSc Clinical Psychology training at the University of Leeds in 1991. He became a member of the Institute of Group Analysis (London) in 2003.

Steven Coles

Steven Coles is a clinical psychologist working across three Assertive Outreach teams within Nottinghamshire Healthcare NHS Trust. He recently became the East Midlands Coordinator for the National Forum for Assertive Outreach.

Steven has a particular interest in equality and diversity; his doctoral research looked at the relationship between ethnic discrimination and mood. He is also involved in a research group looking at black and ethnic minority service users' construction of personal well-being and sources of help and hindrance to their emotional health.

Sarah Davidson

Sarah Davidson is a consultant clinical psychologist at the Gender Identity Development Unit at the Tavistock Clinic and Deputy Clinical Director on the Clinical Psychology Doctorate at the University of East London. She is also the Psycho-social Advisor to the British Red Cross and Vice Chairman of the Board of Trustees. Sarah is also a Patron of Beatbullying, a charity established to change the lives of young people who are being/have been bullied, through facilitation and empowerment. Her interest in working with voluntary agencies has led her to work with such charities as Childline, Saneline and the Samaritans.

Kathryn Dykes

Bristol University was the location for Kathryn's BSc (Hons) in Psychology, which was completed in 2000. After having various voluntary and paid posts she worked as an assistant psychologist in Birmingham for two years before beginning a doctorate in clinical psychology at Sheffield University in 2003. After completing training Kathryn moved to her current position as a clinical psychologist for Barnsley Primary Care Trust. In this post she specializes in working with Older People in Mental Health Services, Memory Services and Cancer and Palliative Care Services.

David Green

David Green qualified as a clinical psychologist over 30 years ago. He has spent the last 20 years of his professional life as Clinical Director of the Doctor of Clinical Psychology Programme at the University of Leeds, where his responsibilities include determining selection policy on the course. He has a long-standing interest in the training of clinical supervisors and has published a number of articles on this and related topics. He used to play a mean game of golf but is frankly pathetic nowadays.

Rebecca Hames

Rebecca Hames graduated from the University of Leeds in 2006 with a doctorate in clinical psychology, having previously worked in primary care mental health and university research settings. She currently works in paediatric psychology in the Department of Clinical and Health Psychology, St James's University Hospital, Leeds, where she has a particular clinical and research interest in involving children and families in treatment decision-making.

Tracey Holley

Tracey Holley describes herself as a mental health educator and a survivor of mental distress. She has battled depression most of her adult life, and after a brief stay in hospital in 2004 is well on the way on her recovery journey. She is an associate lecturer for the University of Worcester and a regular visiting lecturer for Birmingham City University and the University of Birmingham as well as its Centre of Excellence in Interdisciplinary Mental Health. She trains students and professionals alike for nursing, psychology and social work. She is a trainer with Spectrum for the Worcestershire Mental Health Network, of which she is also a trustee. She has published an academic paper entitled 'The Narrative Practitioner – A Service User Perspective, the Narrative Edge'.

Clea Horner

Clea Horner qualified from the Leeds Clinical Psychology doctoral programme in 2007. During training Clea participated in the Personal and Professional Issues sub-committee, taking an interest in how personal and professional development can be supported for trainees. She is currently working in a community multiple sclerosis team in Leeds. Clea's doctoral thesis was an exploratory study of young people and their families' experiences of a first episode in psychosis, and she is interested in pursuing research in this area further.

Jan Hughes

Jan Hughes is Director of Clinical Practice on the Sheffield Doctor of Clinical Psychology course. Prior to this she worked as a clinical tutor at both Leeds and Leicester universities and as a clinical psychologist in a number of adult services. Jan has held a career-long interest in personal development, in particular in relation to training.

Nimisha Patel

Nimisha Patel is a senior lecturer at the University of East London and a consultant clinical psychologist, Head of Clinical Psychology and Head of Audit and Evaluation at the Medical Foundation for the Care of Victims of Torture. She has previously worked in the NHS in a range of adult services.

Simon Platts

Simon studied human psychology at Aston University, Birmingham, and completed his professional doctorate in clinical psychology at the University of East London. Simon is currently employed as a clinical psychologist and is based in a community mental health team in Newham, East London. He works predominantly with people experiencing voices and visions and expressing apparently unusual ideas.

Caroline Rake

Caroline Rake is a consultant clinical psychologist and psychoanalytic psychotherapist. She completed her clinical psychology training at Leeds University in 1991 and has since worked for the NHS in adult mental health. Her training as a psychoanalytic psychotherapist, also at Leeds University, was completed in 2006. Currently, she works in an adult psychological therapies service in Wakefield for South West Yorkshire Mental Health NHS Trust. She is an associate fellow of the British Psychological Society, a registered member of the United Kingdom Council for Psychotherapy and a clinical member of the Universities Psychotherapy and Counselling Association.

Joyce Scaife

Joyce Scaife is a clinical psychologist with a career-long interest in supervision. She particularly values supervision when it encourages the full commitment of personal qualities and creative talents to clinical practice and when it helps to create a sense of fun and excitement at work.

Nick Shelley

Nicholas Shelley qualified as a clinical psychologist in September 2006. Having completed his undergraduate psychology degree at the University of Oxford in 2001, he moved to Yorkshire and worked as an assistant psychologist with older adults and people with learning disabilities. His final year elective placement whilst doing his clinical psychology training at the University of Leeds was with a Tier 2 Child and Family Service. Since October 2006 he has continued to work in CAMHS, now based in Bootle, Liverpool. He is interested in systemic ways of working. He is married and has a two-year-old son.

Stephanie Sneider

Stephanie Sneider is a clinical psychologist working in Child and Adolescent Mental Health Services in Sefton, Merseyside. Stephanie has a specialist interest in working with adolescents and their families. She works in Sefton Youth Offending Team and in SMASH, the Substance Misuse Service for Young People in Sefton. Her research interests include continuity of mental health care for young people engaged in the Youth Justice System and narrative understandings of experience of and recovery from psychosis.

Fiona Smith

Fiona Smith has just completed the Doctor of Clinical Psychology Training Programme at the University of Leeds. Prior to clinical training she worked in research, completing a PhD that investigated the impact of experiencing chronic health conditions in young adulthood. She now works as a clinical psychologist in the specialist psychosis and recovery unit at the Retreat Hospital in York.

Vicky Tozer

Vicky Tozer qualified from the Surrey Clinical Psychology Training Programme in 2006. Prior to clinical training she worked as an assistant psychologist in a specialist autism service and a learning disability team. She now works as a clinical psychologist in a community team for people with learning disabilities in Surrey and has a particular interest in systemic ways of working.

Sheila Youngson

Sheila Youngson is Deputy Clinical Director on the Doctor of Clinical Psychology Training Programme at the University of Leeds, where, over the last 10 years, she has had responsibility for developing the Personal and Professional Development core theme. She is also a consultant clinical psychologist with the Leeds Teaching Hospitals NHS Trust, where she works with children and young people living with chronic illness. Sheila works within the classically oriented person-centred approach.

Acknowledgements

Firstly, our heartfelt thanks to all the contributors to this book who have written chapters or parts of chapters. They managed tight deadlines and last-minute changes without audible protest.

Secondly, further thanks are due to a number of people who have contributed hugely to the process *and* outcome of this book, through conversation and dialogue, reading and commenting on chapters, IT support, formatting and freely giving of time and ideas: Jill Anderson, Clare Dowzer, Chris Harrop, Chris Hughes, Jessica and Mark Lewis, Joyce Scaife, Stephen Morley, Margaret Stark, Mark Woodward, our reviewers, and last but certainly not least, trainees on both the Leeds and Sheffield Clinical Psychology Doctorate Programmes.

We should also like to thank our development editor, Elizabeth-Ann Johnston, who was immensely helpful, patient and supportive.

On a personal note, I should like to thank Mark, Ilona and Chay and my mum for allowing me the time, space and support to make this possible. I would also like to thank many family members, friends, colleagues, service users and carers too numerous to mention by name but who have all affected my personal development journey.

Jan Hughes

I should like to express my personal thanks to the following: all the people who have entrusted me with their stories and their histories – service users and families and carers, supervisees and trainees. It has been a privilege. My colleagues at Leeds University and St James's University Hospital, who have taken on work or allowed the occasional absence to give me time to write. Dawn, Gillian, Nuala, Sarah, and Susan – members of my person-centred personal development group – you continue to move me. Margaret Pinnell, dear friend and Whitby companion, who has been my touchstone on many levels for over 20 years. And to my father, Professor Alexander J. Youngson (1918–2004), who wrote many a book, and instilled in me a love for the written word.

Sheila Youngson

Chapter 1

Personal Development and Clinical Psychology

Jan Hughes and Sheila Youngson

Introduction

This is a book on personal development for the twenty-first century. Our aim is to provide thinking and writing that can appeal, and be useful, to a wide readership – a readership that lives and works in changeable times and has to make sense of multiple epistemologies, governmental and organizational objectives and dictats, theoretical models, financial constraints, challenges to traditional ways of working, new ways of working and expanding roles and more responsibilities and accountability than ever before. We hope to provide a book that encompasses all of this *and* has clarity, direction and inclusivity. So that, whilst acknowledging the individual and idiosyncratic nature of personal development, we hope we also offer thoughts, suggestions and strategies/methods that can be adopted, adapted, changed, considered and debated by most.

Historically, writing around personal development has focused on the individual and therapy and has been within more reflective-practioner models. This book aims to move beyond this – to explore personal development within different realms, within different therapy models and within the different roles of a clinical psychologist. We will offer guidance around these areas and hope that personal development can be embraced within the clinical psychology profession.

There are clear drivers for clinical psychologists to develop personally. In 2004 there was an increased emphasis in the training accreditation criteria for clinical psychology courses to include learning outcomes for

Personal and Professional Development (British Psychological Society 2004). There has also recently been an emphasis within the NHS on Personal and People Development (Department of Health 2004). However, there is very little guidance as to what this may mean and/or how it may be approached and achieved.

This book aims to fill this gap in the literature and to provide a clarity around the concept of personal development, particularly acknowledging the multitude of roles clinical psychologists may have within their working environment. Traditionally, personal development has been linked, in a symbiotic manner, with professional development. In this book, the aim is to arrive at an understanding of what, in its own right, is meant by personal development and make it possible to put that understanding into practice. However, we do recognize that the personal and the professional are closely linked, and over the course of a career are likely to become merged. This separation *and* interlinking may become clearer by considering the answers to the following two questions: what have you learnt about yourself in the role of a clinical psychologist (the more professional emphasis)?; and, what have you learnt about yourself that it is important to know given the work that you do (the more personal emphasis)?

While the focus is on the profession of clinical psychology many of the ideas can be utilized with any professional group working in psychological or physical health. The book aims to bring together the views and voices of many different stakeholders in clinical psychology, including service users and carers, trainees, supervisors and trainers. In the tradition of clinical psychology a wide variety of approaches are used, employing a number of different methodologies (questionnaire survey, focus group, Interpretative Phenomenological Analysis and metaphors). Different styles of writing are also utilized, from the formal and academic to personal reflection, mirroring the range and richness of thinking and writing about personal development. The result of these various discourses and methodologies is a clear construction of our understanding of what personal development means for clinical psychologists in the twenty-first century and a model of personal development processes. We offer this in the hope it will aid the reader to create their own individual and idiosyncratic understanding and model – using individual experience, personality, preferred and new strategies, models, theories and concepts, beliefs and identity – to help individuals move forward in their personal development journeys.

Uses of the book

This book does not offer a quick fix, 'how to do it' approach to personal development. We believe that personal development is an individually constructed process that is different for everyone. However, the book offers guidance on developing personally that can be used for a number of different functions:

1   *Individual personal development*
The book can be used before, during and after training to help individuals understand their own personal development. It offers some clarity around definitions and processes, and the Model of Personal Development Processes (Chapter 4) can be used to guide an individual towards personal growth and application.

2   *Developing others (for example, supervision or mentoring)*
The book can also be used to help guide others. This may be particularly helpful when an individual within supervision or mentoring, for example, is stuck within a personal development process; in this situation the book may help clarify the barriers and provide guidance for moving forward.

3   *Training others (for example, trainee clinical psychologists)*
The book can be used as a core text in clinical psychology training, providing useful information and models and strategies for use with trainees. It can help guide clinical psychology training courses on their approach to personal development and the methods employed. It can also provide useful teaching materials to guide individual teaching sessions and individual meetings with trainees.

The Book

The book begins in Chapter 2 with an historical overview of personal development in clinical psychology on a number of different levels. A brief history of some contextual factors important for the profession of clinical psychology within the NHS is provided, bringing the reader up to date with more recent paradigms within our profession and the reasons why personal development has become more important to our profession. A personal history of development is described and is linked to a journey of promoting personal development within the clinical psychology training community, emphasizing the importance of personal development within the many different roles of a clinical psychologist. This chapter also illustrates the integration of personal development into clinical training. Hopefully, Chapter 2 will help the reader understand and appreciate the different emphases that have been placed on personal development over time and the current need to consider personal development within a multiplicity of roles. Finally, it is hoped that the reader can begin to understand some of the struggles and resistances individuals face in their personal development journeys and to see the roots of the questions as to its relevance and evidence base.

In the third chapter an attempt is made to examine and elaborate the concept of personal development and its importance. Current definitions are too limited and have a tendency to focus only on intra-psychic growth and on the role of therapist. This chapter utilizes psychological theories, knowledge and an understanding of psychological methods, skills and techniques to 'unpack' personal development and indicate how it might be put into practice. The imperative to engage in personal development is underscored by considering the many national and professional codes of practice, guidelines, training accreditation criteria and pieces of documentation, all of which emphasize, if not urge, such engagement.

Chapter 4 presents the Model of Personal Development Processes developed by the editors. It demonstrates that it is possible to describe the processes involved in an accessible way and utilizes a worked-through example as illustration. The model starts with the factors that may prompt an individual to consider that some energy needs to be given to personal development. The model has been developed in partnership with trainee clinical psychologists on both the Leeds and Sheffield training courses, and the feedback is that the model is understandable and helpful. The chapter ends by examining the barriers to personal development and potential ways in which these might be overcome.

The fifth chapter examines the service user and carer perspective on personal development. The limited literature on this topic is reviewed. A focus group of service users and carers is described and the transcript analysed using Thematic Framework Analysis. The service user and carer perspective is clear about the personal and professional characteristics and attributes they need clinical psychologists to demonstrate, as well as the nature of the therapeutic relationship in which they wish to engage. The chapter ends with a contribution from a service user reflecting on her own therapy and the importance of the therapist's personal development.

In Chapter 6 the authors focus on the need always to hold in mind an understanding of power, its operation and its consequences. How power and identity are linked is shown, and also how the way we use language can determine worth and value, on both an individual and societal level. Social disadvantage and privilege in the shaping of identity is also considered. There is a suggestion that clinical psychologists should examine their practice in terms of the way we think and talk about our work and the people we work with, and how this may collude with or maintain social injustices and oppression. The authors include parts of a conversation about their experiences that illustrate some of these points.

The next three chapters focus on methods of personal development, supervison, therapy and personal development groups. In Chapter 7 supervision and personal development are considered. The place of supervision at the heart of personal development is emphasized alongside how detailed contracting can help establish a useful, meaningful and honest relationship. Some of the challenges to bringing personal development issues into supervisory conversations are addressed, and how some models of therapy can determine how this is approached. Insight is offered into opportunities for development through supervision, and for facilitating this development, particularly but not exclusively, in training supervision. The chapter ends with a review of relevant research findings.

In Chapter 8 personal therapy and its relationship to personal development are discussed. The (limited) literature is reviewed that suggests that therapists value personal therapy as a resource in terms of increasing self-esteem, making deeper and more satisfactory relationships and improving professional practice. However, there is little evidence of personal therapy improving client outcome. The author then describes her own qualitative research study, exploring *how* personal therapy influences professional practice. The conclusion of the chapter is a recommendation that clinical psychologists should consider the benefits, if not the necessity, of personal therapy at some point in a career.

Personal development within a group setting is the focus of Chapter 9. A review of the literature is provided by one author and some conclusions and personal reflections are offered. This is followed by two experienced clinical psychologists writing about their experiences of personal development within group settings since qualification. The final part of the chapter addresses the considerable variety of responses to personal development groups, and the mixed reaction from trainees, and offers some *potential* explanations for differing viewpoints.

Chapter 10 turns to the issue of how personal development might be assessed. The importance of developing a culture within the training community that promotes and demonstrates personal development at all levels is stressed. The conflicts and tensions that arise when one tries to assess what is an individual and idiosyncratic and often internal process are considered. The complexity in assessing at the point of selection for training is discussed. Then an example of how one course is currently assessing personal development is described in detail. This is offered as a talking/discussion point and not, in any way, the answer to what is a very difficult and ongoing challenge.

A survey of clinical psychology training courses exploring how they approach personal development is the focus of Chapter 11. It is clear that courses are wrestling with how to meet the new emphasis on personal development in the 2004 training accreditation criteria. The survey reports the activities that are deemed to best promote personal development. This is followed by a chapter focussing on the trainee experience, and six recently qualified clinical psychologists reflect on their experience of personal development during training, including how courses approach personal development and what helped them develop personally. These experiences are then compared to the results in Chapter 11 and used to give guidance for both trainees and trainers.

The book ends by summarizing the emerging themes throughout the chapters. These include the current context, power and identity, service user and carer perspectives and the individual and idiosyncratic nature of personal development. Ideas for 'where next?' are also considered. The final chapter ends with the personal reflections of both editors on the process of writing the book.

Personal Statement – Jan Hughes

I felt an imperative to produce this book. Having had a career-long interest in personal development, I have felt over the years that there has been some resistance to personal development, and I have wondered whether one of the reasons for this was a lack of a framework for people to grasp and help them make sense of the process. I was aware of much work being done in my own local area in training, which seemed to be helping people and trainees in particular. But I was aware that this would potentially never be seen by others. My particular fear was that Sheila would retire and so much would be lost. I hope that this book will help her legacy live on.

Personal Statement – Sheila Youngson

When Jan first mooted the idea of this book, my response was 'absolutely not', knowing the time and effort that would be required. Jan, knowing me well, simply spent the next time she was stuck in a tedious meeting writing the plan of the book, which she then put before me and asked again. Thus she gave shape to her idea and made it surmountable and enticing all at the same time. Clever woman!

I have both a personal and a professional interest and investment in personal development, and various parts of my 'story' are included in this book. I believe that all clinical psychologists have an ethical responsibility to address their personal development needs throughout their careers. Strong words, I know, but I stand firm by them. Our profession requires us to work with people in considerable psychological and emotional distress; it requires us to take responsibility for making decisions that have huge and significant consequences for individuals and those who care for and about them; it requires us to manage and support and advise other workers; it requires us to know ourselves and develop that self-knowledge, so that we do not unwittingly visit on others our own unresolved difficulties, tensions, confusions, assumptions and judgements. Thus I believe there is an imperative to engage in personal development as this is a significant step towards ensuring effective practice and psychologically healthy and robust practitioners.

REFERENCES

British Psychological Society (2004). *Criteria for Postgraduate Courses in Clinical Psychology*. Leicester: British Psychological Society.

Department of Health (2004). *The NHS Knowledge and Skills Framework (KSF) and the Development Review Process*. London.

Chapter 2

Personal Development in Clinical Psychology

The Context

Sheila Youngson

Introduction

Personal development is a difficult concept to define. Indeed, this whole book is an attempt to bring some clarity and substance to the term, to the words. Personal development *in clinical psychology* adds another dimension, as here an ill-defined concept is placed in the context of an ever evolving and changing profession. This chapter will begin with a brief overview of the changing context for the profession, outlining the major paradigms and forces that have been and are at play. It will then consider the place of personal development within these various structures, using the author's own experience as a personal illustration.

Clinical Psychology – The Developing Context

The scientist-practitioner model

Clinical psychology is a relatively 'new' profession when it is contrasted with, for example, medicine and nursing, which have many centuries of history. Perhaps most clinical psychologists would point to the American Psychological Association Boulder Conference on graduate education in 1949 as the time when the profession first made a firm statement about its identity and proposed the adoption of the model of scientist-practitioner. Central to this model was the idea of an empirical approach to clinical work, in which clinicians would assess their clients, arrive at tentative formulations/diagnoses and apply interventions that would test their hypotheses, perhaps leading to modifications, until therapeutic change occurred. It was also emphasized that clinicians must be both expert consumers and evaluators of research, and generators of their own research, thus adding to the scientific evidence base. Now, in the twenty-first century, this is probably still the predominant (but not only) model in training, and in practice, although it could be argued that some emphases have changed, particularly in response to the requirements of the workplace and today's NHS, in which most UK clinical psychologists find employment.

However, a problem has arisen with this model. Whilst it is true to say that clinical psychology training does place considerable emphasis on inculcating research skills, both in critical evaluation and in various methodologies, it is also true to say that the vast majority of clinical psychologists publish no research in the rest of their careers (Pilgrim and Treacher 1992). Thus, one of the basic premises on which the scientist-practitioner model was founded – that clinicians would steadily add to the research and evidence base – has not come to fruition. In talking with today's clinicians, a number of factors arise in explanation, the two major ones being, on the one hand, lack of time as waiting lists grow, alongside the management requirement of a greater and quicker 'throughput' of patients; and, on the other, the time and effort it now takes to submit research proposals and pass them through ethical committees. Even the single case study takes more time than most clinicians feel they have to devote to writing and disseminating their work.

Thus, if the scientist-practitioner model has failed to achieve its full potential as once envisaged, what other models have been proposed? Two that have been debated in recent times are the reflective-practitioner model and the ideas of critical psychology and community psychology. However, before turning to look at these, it is worth considering what other knowledge, experience, movements and forces have helped drive and potentially shape thinking about and within the profession since the 1980s.

A wider view?

For some, there has been a growing dissatisfaction with the notion of psychology as a 'science' in a purist sense, with the idea that there is an objective reality and a 'truth' to be found. However, clinical psychology does not generally hold such a narrow view of its 'scientific' basis, and has moved, in many ways, away from a strictly hypothetico-deductive paradigm (in which theory leads to a deduction of a hypothesis that is then tested to see if it is verified or disproved). Today it can, and does, allow other epistemologies and paradigms and derived models, providing room for more subjective and experiential realities. Thus there is space for invention and creativity. This is reassuring for those clinicians who struggled with the concepts of diagnosis and categorization and the expert model, and were interested and concerned about individual differences and meanings, and a more working-in-partnership model.

Psychotherapy research

The outcome of 40 years of psychotherapy research has provided further food for thought (see, for example, Wampold 2001). This has demonstrated that whatever the therapeutic model utilized, the quality of the therapeutic relationship was a larger factor in positive psychological change. This has led some to question the focus of training, and put more emphasis on developing a deeper understanding of and knowledge about the therapeutic alliance and relationship. Wampold (2001) also argues that the evidence, in fact, demonstrates the importance of the therapeutic relationship *only* when practised by competent and thoughtful therapists adhering to a particular model; that is, the therapeutic relationship cannot be separated from the therapy.

The service user movement

The growth and development of the mental health service user movement has also prompted and required that mental health professionals, and wider society, take a broader and deeper perspective on mental health issues. Although the origins of the movement can be traced back as early as the 1620s (when psychiatric patients came together to speak out about conditions, and produced the Petition of the Poor Distracted Folk of Bedlam), it was in the 1970s that groups critical of the current psychiatric system and treatment began to be vocal. The movement has grown steadily since then, providing support, sharing information, campaigning for change, challenging discrimination and oppression, and promoting opportunities for social inclusion and recovery. From the beginning of this century in particular, government policy has directed that service users be involved in all aspects of health services work, from planning and delivering services through to monitoring services, and planning and conducting research. Although this is a significant step forward, service user networks say that in practice there is a long way to go before services are transformed in direct response to users' needs (Wallcroft and Bryant 2003).

Changes in the NHS

At a macro level, the profession of clinical psychology has been and is always affected by political drivers and changing policies. Since the 1980s, at least, the management structure of the NHS, nationally and more locally, has been reorganized frequently. Many arguments abound as to need, causes, effects, and blame. This frequently results in feelings of uncertainty, instability, anxiety and stress, as the profession feels threatened or invisible. Two initiatives perhaps illustrate this well.

New ways of working
It is probably true to say that the role of psychological therapist is that most often attributed to clinical psychologists. However, they frequently inhabit other roles as circumstances and settings require and as they progress through their careers: supervisor, teacher, consultant, researcher, manager, for example. A current development, New Ways of Working (Lavender and Hope 2007), takes this forward. New Ways of Working for a number of mental healthcare professions, came out of the realization that various professions needed to be clearer about the extent and limitations of their roles and responsibilities in the Health and Social Care arena. New Ways of Working for clinical psychologists aims to clarify and define the essential skills (and by implication roles) that we have in addition to the provision of psychological therapy. These are:

- research, evaluation and audit skills
- training and development, clinical supervision, consultancy and advice
- planning and delivery of innovation and service improvement projects
- clinical leadership which may be clinical capacity building, managerial or research based

In response, training courses need to consider how to be more explicit in beginning to teach these skills, and qualified clinical psychologists need to make sure that their skills in these areas receive continued professional development time.

Improving Access to Psychological Therapies (IAPT)
The national programme IAPT falls under the umbrella of New Ways of Working. It followed on from the unequivocal demonstration of the effectiveness of psychological therapies through the publication of National Institute of Clinical Excellence (NICE) clinical guidelines for a range of common mental health problems, and the recognition that the provision of such psychological therapies, particularly cognitive behaviour therapy (CBT), was inadequate. Lord Layard's report (2006), and the subsequent financial resourcing means that primary care services will be reorganized and restructured, and additional levels of staff trained in delivering psychological therapy, initially CBT. All of this has clear opportunities (management, supervision, provision of high-intensity interventions) and threats (interventions provided by other professions and services) for clinical psychology.

Evidence-based practice and practice-based evidence

As far back as the 1960s, psychologists had seen the importance of evaluating therapeutic endeavour. With a growing interest in behaviour therapy, randomly controlled trials (RCTs) were utilized to test its efficacy. However, it was in the 1970s that the term 'evidence-based practice' first became prominent. Initially, this was concerned with generating and collating a body of research evidence about efficacious treatments for certain conditions. Smith and Glass published a meta-analysis (perhaps the first) to examine the effect of psychotherapy, (defined in the broadest sense) in 1977. In the early 1970s Archibald Cochrane, in the UK, promoted the idea of the RCT as the gold standard of evidence. By 1992 the Cochrane Collaboration was established, and it has become a driving force behind systematic evidence reviews, and a major player in gathering evidence.

It could be argued that evidence-based practice is largely seen in the UK as a 'top-down' imperative, with national policy and guidelines directing what therapies should be offered to whom, based on diagnostic formulation. The various NICE guidelines are a potent example. Quality of services offered and accountability are key issues here.

However, as noted above, there are problems with this paradigm. Clinical psychologists do not often add to the evidence base. Further, noting that some treatments/models of therapy have empirical support is not equivalent to being able to state with certainty that 'this treatment will work for this person with this condition, at this time'. Finally, the absence of evidence is not evidence of the absence of efficacy, and some therapeutic models are more researched and more amenable to research than others. Perhaps it is also true that some practitioners are more willing to put their therapy to the test! Thus, there are enormous gaps in the evidence base.

Roth and Fonagy, in the second edition of 'What Works for Whom' (2006) begin to address some of these concerns, and propose a model that takes into account clinical judgements and clinical consensus in decisions around what form of therapy should be offered. Spring (2007) proposes a model that takes this further. It involves three potentially intersecting circles: research evidence, clinical expertise, all within the context of patient characteristics and preferences. Using information from all these sources, the clinician then makes a decision about what treatment to offer, in collaboration with the patient, thus moving towards the notion of shared decision-making.

This model incorporates the concept of practice-based evidence, that is, evidence rooted in routine clinical practice, and is more of a 'bottom-up' concept. Single case studies, qualitative research and the routine collection of a variety of outcome measures are some of the methods that contribute to the evidence base here. This model also acknowledges some real problems with evidence-based practice, notably the presence of co-morbidities and the many social factors that are known to create and maintain psychological distress and disturbance, for example poverty.

It has been argued that both paradigms – evidence-based practice and practice-based evidence – are necessary to fully understand the complexity of the issues involved, and that a gradation of acceptable evidence needs to be incorporated into practice and what is considered as valid (Charman and Barkham 2005).

These, then, are only some of the drivers and forces with which clinical psychology has to maintain and develop its identity, its position and its goals.

The reflective-practitioner model

This model was first described within the field of education and teaching (Schön 1983), and is more aligned with humanistic and phenomenological approaches to understanding and understanding experiences and their impact. In fact, it has not been well defined and has attracted criticism for being both too nebulous and too difficult to quantify and evaluate. However, it has appealed to those clinicians who give considerable weight to inter-personal factors within therapeutic relationships and place considerable emphasis on them, and who wish to explore inherent subjectivities.

The model requires clinicians to take a metacognitive approach: to stand outside the work and reflect on all that is happening, a reflection that has both cognitive and affective components.

Lavender (2003) describes four principal and interrelated concepts as central to reflective practice:

1   Reflection in action – whereby one reflects both cognitively and emotionally on what one is doing, and what one should do next, in the moment;
2   Reflection on action – in which these reflective processes are engaged in retrospectively;
3   Reflection about impact on others (which will necessarily be subsumed by one or both of the above categories);
4   Reflection about the relationships between the work and the self.

In this context reflective practice is not 'woolly' or unstructured; it is purposeful, considered, thoughtful and goal-oriented.

An interesting question now arises: are these two models, scientist-practitioner and reflective-practitioner, mutually exclusive, based as they are on two very different epistemological paradigms? The July 2003 issue of *Clinical Psychology Forum* (the journal/discussion forum of the British Psychological Society's Division of Clinical Psychology) was devoted to an exploration of reflective practice. Here many authors (for example, Cushway and Gatherer 2003; Lavender 2003; Bennett-Levy 2003) argued for a synthesis of the two models, suggesting that not only can they co-exist but that the result might be a clinician better equipped to function on a number of levels in today's world.

Whittaker summarizes the debate, and a way forward, succinctly:

> Research into reflective practice that incorporates considerations of its subjective and experiential 'realities' fits neatly into a scientist-practitioner paradigm. Likewise clinical practice based upon reflective practices need not be incompatible with an idea of rooting practice in evidence, if our concept of what constitutes evidence broadens too. Whittaker (2004)

Critical and community psychology

Critical psychology is a relative newcomer in terms of the way we think and practise clinical psychology, and currently is at the radical end of the continuum, although a growing and emerging field. There is a confusion of definitions, but a fundamental goal is to help bring about a radically better and transformed society. Fox (2000) proposes four main premises as underlying this approach:

1   Psychology's values, assumptions and practices have been culturally and historically determined.

Thus, what psychology pays attention to, and where it may locate the origins of psychological health or ill-health, will depend on past philosophical traditions, current socioeconomic and political climates and battles over power. Also, because psychology has its own oppressive history stemming from societal norms that have led to an emphasis on measurement, categorization, manipulation and control (think, for example, of the treatment of people with a learning disability, or when homosexuality was finally removed from classifications of mental illness), critical psychology also seeks to transform psychology.

2   Modern society is marked by widespread injustice, inequality and systemic barriers to both survival and meaning.

These injustices, inequalities and barriers are at the heart of individual and community distress; psychology should be working towards changing the dominant ideologies that maintain these injustices and inequalities rather than locating the problem within the individual and/or family.

3   In their everyday work psychologists too often contribute to complacency at one extreme and oppression at the other.

Mainstream psychology is part of the dominant ideology in society, reinforcing the status quo by its emphasis on individualism and personal goals, and maintains different systems from those that are known to create and maintain psychological distress.

4   Critical psychology seeks to alter, and ultimately find alternatives to, both mainstream psychology's norms and the societal institutions that these norms strengthen.

Thus, critical psychology challenges psychology to examine its roots, its beliefs and its applied practices, and to work towards emancipation, social justice, self-determination and participation, using what it already knows and comes to know about the causes and maintenance of psychological distress.

It could be argued that community psychology is one approach that works towards putting some of the ideas of critical psychology into applied practice. A special issue of *Clinical Psychology Forum* in September 2005 was given over to considering how community psychologists could challenge social equalities, thus underlining the growing interest in these ideas. In this issue, as an illustration, Bostock and Diamond (2005) describe some of the ways they have tried to bring a community psychology perspective to their work in the NHS.

So, if that is a very brief overview of the context of clinical psychology in the UK, and a summary of some of the forces and debates that currently exist, where does personal development fit into the picture?

What follows is an individual and personal account of the author's own experience of being a clinical psychologist over the last 30 years, written in the first person so as to feel more immediate. It is hoped that this will not only provide a useful illustration but may also prompt reflection on the part of the reader.

Towards an Individual Understanding of the Importance of Personal Development

Beginnings

I trained to be a clinical psychologist at the end of the 1970s. The box files and ring-binders are now long gone, but I don't recall a module or session entitled 'Personal Development', or even 'Professional Development'. I think the words were used, but they commonly meant the individual accumulation and development of technical clinical skills. Those were the days when the concept of the clinical psychologist as a scientist-practitioner was still relatively new, and the profession was largely rooted in behaviourism, although cognitive approaches were on the horizon. My sense is that we were expected to maintain a detached and objective outlook and stance. We were scientists, using empirically based psychological theory to effect behaviour change. My first job post-qualification was split – I worked in a large institution for people with a learning disability and in an adolescent unit. In the former, my task was to observe behaviour on the wards and day units and devise appropriate behavioural programmes for the staff to implement. In the latter, where child and adolescent psychiatry, in this instance, had a psychodynamic/psychoanalytic approach, one of the clinical psychologists was attempting to bring in some new ideas. Thus, I was introduced to the then new ways of working (!), and learnt about personal construct theory and social skills training in addition to the classical behavioural approaches. Therefore, during training and in my first four years following qualification, personal development was simply not considered.

Even in training supervision, the focus was clearly on what *to do*, and if personal feelings and emotional responses to the work were mentioned, usually this was taken as a sign of over-involvement at best and inappropriate emotional liability at worst. And so I continued in my work, living, professionally, largely in my head. This is not to say that my heart could not be touched; it often was by the stories my clients shared. However, my responses were always within the framework of 'What can I do to/with this person and their difficulties?' and I kept my emotional reactions and responses largely to myself. I thought I was standing predominantly outside any mutually affecting relationship and applying what knowledge I had to provide a solution. Good, sound clinical psychology in the assessment–formulation – intervention tradition. Again, it never really crossed my mind, or not in any great depth, that the relationship itself might be restorative (or damaging) to either or both of us, or that either of us might affect the other.

Recognizing the two-way impact of the work

In the mid-1980s I moved to work in the field of child and adolescent mental health, where I was to remain for the next 14 years. This was the era when the extent and psychological sequelae of child abuse began to be recognized, and I spent increasing amounts of time working with children and families who had experienced abuse, notably child sexual abuse. Two thoughts became persistent through this work. One, I didn't feel as if I had the appropriate clinical skills to be helpful and efficacious with this client group. And, two, I was beginning to struggle emotionally with the accumulating accounts of abusive experiences.

Thus, firstly, I enrolled on a diploma course in person-centred work with children and young people. This was a very different way of being with people therapeutically. This was *all* about the relationship, and creating a facilitative psychological climate. Here there was no role and pretence, no expert persona. The person-centred approach held that my clients were the experts in terms of making sense of their experiences and finding a path towards healing, even when their past relationships and experiences had left them separated from their feelings and their selves. My task was to provide myself in a real relationship, to be fully present in my encounters, to offer empathic understanding, to be open to experiencing. However, it 'fitted' with my politics and philosophy; I'd never been very happy in the expert role, feeling very inexpert; I liked the true and open collaborative stance; and there was an extended theoretical and research basis. I also found that it worked.

Secondly, I sought out support and supervision. This was a time when supervision of one's practice was not mandatory, and one only asked for advice or help when stuck. My sense (which is I think is probably quite accurate) was that I should not get stuck too often, or it would be concluded that I was not competent. Help and advice was always client-focussed, and would involve discussions on what other technique to try. I don't recall a time when it was suggested (by or to me) that we talk about the therapeutic relationship or my feelings. However, as a consequence of my work with abused children, I did now have a sense that I needed regular supervision that involved those elements, and I arranged to self-fund that with a local psychotherapist.

Difficult times and the need to stop for a while

However, even with this support and supervision, I did not take enough care of myself. In retrospect, many personal issues were being triggered, and many patterns and coping strategies, once adaptive but now not so, were being brought into play.

My world view narrowed, and I found myself in dark places, an obvious (now) parallel to the experience of my clients. My body dictated that I stop; I simply did not recover after some minor surgery and was away from work for nine months.

Reflection and an emphasis on personal development

This was a time when reflection was thrust upon me! I realized that I had paid no attention to my own personal development. I had not looked at the road I had travelled or the person I had become; I had no sense of my personal landscape (see Chapter 4); I had not listened to any clues or nudges from inside me or from friends and family and colleagues; I had not acknowledged the patterns I created or in which I became stuck.

I chose to enter personal therapy, which proved enormously helpful. I began to see patterns of being and relating that had been established years ago that did not need to remain set in stone. I began to discover my personal landscape and see that it could and would be fluid and flexible in response to life's experiences. I began to recognize patterns in my work life, some of which were useful, some not so. And I saw and felt, clearly at last, the privilege and the cost of being a therapist; of spending many of my days in deep communication with people experiencing considerable psychological and emotional distress.

Towards the end of my personal therapy, and with the acknowledgement that I had been working full time as a clinical psychologist for 17 years, I decided to change direction. I had had links with the clinical psychology training course at Leeds University for over a decade, providing teaching and placements. A clinical tutor post was advertised, and I applied and was successful. I was also able to move my two clinical days from child and adolescent mental health to a child health setting, and I had the additional responsibility of co-ordinator of supervision for a large clinical and health psychology department. And so began another chapter in my life.

Promoting personal development in a training context

The training course, when I joined it in 1995, did not have an established personal and professional development focus or curriculum, but the core staff team were keen to develop this, and I took on that responsibility. I began by asking a couple of trainees from each year to meet with me every couple of months over my first year. I wanted to hear about their experiences during training: what were the stresses and strains? what were the support needs? did they consider that personal development was important, and, if so, how did they see this being promoted and encouraged? what were the professional issues and challenges they met and with which they struggled? These conversations were remarkably open and honest – perhaps partly because I was a new member of staff and not seen as embedded in the perceived 'establishment'. I remember being struck by the trainees' perception that if they admitted to struggling, particularly emotionally, they would in some way be regarded as not coping and not suitable for training. Over a decade later, I am saddened when new trainees still arrive with this perception, although I think they quickly come to accept our view that we are more concerned when they don't admit to struggling at some point.

This group became known as the Support Issues Forum, perhaps reflecting its early emphasis. After the first year we decided to ask qualified clinical psychologists to join us in our discussions, wanting to learn from their experience, and also to hear whether the conversations we were having had relevance to the post-qualification workplace. Our focus broadened to include proactive ideas about the curriculum and emphases around personal and professional development, as well as reactive responses to trainee need. For example, we looked at the option of establishing reflective groups during training, how to address issues of power and difference and how to incorporate a more explicit consideration of the socio-political context of people's lives.

On reflection I think we felt we were being not a little subversive, and I suspect I willingly colluded with that at the start, quite enjoying feeling more radical in my professional life. We didn't hide what we were doing; indeed we reported back to various course structures. But we did meet in the basement, and we did it quietly! Two years into this process, we had the courage of our convictions, and took a proposal to the Course Management Committee. This was that the Support Issues Forum be renamed the Personal and Professional Issues Sub-committee, and become an established part of the overall management structure of the course. This was agreed.

Acknowledging the impact of the work

By the late 1990s it seemed to me that there was a general consensus that personal development is important in training and beyond – that it is a life-long process. Not everyone opted into this culture, and what was a cultural shift, but in talking to staff and trainees on other courses, there was a general acceptance that we were going in the right direction. This acceptance centred around the recognition that the work impacted on us and we impacted on the work (Scaife and Walsh 2001).

The work can impact on us via a number of routes (and this is not an exhaustive list):

- the social, political, and economic context of the workplace
- the complex and demanding nature of training and the need to develop multi-tasking skills
- relationships with colleagues
- team dynamics
- the pressure of waiting lists
- seeing or knowing of changes that would improve a service and there not being the time or funding to implement them
- the emotional impact of being with many people in psychological distress
- the emotional impact of personal stories

We can impact on the work via a number of routes (and again this is not an exhaustive list):

- beliefs
- attitudes
- values
- expectations
- prejudices and assumptions
- perceptions of others based on past experiences
- the emphasis placed on and weight given to certain principles
- overall, the influence of personal life history

Given this general acceptance of the two-way impact of our work, came the realization that the sub-committee, and the course, had to develop a programme that addressed and promoted personal development if we were to produce psychologically and emotionally knowledgeable and robust practitioners who would remain effective and healthy.

Developing the programme

This sub-committee has significantly broadened its remit over the decade since its formation. It oversees the taught Personal and Professional curriculum, comprising nine half-day workshops in each of the three years. Some workshops have a more professional development focus, some a more personal development focus, but each, of course, has an element of the other. It closely monitors and evaluates feedback from these sessions, and I think we have finally reached a programme that has cohesion and progression. It has wrestled with the reflective groups, and again we seem to have reached a format and structure that works – at least for some. It has ushered in a variety of methods for promoting personal development. It continues to be reactive to expressed needs, and pro-active in terms of always searching for new and different ways of delivering the overall programme; for example, we are currently working on how to involve service users appropriately in all aspects of the work of the sub-committee, including the taught curriculum. Finally, it has produced documentation to explain the rationale for the programme in its entirety, to describe it fully and to link it to core competencies and associated learning outcomes and elements. (See Chapter 10 for further elaboration.)

In the next two chapters we will consider a further exploration of personal development – what it is and why it is important – and then propose a model of personal development processes that we hope will aid the reader construct and develop an individual, meaningful and useful understanding.

REFERENCES

Bennet-Levy, J. (2003). 'Reflection: A Blind Spot in Psychology?' *Clinical Psychology*, 27 (16–9 July).

Bostock, J. and Diamond, B. (2005). 'The Value of Community Psychology: Critical Reflections from the NHS'. *Clinical Psychology Forum*, 153 (22–5 September).

Charman, D. and Barkham, M. (2005). 'Psychological Treatments: Evidence-based Practice and Practice-based Evidence'. *InPsych, Australian Psychological Society* (December).

Cushway, D. and Gatherer, A. (2003). 'Reflecting on Reflection'. *Clinical Psychology*, 27 (6–10 July).

Fox, D. (2000). 'The Critical Psychology Project: Transforming Society and Transforming Psychology'. In T. Sloan (ed.), *Critical Psychology: Voices for Change*. London: Palgrave.

Lavender, T. (2003). 'Redressing the Balance: The Place, History and Future of Reflective Practice in Clinical Training'. *Clinical Psychology*, 27 (11–15 July).

Lavender, T. and Hope, R. (2007). *New Ways of Working for Applied Psychologists in Health and Social Care – The End of the Beginning. Summary Report.* Circulated to DCP Managers Group, 24 July, 2007.

Layard, R. (2006). *The Depression Report: A New Deal for Depression and Anxiety Disorders.* The Centre for Economic Performance's Mental Health Policy Group, London School of Economics.

Pilgrim, D. and Treacher, A. (1992). *Clinical Psychology Observed.* London: Routledge.

Roth, A. and Fonagy, P. (2006). *What Works for Whom?* (2nd edn.). New York: Guildford Press.

Smith, M. L. and Glass, G. V. (1977). 'Meta-Analysis of Psychotherapy Outcome Studies'. *American Psychologist*, 32: 752–60.

Scaife, J. and Walsh, S. (2001). 'The Emotional Climate of Work and the Development of Self'. In J. Scaife, *Supervision in the Mental Health Professions.* London: Brunner-Routledge.

Schön, D. A. (1983). *The Reflective Practitioner.* New York: Basic Books.

Spring, B. (2007). 'Evidence-Based Practice in Clinical Psychology: What It Is, Why It Matters, What You Need to Know'. *Journal of Clinical Psychology*, 63: 611–31.

Wallcroft, J. and Bryant, M. (2003). *The Mental Health Service User Movement in England*, Policy Paper 2, London, The Sainsbury Centre for Mental Health.

Wampold, B. E. (2001). *The Great Psychotherapy Debate: Models, Methods, and Findings.* Mahwah, NJ: Lawrence Erlbaum.

Whittaker, R. (2004). 'The Scientist-Practitioner Model and the Reflective-Practitioner Model are Two Opposing Paradigms in Clinical Practice. Discuss'. Unpublished essay, Doctor of Clinical Psychology Programme, University of Leeds.

Chapter 3

What is Personal Development and Why is it Important?
Jan Hughes

Introduction

What *is* personal development? Who defines it and how? Are there different meanings in different contexts? And why do *you* need to consider personal development? This chapter aims to begin to address these questions and more.

The importance accorded to personal development in clinical psychology can be linked to the historical factors described in Chapter 2. Within the traditional empiricist scientist-practitioner model, in which the main educational approach has been to develop clinicians whose work benefits from the use of scientifically valid methods, tools and techniques, the 'person', and therefore personal development, has not taken centre stage. However, moves within clinical psychology to embrace additional epistemologies have made room for the *person* in the work to take a more central role. This is relevant for clinical psychologists working primarily from the perspective of a reflective-practitioner, and also for those working in the frame of scientist-practitioner, because the evidence base attests to the importance of the therapist–client relationship in therapy outcomes within different models (Horvath and Bedi 2002: 37–69; Martin, Garske and Davis 2000). Research evidence also gives testimony to the importance of therapist characteristics in psychotherapy outcome, over and above model and technique (for example, Wampold 2001).

This chapter begins with some definitions of personal development that have been adopted in relevant literature, and describes some frameworks and models that can aid understanding and research within the topic. There follows an overview of the context in which personal development has become an imperative within the profession of clinical psychology and exploration of the reasons why personal development is useful to clinicians, not only in their role as therapists but also in relation to their other responsibilities. Outcomes of methods addressed to personal development are described. The chapter ends, in keeping with the traditions of clinical psychology, by integrating a cross-section of relevant ideas, theories and concepts to produce a contextual model intended to further understanding of personal development in clinical psychology.

Definitions and Models of Personal Development

Popular psychology

Within popular psychology there is a vast literature on personal development, with a huge array of self-help books testifying to its use in self/personal development (for example, Burn 2007). There are key themes related to the meaning of personal development within this arena:

- self-awareness
- spiritual growth
- pursuit of happiness
- quality of life
- changing personal habits
- meaning and understanding in life
- positive thinking and goal-setting

It can be seen from this that these issues are wide-reaching and hard to define in themselves. In the clinical professions there has been much discussion and debate about 'personal development', and 'personal and professional development' with the same terms being used to describe different processes. Authors have used the phrases 'personal and professional development', 'personal development', 'personal growth' and 'self-awareness/knowledge' to define the same concept and the literature can appear somewhat confusing. In terms of defining professional development, Wilkins (1997) states that this is the area 'which addresses the extensions and skills of the clinician'. Donati and Watts try to unpick the meaning behind the different terms and conclude that personal development has an impact on both professional development and on personal growth. A helpful distinction that is made is that personal development is the process that results in the outcome of personal growth (Donati and Watts 2005). This fits with Irving and William's understanding of personal development, that it is a purposeful process which can be experienced as positive or negative, whereas personal growth can be incidental but is always positive (Irving and Williams 1999).

Person-centred approaches

In the counsellor training literature, in which there is a history of the centrality of personal development in the training/work, with its roots in a person-centred approach, definitions include the following: '[personal development is the] consistent and continual striving for self and other awareness, knowledge, understanding and acceptance' (Johns 1996: 3), 'personal growth (as it is relevant to development as a therapist) is the process of attending to our own needs in such a way as to increase our ability to be with our clients in a way that is not only safe for both parties but which incrementally improves our effectiveness' (Wilkins 1997: 9) and 'personal development is a process of recursive and ongoing integration' (Cross and Papadopoulos 2001: 1). These definitions are limited in their intra-psychic approach to personal development. David Mearns (1997) has developed a more holistic approach, identifying the following four basic domains in which we may personally develop.

Self-structure
This includes introjected beliefs, personal constructs, self-concept, personal identity, degree of self-acceptance, maturity and personal responsibility. All of these features are concerned with how we have developed into the person we are and will play a part in determining what we might become.

The following aspects are concerned with more specific parts of the self which have relevance for identity as therapists/clinical psychologists as well as people.

Self in relation
Mearns states that we need to understand how and why we behave towards others as we do. Important here are our beliefs about others, our past patterns of interpersonal relating, assumptions and prejudices, understanding of roles, and how we appear or want to appear to others.

Self as therapist

This represents one important role that a clinical psychologist may occupy. Here there is a need to develop the ability to monitor and evaluate the personal impact of client work, the impact of personal life on work with clients, blocks/barriers from ourselves that may impact on therapy, the overall influence of personal life history, values, beliefs and personal characteristics.

Self as learner

This is emphasized not only in training but also in the continued journey into professional life and career. Important here is our ability to develop personal learning goals, a willingness to critically appraise our learning, confidence to tolerate uncertainty that follows challenge, owning responsibility for our learning and behaviour, and the capacity to openly and accurately appraise all aspects of our selves.

Personal development within this model means increasing self-awareness and self-knowledge within one or more domains, all of which may overlap.

Cognitive behaviour therapy (CBT) and the therapeutic relationship

The meaning of personal development within CBT can be linked to the importance of developing positive therapeutic alliances. While this has always been a focus for some working within the field of CBT, it has gradually gained more of an emphasis in the field (for example, Gilbert and Leahy 2007). In a review of the empirical CBT literature Waddington (2002) found that 'an association between the therapy relationship and outcome has been observed more often than not'. Holtforth and Castonguay (2005) state that 'The therapeutic relationship deserves a central position in CBT research, training and practice.'

As highlighted above, research findings consistently show that the therapeutic alliance is the most important predictive factor in psychotherapy outcome regardless of therapeutic model (Horvath and Bedi 2002: 37–69) and that the most important predictive aspect of the alliance is the therapist's contribution (Norcross 2002). These findings support the view that the most important issues in outcome research are therapist common factors – related to the shared goals of therapy, consensus on method, means and techniques of treatment and the emotional bond (Wampold 2001). Developing personally can be seen as just as important within a CBT approach as in any other model. Indeed, this is stated specifically by Bennett-Levy in his cognitive model of therapist skill acquisition: 'The model also clearly indicates a role for the therapist's personal development in the development of their therapeutic skills' (Bennett-Levy 2006: 73).

Psychodynamic approaches and personal therapy

Personal development in terms of self-awareness and insight is a fundamental concept within psychoanalytic therapy, with the emphasis on the link between personal and professional development. This is evidenced by the key requirement to engage in long-term therapy as part of the criteria for qualification as a psychoanalytic psychotherapist (Clark 1986). The research into the effects of personal therapy on therapists show largely positive results, both in terms of the therapist's personal development (for example, Orlinsky, Norcross, Ronnestad and Wiseman 2005) and their professional development (for example, Orlinsky, Botermans and Ronnestad 2001). Personal therapy and the implications for personal development are explored in more depth in Chapter 8.

Consultancy approaches

Many clinical psychologists work within an indirect or consultancy-based framework. Historically there have been a number of approaches to consultancy, ranging from Caplan's (1970) four types (client-centred case, consultee-centred case, programme-centred administrative, consultee-centred administrative), to recognizing the different roles of expert versus process consultants. Consultancy approaches in clinical psychology have utilized generic frameworks and therapy-specific frameworks (for example, systemic, psychoanalytic etc.). Within all of the different approaches there is an emphasis on awareness of the consultant's role and position, for example, expert and removed or integral (for instance, Campbell's social construct approach (Campbell 2000)). All roles are in relation to others and have elements of power embedded within them. It is therefore important for the clinical psychologist to have developed personally in order to guide them in these roles.

Models of therapist development

There have been a number of empirically tested models of therapist development employing large numbers of therapists. Ronnestad and Skovholt (2003) summarize a longitudinal study examining 100 therapists which outlines six stages of development: the lay helper, the beginning student, the advanced student, the novice professional, the experienced professional and the senior professional. The themes related to personal development that emerge within the model are attentional focus and emotional functioning, the importance of continuous reflection for personal growth and a lifelong personal/professional integration process. Orlinsky has been at the forefront of major studies of nearly 4000 therapists looking at personal development across career, resulting in another six-stage model including novice, apprentice, graduate, mature (for example, Orlinsky and Ronnestad 2005). This research attempts to operationalize and test the common issues across the development of therapists, including themes around experience linked to professional mastery and currently experienced growth.

Clinical psychology training programmes

The profession of clinical psychology has tended to focus on personal development not as a separate entity, but as a linked concept: 'personal and professional development'. Gillmer and Marckus (2003) surveyed clinical psychology training courses to ascertain how courses were defining, teaching and assessing personal development. The conclusion of this research was that personal development is 'that part of the curriculum that is dedicated to developing in trainees a capability to reflect critically and systematically on the work-self interface. This process is directed towards fostering personal awareness and resilience' (Gillmer and Marckus 2003: 23).

Horner, Youngson and Hughes have since tried to build on this survey with an emphasis on personal development, particularly in light of the new British Psychological Society (BPS) accreditation criteria, and have found that some clinical psychology programmes continued to use this definition. Chapter 11 provides further detail on the survey by Horner, Youngson and Hughes. One course had taken a definition from a paper written by clinical psychologists which states that personal development is 'the process of developing understanding of the relationship between one's own life history and clinical work' (Walsh and Scaife 1998: 21). Another course uses the definition of personal development devised at the Group of Trainers

Clinical Psychology Conference Oxford in 2001: 'an ability to be continually reflective about our own practice; to be respectful and curious about others (clients and colleagues); and to change and develop as appropriate'. Finally, another course team had developed their own definition: 'clinical work requires some understanding of the complex inter-relationships between professional and personal issues . . . (that) essentially revolves around a process of interpersonal exchange and of developing acquaintanceship between practitioner and client(s)'. On the Leeds Clinical Psychology Programme, where there has been a particular emphasis on personal development, it has been acknowledged that personal development 'is a highly complex, multi-faceted, ill-understood, under-researched, very individually based, concept'.

The Leeds Programme suggests there are three key features of personal development (following Mearns 1997):

1   A preparedness and willingness to become more and more aware of self;
2   A preparedness and willingness to try to understand one's self;
3   A preparedness and willingness to explore and experiment with one's self, i.e. to risk doing things differently, face fears, invite challenge, examine one's character and personality, learn to confront, etc.

More recently within clinical psychology an integrative model of personal and professional development has been developed by Sheikh, Milne and MacGregor (2007). Gillmer and Marckus's definition is used in this chapter in conjunction with the following characterization: personal development is 'about knowing yourself and understanding how your experience shapes your subsequent encounters with the world. It is of critical importance for counsellors and therapists' (Cross and Papadopoulos 2001: 1).

Limitations of definitions

There are limitations to current understandings of personal development. The first is that all the definitions and understandings described have been developed within predominantly White-Eurocentric cultures. Secondly, personal development is described as a primarily intra-psychic process with less emphasis on interpersonal processes. The definitions of personal development do not emphasize the impact of and on others around the individual who is engaging in a personal development process.

There is also little acknowledgement of the impact of the context on the individual.

Clinical psychologists may consider that there are limitations for them in the definitions of personal development as the focus is often on therapy, only one of the many roles that they occupy. There is a need to consider the place of personal development for clinical psychologists within multiple roles.

The Context for the Developing Importance of Personal Development in Clinical Psychology

The NHS

Ten Essential Shared Capabilities (ESC)
At the beginning of the twenty-first century a number of changes within the NHS emphasized the importance of personal development for all NHS staff. For example, the 10 ESC (Department of Health 2004a) were developed by the Department of Health, the Sainsbury Centre for Mental Health and the National Institute for Mental Health in England and the NHSU. The 10 ESC set out the values and principles for service delivery in the field of mental health. All clinical psychologists within this field should be using the 10 ESC to guide their work. One of the 10 ESC is Personal Development and Learning, which is defined as 'keeping up-to-date with changes in practice and participating in life-long learning, personal and professional development for one's self and colleagues through supervision, appraisal and reflective practice'.

Knowledge and Skills Framework (KSF)
All NHS employees and therefore all clinical psychologists working in the NHS have to have a Personal Development Plan (PDP) within the KSF (Department of Health, 2004b), on which they are reviewed on an annual basis. Every employee has a number of dimensions which are specific to their post. However, all employees have to show evidence that they are meeting criteria on six core dimensions. Depending on the level of responsibility of the job the individual will have to meet criteria on one of four levels on each dimension. One of the six core dimensions is personal and people development. At all levels on this dimension individuals must show they can contribute to their own development. The KSF handbook describes this core dimension as 'developing oneself using a variety of means and

contributing to the development of others through ongoing work activities'. Progression through the levels on this dimension is characterized by:

- taking greater responsibility for your own personal development – this includes more reflectiveness and self-evaluation, and addressing own development needs
- increasing involvement in supporting others and their development including a wider range of people with different backgrounds
- having a greater understanding of own and other's learning needs and preferences, styles of learning and how to facilitate learning and development

The examples of application which could be relevant at any level include 'on the job' learning, reflective practice, learning from others and supervision. For psychologists the levels on this dimension range from 2 (assistant psychologist) to 4 (consultant), and the implications for this are that any psychologist working in the NHS should be able to show evidence that they have developed personally.

The profession of clinical psychology

For clinical psychology training programmes to gain and keep their accredited status they must meet all the British Psychological Society's Committee on Training in Clinical Psychology criteria for accreditation (BPS 2007). In 2004 there was a change in the accreditation criteria to give greater emphasis to personal development. The learning objectives that trainees must meet show the meaning of personal development in clinical psychology training at the level of accreditation as follows:

B.1.1.6 High level skills in managing a personal learning agenda and self-care, and in critical reflection and self-awareness that enable transfer of knowledge and skills to new settings and problems

B.1.2.4 Professional competence relating to personal and professional development and awareness of the clinical, professional and social context within which the work is undertaken.

The criterion includes nine areas of competence, one of which is entitled 'Personal and Professional Skills'. Guidance is also given on how to achieve personal development, for example:

12.2 Programmes should ensure that trainees monitor and review their own progress and develop skills in self-reflection and critical reflection on practice.

Personal Development and the Multiple Roles of Clinical Psychologists

There is little empirical evidence for the effectiveness of personal development in the roles of a clinical psychologist *per se*. However, there is literature that gives evidence of the importance of personal characteristics to a number of different professional roles. It can be inferred that these characteristics could arise through personal development. These include the personal characteristics that have been linked to effective leaders, for example, emotional intelligence (Goleman, Boyatzis and McKee 2003); effective team players, for example, communication skills, collaboration (West 2004); effective teachers, for example, reflexivity (Ghaye and Ghaye 1998); effective supervisors, for example, boundaried, open, supportive (Beinhart 2004) and researchers, for example, functional and personal reflexivity (Thompson 2007).

Reasons Why Personal Development is Important in Clinical Psychology

For a number of years I have run sessions with colleagues for first-year trainees on clinical psychology courses exploring personal development. The answer to the question, 'Why is personal development important?' consistently receives answers within the following themes:

- it contributes to self-awareness and increasing knowledge of gaps in awareness;
- being aware decreases the risk of harm to others;
- it gives a resilience in dealing with problems and dilemmas;
- we should practise what we preach – we ask our clients to reflect on themselves so shouldn't we be able to do this too?
- it can help us take care of ourselves;
- developing personally helps us contribute to our profession.

There has been a unanimous sense in these sessions of these fundamental themes and that personal development is important, whilst the difficulties inherent in putting them into practice are recognized.

This section aims to summarize the numerous reasons why personal development is important for clinical psychologists.

Professional context

In the current context, working and training clinical psychologists in the NHS, there is an increased emphasis on formal accountability. Since the 2000s there has been an increased emphasis on protecting the public through statutory registration under the Health Professions Council, and chartered status. To gain entry to and remain on the register, clinical psychologists must complete annual continued professional development (CPD) logs. As Golding and Gray (2006) state, in the past CPD has been a rather *ad hoc* activity. Now there is a requirement to keep, and submit records of CPD undertaken, and to map these on to National Occupational Standards (NOS) for psychologists. The first NOS is entitled: 'Develop, implement and maintain personal and professional standards and ethical practice', and one of the units within this NOS is:

> 1.3 Contribute to the continuing development of self as a professional applied psychologist.

We are accountable for our personal development to our employer through clinical governance. We are accountable to the BPS through their accreditation criteria for clinical psychology programmes to ensure trainees are enabled to develop personally. It is important we are aware of our responsibilities to develop personally within all of these professional contexts and in relation to the many roles of a clinical psychologist discussed above.

The personal context

It is important also to balance this with the personal context. There are many reasons why an individual may want to develop personally. These may be an attempt to move away from 'negative' aspects, that is, the need to change unhelpful or uncomfortable thoughts, feelings or actions. There may be positive reasons, for example, the desire to expand understanding of self and the application of that understanding within different settings. In his hierarchy of needs, Maslow states that it is every human's desire to reach a state of self-actualization with the need for development and creativity (Maslow 1943).

Resilience and robustness

There are a number of different stressors involved in working as a clinical psychologist. There is a heavy emotional load from working with service users and their carers and holding the level of distress on a day-to-day basis. Many stressors arise from the different roles that clinical psychologists occupy and the inherent responsibility they place upon us. Personal growth can enhance resilience and robustness within the demanding roles clinical psychologists are required to take.

Potential of harm to self

One of the risks of a failure to develop the necessary resilience is the potential for psychological or physical harm to one's self or 'burn out'. It is not uncommon for clinical psychologists to be on long- or short-term sick leave either for psychological problems or psychologically related physical problems. The more we develop our self-knowledge and awareness (and our ability to act on this and care for ourselves) the better placed we will be to avoid these problems and provide care for others.

Potential harm to others

The other main risk in not developing personally as a clinical psychologist is the potential we have to hinder the progress of, or even cause psychological harm to, others. The potential to cause damage is great if we have major areas of difficulty with self-awareness and how we relate to others. This may include the service users and carers with whom we work, and may also include our colleagues, trainees and people within our wider work system. We cannot ignore our position of power and with this the potential to do harm that comes with our roles.

Modelling: 'practicing what we preach'

As clinical psychologists it is our responsibility to ensure that we model personal development. We ask the service users and carers with whom we work to do this within our direct and indirect clinical work. We ask our colleagues to do this within supervision/mentoring. We ask our trainees to do this within their training – in many different ways. To have face validity we must 'practise what we preach' and show not just by what we say, but also by what we do, that developing personally is imperative.

Effectiveness – helping ourselves and others
By focussing on personal development our profession is helping us to help ourselves and to help others. There is great potential for this to snowball – the more we develop ourselves the more we are able to gain help to develop further. The more confident we are in knowing ourselves, understanding how we relate to others and recognizing aspects of our hidden selves, the more confident we will be to explore this further. This in turn will help us to understand more fully the service users and carers with whom we work, and our colleagues, and enable us to work alongside them in a more effective manner.

Ethical practice

In summary, the importance of developing personally as a clinical psychologist is to be able to engage in ethical practice. This is in line with the BPS Code of Ethics and Conduct (2006), particularly sections 2.3 (Standards of Recognising Limits of Competence) and 2.4 (Standards of Recognising Impairments). If we are in a process of continuing to personally develop, whatever our role as a clinical psychologist, we can be confident we are doing the best we can to practise as safely and ethically as possible.

Methods in Personal Development

There are a number of studies that show evidence that a variety of methods can be helpful in developing personally. These include:

- therapy (for example, Orlinsky, Norcross, Ronnestad and Wiseman 2005)
- supervision (for example, Arvidsson, Löfgren and Fridlund 2000)
- groups (for example, Lennie 2007)
- mentoring (for example, Melnyk 2007)
- coaching (for example, Guthrie and Alexander 2007: 63–70)

Later chapters will focus in more depth on the effectiveness of supervision (Chapter 7), therapy (Chapter 8) and groupwork (Chapter 9) in personal development.

Theories of Change and Development Relevant to Personal Development

Theories of change

There are a number of different theoretical models of change which may add to our understanding of how we develop. The two most well-known models are Prochaska and DiClemente's (1983) Trans-theoretical Model of Change and the Assimilation Model (Barkham, Stiles, Hardy and Field 1996). The stages of change within Prochaska and DiClemente's model are:

* *precontemplation* – no action for change is planned in the foreseeable future;
* *contemplation* – intention for change is planned within the next few months and the advantages and disadvantages of change are being considered;
* *preparation* – action is planned in the next few weeks and a plan has been made;
* *action* – specific and overt actions for change are taken;
* *maintenance* – relapse prevention is the focus and confidence in continued change is high.

The stages of change in the Assimilation model are:

0   *Warded Off*: individual is unaware of the problem;
1   *Unwanted Thoughts*: individual prefers not to think about the problem;
2   *Emergence*: individual acknowledges problem but cannot formulate;
3   *Problem Clarification*: clear statement of problem;
4   *Insight*: problem is formulated and understood;
5   *Application*: understanding is used to work on problem;
6   *Problem Solution*: successful solution to a particular problem;
7   *Mastery*: individual successfully uses solutions for new problems.

Both models emphasize that in order to change (or personally develop) there are a number of processes that occur, moving from insight or awareness of the problem through to behavioural change.

Learning theories

There is a vast literature on differing learning theories, with some parallels and themes merging with the models of change literature. It is not possible within the scope of this chapter to cover all relevant theories, rather to provide some highlights for the reader. In particular, there are links with experiential learning theory, for example, Kolb's experiential learning cycle (1984). There is a similar process of moving through stages in a process of learning (and therefore change). This model describes how individuals learn new knowledge through a cyclical process of experiencing, reflecting, abstract conceptualization and active experimentation. Moon reviews a number of papers on experiential learning and compares the stages of reflection identified in each. She concludes that although the authors come from very different backgrounds it is possible to identify stages of reflection common to them all (Moon 1999).

Within learning theories there is a continuum of learning. In surface learning the process that occurs is rote learning or the reproduction of ideas with little linkage between them. At the other end of the continuum, deeper learning occurs where learning is meaningful, the world is restructured and information is assimilated. This has also been termed transformational learning (Mezirow and Associates 2000). To achieve transformational learning the change must occur 'as a person', in a holistic manner, or in other words, the person must personally develop.

Reflective practice

It was evident from the special edition of *Clinical Psychology* in July 2003 (Special Issue: 'Reflective Practice') that the term 'personal development' has, for many clinical psychologists, been synonymous with reflective practice. The term 'reflective practice' has been used within education for many years with an emphasis on the original and developed work of Schön (Schön 1983, 1987). As cited in Chapter 2, within psychology Lavender has expanded Schön's work for utilization in clinical psychology training (Lavender 2003). Lavender uses Schön's concepts of reflection in action and reflection on action and adds reflection about impact on others, and reflection about self (awareness and development). Other authors within education advocate reflection within a number of dimensions, including Ghaye and Ghaye's model of reflection on values, practice, improvement and context (Ghaye and Ghaye 1998). In terms of the operationalization of these models or concepts there can be problems with the terms being applied either too loosely or rigidly. At one end of the continuum there have been criticisms within clinical psychology of reflective practice being too woolly, unscientific and nebulous a concept to be useful. At the other end of the continuum the term has been used too prescriptively and in an instrumental manner, as a way of 'ticking the box' to ensure personal development has been undertaken, but not taking into account the individual. Boud reflects on whether the individualistic notion of reflective practice is now an out-dated concept, with current emphasis in education being about learning in context. He concludes that rather than the wholesale rejection of the notion of reflective practice we should adapt the concept to be reflection in practice/context, with the acceptance that reflection is conducted within groups or team settings (Boud 2007).

The Johari window

The Johari window (illustrated in Figure 3.1) was developed by two American psychologists exploring group dynamics, Joseph Luft and Harry Ingram. It has since been used in many different arenas to explore

	Known to self	Unknown to self
Known to others	Public Self You and others know	Blind Self Others know but you don't
Unknown to others	Hidden Self You know but others don't	Unknown Self You and others don't know

Figure 3.1   Johari window

individual development, group processes and management development. The Johari window consists of four 'panes'. The first is the part of the self that is open to ourselves and open to others: it is that which is in the public arena, the Public Self. There are other parts of ourselves of which we are aware but that we prefer to keep hidden from others. This is the Hidden Self. We all have a Blind Self, the parts of ourselves that other people may know but of which we are unaware. The final pane is called the Unknown Self, those aspects of our selves which neither we nor others know. The function of personal development within this model is to increase the public self, to allow the self to become more known to others and to oneself.

Integrated Model of Personal Development

This section aims to integrate the above definitions, models, concepts and theories and to build on them in the context of clinical psychology. Ideas from the reflective practice literature suggest that development be located in the wider context or community within which the individual works. Figure 3.2 illustrates the many realms within which personal development can take place, building and expanding upon Mearns's model. It is inherent within the model that each realm overlaps and affects the other realms.

At the heart of this diagram is the self: self-knowledge, awareness and understanding. Some aspects of the self may be conscious and others may be unknown or hidden (see Johari window). Inherent to this is the individual's self-identity, including aspects of difference and diversity – ethnicity, disability, sexuality, class, etc. This is the focus of Chapter 6 by Davidson and Patel. In the next realm there is understanding (and being able to act on this understanding) one's self in relation to others. Some of this process may be shown to others and some may be kept hidden. The wider realm is personal development in the context of the individual's life. Included within this are the individual's identity with the community within which they live, that is, all the groupings with whom we clearly identify (see Chapter 6), and also the effect of the community on the individual. In the widest realm there is personal development in relation to differing and multiple roles at work. The argument for developing personally has been put forward by other professions with a primary role as a therapist/counsellor. The same should surely apply to clinical psychologists for whom this is also a primary role. But what about the other roles in which we are

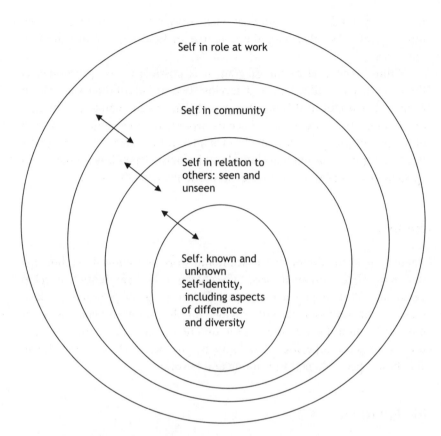

Figure 3.2 Realms of personal development

trained to engage: supervision, team working, consultancy, leadership, organizational work, managing, teaching, training and researching?

Reflecting on these roles, it is clear that none of them are possible in isolation. To be a clinical psychologist is to work in partnership and to work in relation to others. Who we are in relation to others and our community, and our awareness of this, has been highlighted as a major issue in personal development. Often these roles involve being in a position of power, with levels of responsibility for others. Clinical psychologists may face challenges, conflicts, dilemmas and strong dynamics and projections. In order to be effective we need to be aware of ourselves and our patterns of relating to others. We need to know how we operate and how we are perceived. We need to be able to contain high levels of stress or anxiety or uncertainty. We have the potential when working in partnership to help others greatly. We also have the potential to hinder or harm others or ourselves.

Within every level of the diagram it is possible to use psychological theory to help us understand and develop. Two strands of theory have been proposed as useful in this process, namely models of change and models of learning. These theories have been incorporated into a model of personal development processes described in Chapter 4. But others may be equally important for any individual clinical psychologist, depending on their own epistemological position, training, model or personal experiences.

Summary

There seems little doubt that to train and work as a clinical psychologist within the NHS individuals need to be able to show their ability to develop personally. This chapter has explored the meanings of personal development in different contexts and provided an illustration of personal development in clinical psychology within different realms. In Chapter 4 this is used to map out a personal development process which, it is hoped, will aid clinical psychologists in training and beyond.

REFERENCES

Arvidsson, B., Löfgren, H. and Fridlund, B. (2000). 'Psychiatric Nurses' Conceptions of How Group Supervision in Nursing Care Influences Their Professional Competence'. *Journal of Nursing Management*, 8: 175–85.

Barkham, M., Stiles, W. B., Hardy, G. E. and Field, S. D. (1996). 'The Assimilation Model: Theory, Research and Practical Guidelines'. In Windy Dryden (ed.), *Research in Counselling and Psychotherapy: Practical Applications*. Thousand Oaks, CA: Sage Publications, Inc.

Beinart, H. (2004). 'Models of Supervision and the Supervisory Relationship and Their Evidence Base'. In I. Fleming and L. Steen (eds.), *Supervision and Clinical Psychology*. Hove: Brunner-Routledge.

Bennett-Levy, J. (2006). 'Therapy Skills: A Cognitive Model of Their Acquisition and Refinement'. *Behavioural and Cognitive Psychotherapy*, 34: 57–78.

Boud, D. (2007). 'Rehabilitation or Rejection? Relocating Reflection in the Context of Practice'. Paper presented at Standing Conference on University Teaching and Research on the Education of Adults. University of Leeds.

British Psychological Society (2006). *Code of Ethics and Conduct*. Leicester: British Psychological Society.

British Psychological Society (2007). *Criteria for Postgraduate Courses in Clinical Psychology*. Leicester: British Psychological Society.

Burn, G. (2007). *Personal Development All-In-One for Dummies*. Chichester: Wiley.

Campbell, D. (2000). *The Socially Constructed Organisation*. London: Karmac Books.

Caplan, G. (1970). *The Theory and Practice of Mental Health Consultation*. London: Tavistock Publications Ltd.

Clark, M. (1986). 'Personal Therapy: A Review of Empirical Research'. *Professional Psychology: Research and Practice*, 17: 541–3.

Cross, M. and Papadopoulos, L. (2001). *Becoming a Therapist: A Manual for Personal and Professional Development*. Hove: Brunner-Routledge.

Department of Health (2004a). *Ten Essential Shared Capabilities: A Framework for the Whole of the Mental Health Workforce*. London: HMSO.

Department of Health (2004b). *The NHS Knowledge and Skills Framework (KSF) and the Development Review Process*. London: HMSO.

Donati, M. and Watts, M. (2005). 'Personal Development in Counsellor Training: Towards a Clarification of Inter-Related Concepts'. *British Journal of Guidance and Counselling*, 33(4): 475–84.

Ghaye, A. and Ghaye, K. (1998). *Teaching and Learning through Critical Reflective Practice*. London: David Fulton.

Gilbert, P. and Leahy, R. L. (2007). *The Therapeutic Relationship in the Cognitive Behavioural Psychotherapies*. New York: Routledge/Taylor & Francis Group.

Gillmer, B. and Marckus, R. (2003). 'Personal Professional Development in Clinical Psychology Training: Surveying Reflective Practice'. *Clinical Psychology*, 27: 20–3.

Golding, L. and Gray, I. (2006). *Continuing Professional Development for Clinical Psychologists: A Practical Handbook*. Oxford: Blackwell.

Goleman, D., Boyatzis, R. E. and McKee, A. (2003). *The New Leaders: Transforming the Art of Leadership*. London: Time Warner.

Guthrie, V. A. and Alexander, J. R. (2007). 'Coaching for Effective Action: A Core Leadership Process'. In M. Goldsmith and L. Lyons, *Coaching for Leadership: The Practice of Leadership Coaching from the World's Greatest Coaches* (2nd edn). San Diego, CA: Pfeiffer & Company.

Holtforth, M. G. and Castonguay, L. G. (2005). 'Relationships and Techniques in Cognitive Behaviour Therapy: A Motivational Approach'. *Psychotherapy: Therapy, Practice, Research, Training*, 42(4): 443–55.

Horvath, A. O. and Bedi, R. P. (2002). 'The Alliance'. In J. C. Norcross (ed.), *Psychotherapy Relationships That Work*. New York: Oxford University Press.

Irving, J. A. and Williams, D. J. (1999). 'Personal Growth and Personal Development: Concepts Clarified'. *British Journal of Guidance and Counselling*, 27(4): 517–26.

Johns, H. (1996). *Personal Development in Counsellor Training*. London: Cassell.

Kolb, D. A. (1984). *Experiential Learning – Experience as the Source of Learning and Development*. Englewood Cliffs, NJ: Prentice Hall.

Lavender, T. (2003). 'Redressing the Balance: The Place, History and Future of Reflective Practice in Training'. *Clinical Psychology*, 27: 11–15.

Lennie, C. (2007). 'The Role of Personal Development Groups in Counsellor Training; Understanding Factors Contributing to Self Awareness in the Personal Development Group'. *British Journal of Guidance and Counselling*, 35(1): 115–29.

Martin, D. J., Garske, J. P. and Davis, M. K. (2000). 'Relation of the Therapeutic Alliance with Outcome and Other Variables: A Meta-Analytic Review'. *Journal of Consulting and Clinical Psychology*, 68: 438–50.

Maslow, A. H. (1943). 'A Theory of Human Motivation'. *Psychological Review*, 50: 370–96.

Mearns, D. (1997). *Person-Centred Counsellor Training*. London: Sage.

Melnyk, B. (2007). 'The Latest Evidence on the Outcomes of Mentoring'. *Worldviews on Evidence Based Nursing*, 4(3): 170–3.

Mezirow, J. and Associates (2000). *Learning as Transformation. Critical Perspectives on a Theory in Progress*. San Francisco: Jossey-Bass.

Moon, J. (1999). *Reflection in Learning and Personal Development: Theory and Practice*. London: RoutledgeFalmer.

Norcross, J. N., (ed.) (2002). *Psychotherapy Relationships That Work*. New York: Oxford University Press.

Orlinsky, D. E., Botermans, J.-F. and Ronnestad, M. H. (2001). 'Towards an Empirically Grounded Model of Psychotherapy Training: Four Thousand Therapists Rate Influences on Their Development'. *Australian Psychologist*, 36(2): 139–48.

Orlinsky, D. E. and Ronnestad, M. H. (2005). 'How Psychotherapists Develop: A Study of Therapeutic Work and Professional Growth'. Washington, DC: American Psychological Association.

Orlinsky, D. E., Norcross, J. C., Ronnestad, M. H. and Wiseman, H. (2005). 'Outcomes and Impacts of the Psychotherapist's Own Psychotherapy: A Research Review'. In: J. D. Geller, J. C. Norcross and D. E. Orlinsky, *The Psychotherapist's Own Psychotherapy*. New York: Oxford University Press.

Prochaska, J. O. and DiClemente, C. C. (1983). 'Stages and Processes of Self-Change of Smoking: Toward an Integrative Model of Change'. *Journal of Consulting and Clinical Psychology*, 51: 390–5.

Ronnestad, M. H. and Skovholt, T. M. (2003). 'The Journey of the Counselor and Therapist: Research Findings and Perspectives on Professional Development'. *Journal of Career Development*, 30(1): 5–44.

Schön, D. A. (1983). *The Reflective Practitioner*. London: Basic Books.

Schön, D. A. (1987). *Educating the Reflective Practitioner*. London: Basic Books.

Sheikh, A. I., Milne, D. L. and Macgregor, B. V. (2007). 'A Model of Personal Professional Development in the Systematic Training of Clinical Psychologists'. *Clinical Psychology & Psychotherapy*, 14(4): 278–87.

Sheikh, A. I., Milne, D. L. and MacGregor, B. V. (forthcoming). 'A Model for Improving Psychological Therapy Services through "Personal Professional Development"'. *Clinical Psychology and Psychotherapy*.

Thompson, A. R. (2007). 'Supervision of Qualitative Research: Towards a Competency Framework'. Paper delivered at the Annual Interpretative Phenomenological Analysis Conference, Brighton.

Waddington, L. (2002). 'The Therapy Relationship in Cognitive Therapy: A Review'. *Behavioural and Cognitive Psychotherapy*, 30: 179–91.

Walsh, S. and Scaife, J. M. (1998). 'Mechanisms for Addressing Personal and Professional Development in Clinical Training'. *Clinical Psychology Forum*, 115: 21–4.

Wampold, B. E. (2001). *The Great Psychotherapy Debate: Models, Methods and Findings*. Mahwah, NJ: Lawrence Erlbaum Associates.

West, M. (2004). *Effective Teamwork: Practical Lessons for Organisational Research (Psychology of Work and Organisations)*. Oxford: Blackwell.

Wilkins, P. (1997). *Personal and Professional Development for Counsellors*. London: Sage Publications Ltd.

Chapter 4

A Model of Personal Development Processes

Sheila Youngson and Jan Hughes

Introduction

In this chapter a proposed model of personal development processes is gradually built, utilizing the information provided in the preceding chapters. This is not an attempt to prescribe a fixed process, rather to offer some guidance it is hoped will aid the reader. This is linked to our assertion that personal development is an individual and idiosyncratic process. At first glance the model can seem linear; however, it is, in fact, circular at many points, and this is the emphasis. The reader is guided through the process using an illustrative example. Examples are also used throughout to illustrate the use of this model within different realms of personal development (self, self in relation, self in community, self in role) and within the different roles of a clinical psychologist. Potential barriers to personal development and ways to overcome them are offered. Finally, an extended metaphor is used to illustrate personal growth.

The Model

Clues

The first hint that an issue may need attention can be described as a 'clue'. Clues come in a whole variety of guises and may not be immediately obvious to the individual, while others are an inescapable message. They may be internal, within us, a message from our selves, or external, a message from others. They may be an intense single experience or an ongoing sense

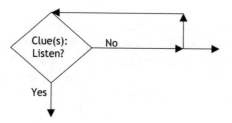

Figure 4.1   Clues in personal development

that something is 'not quite right'. Examples of clues within the four realms of personal development include the following:

Self
- a feeling that threatens to overwhelm, e.g., sadness, anger
- physical tension and pain, e.g., recurrent headaches
- intrusive thoughts, e.g., I can't manage this
- a sense of existential discomfort, e.g., I'm not good enough
- an unhelpful coping strategy, e.g., drinking too much
- a wish to learn more about self

Self in relation
- a feeling of dissatisfaction, e.g., with partner
- intrusive thoughts, e.g., I'm compromising too much with my parent
- a sense of existential discomfort, e.g., relationships never work for me
- a damaging action in relation, e.g., withdrawing from friends
- a wish to learn more about self in relation

Self in community
- feelings of guilt about oppressing others, e.g., I have excluded others; feelings of anger about being oppressed, e.g., I have been excluded
- persistent thoughts, e.g., I need to know about identity and its importance
- an existential discomfort, e.g., where do I fit and what is my role?
- acting in a discriminatory way, e.g., a member of my community tells me that I have made many assumptions and acted on prejudice
- a wish to learn more about self in relation to community

Self in multiple roles
- panicky feelings when faced with a new service user
- thoughts of inadequacy, e.g., my supervisee knows more than me
- a sense of existential discomfort, e.g., I'm not able to lead others
- compulsive actions, e.g., always over-preparing for teaching
- a wish to learn more about self in relation to self in multiple roles

Some of the clues involve a negative driver – a need to change negative feelings, thoughts, senses and actions. Another aspect of personal development may be proactively searching out 'clues'. This could involve the individual putting him- or herself in the position of gaining new clues, for example, of experimenting with new situations, relationships, groups or engaging in training that will by its very nature challenge the person's sense of self.

Clues may be intermittent or persistent, quiet or loud, subtle or inescapable. Individuals may respond immediately or wait a while or simply not be able to 'hear'. If a clue is heard – what next?

Worked example: clue

Ann would often turn up late for her supervision session. I noticed my irritation but did not make comment. (Did not listen to internal clue - feeling.)

Ann cancelled a session and I did not immediately contact her to offer a replacement time. (Did not listen to internal clue - behaviour.)

A colleague described a supervision group he was facilitating. I reflected on what a useful service he was providing. In comparison I felt a sense of guilt over the poor service I was offering Ann. I decided to reflect more on this. (An external prompt triggered an internal clue to which I did listen.)

Internal reflection

In listening to the clue we enter in to a phase of reflection, considering the meaning of the clue. This may occur over a short or prolonged period. As a general or common-sense definition of reflection, Moon (1999) states that reflection involves thinking that is driven 'either by a purpose or by the expectation of some form of desired outcome'. Within this model the purpose of reflection is to try and to assimilate this clue within the sense of self: 'Do I understand what this clue is all about and is that enough?'

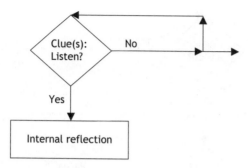

Figure 4.2   Internal reflection in personal development

Worked example: internal reflection

I reflected on my work with Ann and wondered why I was behaving differently with her by not exploring why she was late and not offering an alternative appointment for the cancelled one? I asked myself, 'What makes Ann different?'

I also asked myself, 'Are you affording Ann less respect and value because she is a nurse? and do I have an unconscious value system in operation?' I reflected on all my interactions and working relationships with other nurses, and concluded that this did not feel right. I felt that the problem lay in something that was happening between the two of us. Thus, whilst I had ruled out one possibility, I was no nearer knowing or understanding what this was about.

I resumed internal reflection and asked myself, 'What are your feelings towards Ann?' I reflected that I respected the person and the work that she did, and I felt warmth towards her. However, I also felt irritation and frustration within supervisory sessions and I questioned what that was about.

Awareness and understanding

The internal reflection process may result in a good knowledge and understanding of the issue ('I know what this is about and I know what to do'). This may require no further action and this knowledge and understanding can be assimilated, resulting in personal growth and application. However, the individual may have a partial knowledge and understanding of the issue ('I have some sense of what this is about, but it's not clear, and I'm not sure what to do about it'). In this situation there is a need to engage in further internal reflection, to try and gain further insight. Individuals may

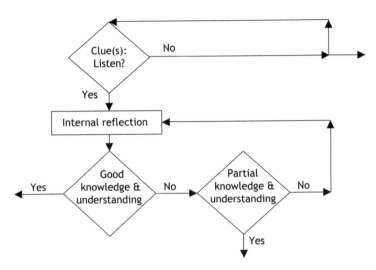

Figure 4.3 Awareness and understanding in personal development

revolve around this loop several times, gradually gaining (and possibly losing at times) insight into the issue. At a point in this process the individual has a decision to make about the impact of change.

Worked example: awareness and understanding

I came up with a list of things Ann didn't do in supervisory sessions. She didn't stay on topic, she didn't self-reflect, she didn't sit and think, and so on. I gradually realized that I have a somewhat rigid sense of how people should be in supervision and how they should use the time. I also realized that Ann's prior experience of supervision would have been very different from mine. I concluded that I needed to explore with Ann how we could use the supervision time, and I needed to explore my potential rigidity around supervision. I had reached the point of some partial knowledge and understanding.

Assess the impact of change

At this juncture an individual enters into a decision-making process about if/how much to invest in a course of further change. A number of factors may influence this decision, including the impact on self and the impact

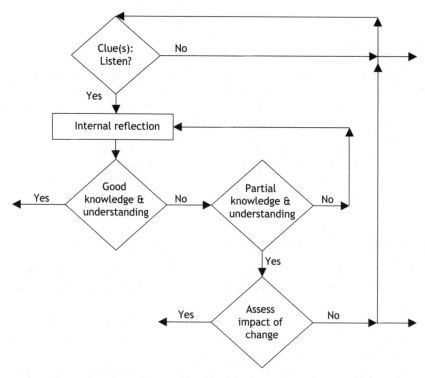

Figure 4.4   Assessing the impact of change

on others. Some issues may be so strong or have reached such a crescendo that there is really very little choice – the impact on self and/or others of not acting may be untenable. Alternatively, this may be something the individual has lived with for a long time and making a decision to change may include overcoming some of the barriers described below. The individual may decide at this point not to attend to the clue any longer; to try and let it dissipate and dissolve away. This may work, particularly in the short term, or it may re-emerge as the same or a different clue. Considering stages in the process of change described in Chapter 3 may help the individual make this choice; for example, in terms of the Prochaska and DiClemente (1983) model, is the individual in the contemplative or preparation stage? If an individual decides to focus on the clue and engage further in the change process this can be done using a variety of methods.

Worked example: assessing the impact of change

I was now feeling increasingly uncomfortable, as I questioned my perception of myself as fluid and flexible. I realized it was possible that I might have to face a significant reappraisal of my sense of self. However I also had a sense that in exploring this further, I might become a better supervisor overall, and I certainly hoped I might become a better supervisor for Ann.

I was also aware of an inner voice that was trying to minimize the impact of change by saying that other supervisees liked my model of supervision. I decided to pursue an external method of personal development and to discuss this situation in my own supervision.

Internal and external methods of personal development

Methods of focussing on change may differ in the four realms of personal development and include internal/intra-psychic processes and/or external methods. Some examples of personal development methods are provided in Chapter 7 (supervision), Chapter 8 (therapy) and Chapter 9 (personal development groups). An individual may decide to focus on one method (either internal or external) to see if this helps aid good knowledge and understanding. If this does not work another method may be chosen, again either internal or external. Alternatively, more than one method of personal development may be engaged at the same time. For some, internal methods of personal development may be more attractive, for example, for individuals who learn more through the reflective process. For those who prefer learning through action, the external methods of personal development may be more appealing. Whilst it is understandable for someone to choose an approach with which they personally feel easier, it may be that engaging in less comfortable and familiar processes could help encourage change. An individual may go around this loop a number of times until eventually they have a good knowledge and understanding of the issue – leading to personal growth and application.

Some key personal development methods include:

Self (internal)
- reflection
- meditation
- creative writing, e.g., journals/diaries

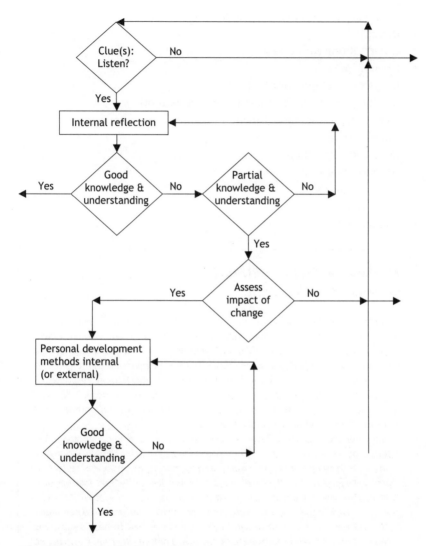

Figure 4.5   Methods of personal development

- reading
- prayer
- problem-solving
- literature and music
- sport
- specific personal development exercises, e.g., timelines, genograms

Self in relation/community/multiple roles (external)
- therapy
- conversations with others
- supervision
- personal development groups
- specific personal development exercises with others
- comparing to role model/mentors within work or community
- training courses
- feedback from others
- community groups
- religious groups
- social action
- political action

Worked example: methods of personal development

My preferred style of being in my own supervision is to take to each session 'myself in relation to my work'. Thus, in my next supervision session, I gave voice to my reflections concerning my supervision of Ann, along with all my thoughts and feelings. Together, my supervisor and I explored possible underlying meanings for me. This involved both internal musings in response to prompts and further voicing, and more straightforward dialogue. Thus you could say that supervision, for me, is a bringing together of internal and external methods of personal development.

Together we reached a level of more knowledge and understanding. We agreed that there were some good practice standards relating to supervision, for example, turning up on time, being prepared, demonstrating a level of reflective capacity. Beyond those, there was room for more flexibility, and just because most of the people I supervised 'fitted in' with my ways in supervision, that didn't mean it was the only way. I reflected more on this and wondered how much I had 'required' others to fit in with my way, and resolved to have discussions around this at reviews. I realized that I did have a potentially rigid construct or schema about how supervisees should be in supervision, related to my person-centred model, and that this needed to be more flexible. I saw from where this had evolved based on past personal and professional experiences.

We resolved to talk more about this, considering whether some of this needed further exploration in personal therapy.

We also talked about Ann's professional background, and her past experiences and expectations of supervision and its meaning, and I decided to talk with Ann about this.

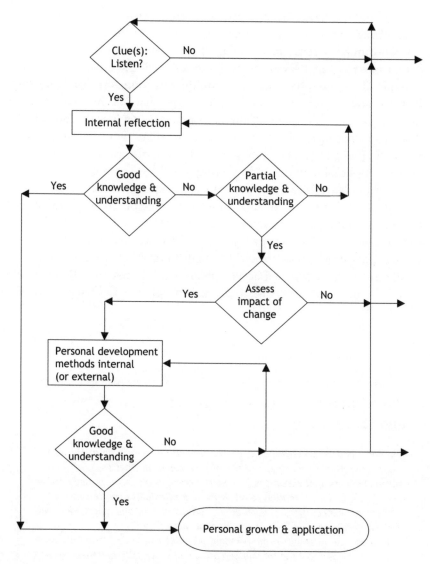

Figure 4.6   A model of personal development processes

Personal growth and application

This leads to the end of the flow diagram. An individual may have gone
through many different processes (or not) and used many different methods

(or not) and will have reached a place of personal growth and application. Here, change will have occurred on many levels and the person will have a new/assimilated sense of self. The change can have occurred mainly within one realm; however, this will also affect all the other realms. For example, change may have occurred with the first realm, involving internal methods and resulting in intra-psychic change, new insights and perceptions of self. This, however, will also have an impact on how the individual develops within their relationships, in their roles and in their community. Similarly, the change may have occurred primarily within a work role involving external methods and resulting in a change in behaviour within role. However, this will also have an impact on intra-psychic processes. The individual will have experimented with a new sense of self, that is, applied this understanding and knowledge to new situations and taken risks to act and be different. Personal development therefore involves both intra-psychic and interpersonal change. But that is not the end. We are all constantly in a state of personal development, and it is just a matter of time before the next clue shows itself and we engage in a further process of change.

Worked example: personal growth and exploration

Ann and I had a conversation about our supervisory relationship. She talked about supervision in nursing, and the differences from what I was offering. I talked about my realization that my way of being as a supervisor had become quite fixed, and my intention to allow for more flexibility. We re-contracted, with clearer expectations of each other, and it felt that our supervisory relationship deepened, and both of us valued it more.

In summary, in terms of my personal growth I had learnt that I did have quite fixed ideas about the content and process of supervision and these needed to become more flexible. It also made me reflect on whether I had fixed views on other aspects of my working relationships and life generally. In terms of the application of this learning I decided to ask for feedback from my supervisees about my style and model of supervision and whether it felt useful to them. I also decided to talk further about this in my own supervision (external method). Finally, I decided to reflect further on my approaches to other relationships (internal method).

Barriers to Personal Development

Whilst personal development frequently results in personal growth, it can also be a difficult and painful process. Personal growth can follow a time of individual crisis and thus become associated with emotional distress. Therefore hesitation, anxiety and avoidance are understandable occasional responses. It is important to acknowledge that with any change process there can often be a sense of loss; individuals can frequently move around the cycles of change described above (Prochaska and DiClemente 1983; Barkham, Stiles, Hardy and Field 1996) until something shifts to make them able to stay with 'action' and 'maintenance'/ 'mastery'. Finally, there can be a real sense of trepidation and fear, as we ask the question 'What will I uncover and how will it impact on my life?'

There may be tangible and actual barriers to engaging in personal development, which are explored below using the realms of personal development:

Internal barriers (self)

- Limited personal resources. Engaging in a personal development process requires a number of elements to be in place. The first (relating to self) is that the individual has enough physical and psychological reserves to engage in a change process.
- Limited knowledge/guidance. Individuals may struggle with knowing *how* to develop personally. There may be little guidance available for individuals regarding the processes and methods involved in personal development.
- Individual temperament/personality. There are a number of personality and learning style theories that may help us understand why developing personally may be more difficult for some people. For example, according to Honey and Mumford's (1984) classification of learning styles there are four primary styles of learning: Activist, Reflector, Theorist, Pragmatist. For those with a primary style as Reflector, personal development may seem more natural. For those with a different primary style, in which the focus is on learning through experience or developing theories, some difficulties may be experienced in learning to reflect and learning from reflection. Whilst reflection is not the only process in personal development, it is immensely helpful

and some individuals may have to actively adapt/learn/practise the art of reflection.

- Self-appraisal. A barrier to accurate appraisal on the need to change is self-appraisal. The literature suggests there is little evidence that any individual is a naturally accurate self-appraiser (Collins 2002). There are a number of potential biases in self-appraisal, including being over-confident about abilities or basing judgements on select memories (Collins 2002). This highlights the need to be engaged in processes that continually require receiving feedback from others.

External barriers (self in relation, self in community, self in multiple roles)

There may be a number of external barriers to personal development:

- Limited personal space. Looking after others (in relation, within community, within work roles) may make it hard to take time for one's self.
- Lack of financial resources. Support may be needed/wanted to develop personally, for example, supervision or therapy, but this may be financially difficult.
- Lack of managerial support. Personal development goals may not necessarily fit with those from management or within the wider system.
- Limited personal support. Significant others may not place as much importance on personal development: 'what's the point of all this navel gazing?'
- Difference within communities. The importance of and emphasis on personal development may vary between different groupings, for example, gender, class, ethnicity at any point in social history.
- Managing multiple and complex demands. Balancing the complex demands within family and social network, within community, with multiple workloads may mean that priority is shifted away from personal development.

Overcoming barriers

There may be ways that these barriers can be overcome. The first step is to acknowledge the existence of a barrier and to consider whether it is an internal or external, practical or resource barrier. Overcoming some barriers may involve organizing time for self, for reflective purposes, but will often also involve utilizing guidance and support from others. If there is an external resource barrier this may be overcome with a practical solution, for example, looking for therapists who offer a sliding scale of charges. If the barrier is in relation to others (significant others within family and/or community, work colleagues and managers) this may mean some negotiation and potential compromise. If the barrier(s) is an internal barrier, particularly around lack of information and guidance, then utilizing the above model may be helpful. This model may also help supervisors and managers understand the processes involved in personal development to aid their understanding of colleagues and help provide solutions to any barriers.

Personal Development and Growth: An Extended Metaphor

In discussing the model and trying to 'bring it to life' we have had many conversations using metaphors. One included the use of an orchestra, in which many different instruments are all striving to play the same symphony but in which some instruments are louder than others and some definitely in need of tuning. One method of considering your personal development is to imagine your own metaphor and allow some creative process around extending this. We offer the following extended metaphor, written by Sheila, as one example.

My archipelago – Sheila Youngson
I have a tendency to conceptualize in a visual way, and to use metaphors. Hence, for me, my personal development and the resulting growth is all about negotiating my way round my archipelago.

Today is bright and the seas are calm, and many of the islands can be seen. The tide is low so that the bridges, the connections between the islands, can be seen, and I can walk around most of the landscape without getting my feet wet. It's familiar to me, and I feel at home. Indeed I can sit and admire the view.

I can see that some bridges are just being constructed, whilst others are solid and reinforced. Some bridges are architectural flights of fancy; others are utilitarian and used to heavy traffic.

Some islands are very well known to me, and I can dare to take a different path as I wander round, sometimes discovering places I didn't know existed. Sometimes these places are very beautiful; sometimes they are overgrown and it feels like a swamp beneath my feet, but I feel carefree.

Some islands are less known, and I tend to plan my journey, tread a careful path, and take a rucksack filled with items in case of emergency. I can feel anxious here, as well as keen to explore.

Some islands are hardly known at all, and I wouldn't visit unless it was a clear day, and I'd told someone where I was going. I can feel trepidation on these days, as well as excitement at the potential for discovery.

Some islands out there I've only seen in the distance, and would only contemplate a journey if I took a companion with me. I don't know what to feel, and may not go unless I feel an imperative.

I also know that parts of every island are under water, and deep below the surface almost every island has some connection.

Many years ago, I lived on just one of these islands and tended not to explore. Now I know many of them and cross the bridges daily. About 15 years ago I consulted with a well-known architect who helped me see the best place to build connections, and that has been very helpful. Since then, I have built a number of new bridges, and I have a crew of people who will help me make the links.

Of course, it is not always calm and clear on my archipelago. Sometimes it is dark and cloudy, and the journey around the islands takes time and effort. Sometimes there can be a storm, and violent or prolonged storms can bring down bridges. However, such storms can sometimes reveal new islands to be explored, and can change the landscape so that islands are now connected without the need for a bridge.

When a clue pops up, or I uncover one, I will take it with me and walk round the archipelago, and see if it finds a home. If it doesn't I may need to go and visit that very distant island, or I may need to don the scuba gear and go diving, and, of course, one always goes diving with a 'buddy' (British Sub-Aqua Club 2007).[1]

Personal development and growth, for me, is a dynamic, ever-changing, always involving, and evolving process. It can be exhilarating, exciting, wearying, painful, absorbing, astounding, comforting, ugly, beautiful – but never, ever boring.

NOTE

1. Jan is fond of references, whilst admiring of the lyricism.

REFERENCES

Barkham, M., Stiles, W. B., Hardy, G. E., Field, S. D. (1996). 'The Assimilation Model: Theory, Research and Practical Guidelines'. In Windy Dryden (ed.), *Research in Counselling and Psychotherapy: Practical Applications.* Thousand Oaks, CA: Sage Publications, Inc.

British Sub-Aqua Club (2007). *Safe Diving.* www.bsac.org

Collins, S. (2002). 'Are Clinical Psychologists Likely to be "Naturally" Accurate Appraisers of Their Own Performance? In What Ways Can Individuals Develop and Maintain Critical Appreciation of Their Strengths and Weaknesses throughout Their Careers?' Unpublished essay. University of Leeds.

Honey, P. and Mumford, A. (1984). *A Manual of Learning Styles.* Maidenhead: McGraw-Hill.

Moon, J. A. (1999). *Reflection in Learning and Personal Development: Theory and Practice.* London: RoutledgeFalmer.

Prochaska, J. O. and DiClemente, C. C. (1983). 'Stages and Processes of Self-Change of Smoking: Toward an Integrative Model of Change'. *Journal of Consulting and Clinical Psychology,* 51: 390–5.

Chapter 5

'If They Don't Know Themselves, They Can't Help You Find Yourself, Can They Really?' Service User Perspectives on Personal Development of Clinical Psychologists

Sheila Youngson, Rebecca Hames and Tracey Holley in collaboration with Charmaine Riley, Geoff, Judy and Margaret

Introduction

Recently a mental health service user said to me, 'If it wasn't for people like me, there would be no need for people like you.' I have reflected on that moment many times. The statement is, of course, simply and profoundly true. It also reminds me, redolent as it is with the notion of a 'them' and 'us', of how very, very far there is to go, in terms of understanding power and its inequalities and all the stigma and oppressions that follow, it would seem inevitably. (See Chapter 6 for further elaboration.) How very, very far away are services that match the needs, wishes and expectations of their users. How very, very far away is a mutuality that, in reality, sees, believes and acts as if we are all on a continuum that means that at different times and stages in our lives sometimes we are the helper, and sometimes the helped.

Clinical psychology, as a profession, has been lamentably slow to address the exhortations of various governmental policies (for example, the

Disability Discrimination Act (1995), the National Service Framework for Mental Health (1999) and The Health and Social Care Act (2001)) to engage with and respond to people who use services in the planning, delivery and evaluation of those services. Further, to involve service users and carers in the planning, delivery and evaluation of the training of the workers who staff those services. However, it is true to say that some clinical psychology training courses are much more advanced than others in this respect. See, for example, the work undertaken by the universities of Surrey and Canterbury Christ Church (Goodbody, Hayward, Holttum and Riddell 2007).

However, to us it seemed vital to include service users' and carers' voices. It is clear in Chapter 3 that personal development is a requirement for clinical psychologists, from a national level (Department of Health), from a professional level (British Psychological Society, Division of Clinical Psychology) and from the level of the employer (Trust policy in line with the Knowledge and Skills Framework). However, this requirement comes largely, but not exclusively, from the practitioner frame of reference, from theory and from lived professional practice. What about the perspective of the service user and carer? It felt crucial to avoid making assumptions about the importance of personal development to those that use our services, and, instead, to gather some opinion and understand, appreciate and value their perspective.

The Search for Service Users' and Carers' Voices - Sheila Youngson

This task proved much more difficult than anticipated. A literature search initially provided over 150 potentially relevant papers. However, whilst a few looked at gender and ethnicity mix in therapeutic dyads, and a few looked at desired qualities in therapists, none directly addressed the beliefs of service users and carers of the importance or otherwise of personal development for those with whom they worked. The literature, such as it is, on service users' and carers' beliefs about the personal characteristics and qualities they wish in their therapists, have been elegantly summarized by Goodbody:

> Service users generally argue for needs-led services, for a voice in definitions
> of need, for relationships with services where power differentials are worked

with and their experiences, identities and lives beyond patienthood are acknowledged, and for a holistic view of well-being involving warmth, humanity and relationship. Broadly speaking, the focus is on the need for and value of non-specific processes and principles reflecting the human rights agenda (e.g. for dignity, respect, privacy, safety, information, cultural appropriateness, freedom from stigma and discrimination), and for recognition of the social context of people's lived experience. (Goodbody 2003)

That said, it would be a mistake, and, as Goodbody says, to miss the point, to assume this is true for all. David Green, Clinical Director, and the selection sub-committee on the clinical psychology training course at Leeds University have for a number of years increasingly involved service users and carers in the selection process. Various groups of service users and carers have been involved in consultation exercises around this process, and asked the question 'What kind of person should we be selecting for clinical psychology training?' Whilst, generally speaking, these service users and carers have highlighted characteristics involved in making friendly, non-judgemental relationships and the ability to listen, there have been some interesting and notable differences. A consultation with users of forensic services, for example, demonstrated major concerns around issues of confidentiality; and for users of services for people with learning difficulties the 'top' requirement in their clinical psychologist was that they should be reliable and turn up on time. How very telling.

We would argue that a number of the personal characteristics specified in some of these articles and consultation exercises (for example, an understanding of power and inequality, a non-judgemental attitude, cultural awareness) will be expanded through attention to personal development (see below), but the link is not clearly made.

I next went to numerous websites (for example, Mental Health in Higher Education and the Higher Education Academy, Care Services Improvement Partnership and National Institute of Mental Health in England, Mind), and still found nothing directly related to the personal development of healthcare professionals. I then approached colleagues, including service user colleagues, on a national basis, whom I knew to be heavily involved in service user and carer research, involvement projects and training, and asked if I had missed any literature. Postings were also put on various web-based discussion forums. I was directed to some interesting review articles and project reports. One was Repper and Breeze (2007), who reviewed the literature on user and carer involvement in the training and education of health professionals. As part of this review they reported three studies that looked at consumer views of what should be taught to mental health nurses. Again, the findings are that service users and carers stress humanistic qualities: warmth, care, and respect, as well as awareness of their (the professionals) own value conflicts, a non-labelling attitude and an awareness of individual differences. Thus, the emphasis is on how users wish to experience the therapeutic relationship and how they wish to be approached and perceived by the health professional. Nothing I was directed to explicitly stated that this might be achieved through personal development strategies, nor considered the importance of personal development, *per se*, for the individual health professional.

However, by good fortune, through the web postings I was put in touch with Tracey Holley, who, I discovered, was keenly interested in the work of Daniel Goleman (1995) and his concept of the 'emotionally intelligent practitioner'. In the course of talking with Tracey it seemed only right that I hand over to her the final part of this chapter for her to comment on what I had written and offer her own views and experience.

As I had found little that was directly relevant to the question 'What do service users and carers think about the importance of personal development for clinical psychologists?', it seemed useful to try and access any answers directly. Thus it was decided to convene a focus group.

A Focus Group

It was decided that we would invite a number of service users and carers to a focus group, which would be audiotaped, and to utilize a semi-structured interview schedule to elicit feelings, thoughts and beliefs about personal development and its perceived importance. Individuals were invited from the pool of service users and carers who have been involved in selection panels for the Doctoral Clinical Psychology Programme at the University of Leeds. Thus participants would have some knowledge about the training of clinical psychologists, although it is acknowledged that this might make them less representative of service users and carers at large. One of the authors of this chapter (SY) conducted the focus group, which lasted for 75 minutes. Four participants attended, admittedly a small number, although it transpired that there was a (relative) consensus in their views. All had been in a therapuetic relationship with a clinical psychologist in the past. The design and content of the semi-structured interview was piloted with a researcher who is also a former service user.

The participants were provided with a definition of personal development and then asked whether they thought it was important that the clinical psychologist they had seen (or might see) to have completed some personal development. This led to a discussion of their own experiences of clinical psychologists, and further developed into sharing ideas about what qualities and characteristics were helpful in a clinical psychologist, both personally and interpersonally. Finally, there was discussion around the different roles psychologists might have: supervisor, teacher, researcher, consultant, leader and manager.

Analysis of the transcript – Rebecca Hames

The focus group transcript was analysed using Thematic Framework Analysis (Ritchie and Spencer 1994). This is an approach that has been developed for applied qualitative research, in which it has been used to meet specific information needs and facilitate actionable outcomes. The process involves identifying emerging themes with a sub-sample of the raw data in order to develop a coding framework that is then applied to the complete transcript. This approach to analysis allows reconsideration and reworking of ideas, following an iterative method, and is facilitated by a clearly documented and accessible process.

The full analysis of the transcript will not be detailed here, but rather the major emerging themes will be outlined and discussed.

Summary of the focus group discussions

These were rich discussions. What can we draw from them?

Firstly, personal development is also a difficult concept for service users and carers to define and articulate.

'I think the skills and techniques were definitely there, um, it was hard to explain.'

'Some of the psychologists [I have seen] in the past definitely needed some personal development, I mean it's a tricky one for me, is that.'

'Personal development, it was there; I mean I don't think there was anything to develop.'

For these participants, concerns about whether a clinical psychologist had undertaken any personal development had not been relevant when they had commenced their therapy, their own psychological distress being paramount.

'To be honest, no, [personal development] wasn't important to me . . . when I first started seeing the psychologist I was too wrapped up in myself in a way.'

'My own thoughts were [my priority] in the first instance, cos I had seen quite a few psychologists in my time.'

It would seem that personal development is largely assumed, and sub-sumed under the notion of professional competency. Thus, if an experience of therapy with a clinical psychologist had been helpful, and the participants were clearly able to determine when this was so, then that psychologist had probably developed personally. Equally, participants were well able to tell when their therapy had not been helpful, and identify characteristics in the clinical psychologist that contributed to that outcome, for example, being incomprehensible, not listening, having their own agenda.

'I think understanding is one of the words I would use, [the psychologist] didn't have that, he didn't seem to appreciate what I was saying to him.'

'I got the impression that they didn't understand my problems, my struggles.'

'A lot of the things he asked went way over my head . . . I didn't understand half the things he was saying to me, he was a little bit too technical, and I just couldn't understand what he was talking about.'

Having understood that, there was a sense, a feeling, that personal development could be important. There was a need for the clinical psy-chologist to contain and 'stay with' strong emotions.

'I think it is important, but only like . . . it's about them [the psychologist] being strong enough themselves . . . so they know they can cope with what-ever the pain is.'

'I needed someone who I felt could manage the amount of upset and sadness and fear that I felt at that time.'

And, relatedly, the psychologist needed to be emotionally robust and manage their own stress, and there was a concern that what the service user needed to say might be 'too much', and almost a sense of taking it slowly so as not to overwhelm the psychologist.

> 'I suppose that these worry me a few times as well when I ask myself have I just made them feel uncomfortable or whatever?'

> 'When I first saw a psychologist one of the things I worried a lot about was whether I was too much for this person, whether they could actually cope with what I was talking to them about.'

Interestingly, what was not clearly vocalized was the possibility that a clinical psychologist might be ineffectual or even damaging if they had not paid attention to their own personal issues, difficulties and attitudes. It seems that personal development, or the desired outcome of personal development, is regarded as very much a relational, interpersonal issue, rather than an internal one.

However, what does seem clear is that central for these participants were a number of personal qualities in the clinical psychologist, and the quality of the interactions between the clinical psychologist and others. These are outlined in Table 5.1. This list of desired essential characteristics and interpersonal abilities are similar in many respects to those mentioned above. Many, if not all these essential qualities are related to the ability of the clinical psychologist to make and maintain containing, non-judgemental and safe therapeutic relationships, and relationships where difference and power imbalances are addressed. It is argued that these are all abilities and skills in which personal development plays a central role.

Finally, when the group was asked to consider the various roles clinical psychologists might undertake, personal development was seen as very important in at least three respects. Firstly, that without it, individual assumptions and prejudices could affect what is considered as important, the approach to others, and the direction taken.

> 'If you were a clinical psychologist and you were supervising and you haven't really any personal development then you might not give space to the person you're supervising.'

> 'And if you're going into a team, say you're going into a team and they're struggling, perhaps they're not getting on, you know they're not getting on

Table 5.1 Desired qualities of a clinical psychologist from a service user perspective

Desired qualities of the psychologist	Illustrations from focus group discussion
Personal qualities	
Respectful approach	'I think it takes a special kind of person to be a psychologist; you know, in the way you have to treat people and your attitude towards them.'
	'Respectful; you know, they treat you with respect.'
Strength and experience	'There is something about just feeling that the person is going to be strong enough somehow, or is experienced enough.'
	'I needed to feel they were robust.'
	'In my view that person needs to be psychologically mature to be able to support you.'
Attitude towards work	'You need to basically feel that it's a vocation for them, not just a job where they are getting paid to listen to you or whatever.'
Calm approach, no anxiety	'If the psychologist is very anxious then it's difficult to communicate confidence.'
	'Someone who is fairly centred as well, calm.'
Confidence	'Helping somebody set goals, that takes quite a bit of confidence from the psychologist, it's quite an active approach really.'
Knowing themselves	'I think knowing yourself can give you extra strength.'
	'If they don't know themselves they can't help you find yourself, can they really?'
Interpersonal qualities	
Creating a safe space	'When I saw a therapist it was important to feel safe.'
Listening	'A good listener . . . um . . . attentive as well to everything.'
	'Someone who can recognize what you might not be able to say.'
Being non-judgemental	'Um . . . non-judgemental, so you feel you can say almost anything without feeling that you've said something wrong.'
Being objective	'Um . . . be objective'
	'If they [psychologists] identify with me too much then they wouldn't be able to know what difficulties I was having.'

Table 5.1 *Continued*

Desired qualities of the psychologist	Illustrations from focus group discussion
Being trustworthy	'Trust, trusting the person, confidentiality that they showed you, so you know you were okay saying something.'
Being aware of difference, and of power	'I definitely at times have needed somebody that could be . . . knew we were different as well as how we were the same, to be able to put themselves in my shoes in some ways but not carry all their stuff with them.' 'There's something about recognizing the position of power they are in . . . and feeling unable to say something.'

with the people they're working with . . . then if you go in as a consultant, or a clinical psychologist is brought in, they can get drawn into that disagreement if they don't know themselves.'

'If there is a prejudice which is already established within the staff team towards perhaps a client they are working with, then if it's coming back to the clinical psychologist and they hold the same prejudice, then in the end who is going to stand for that client because what you've got is a group of people representing them.'

'You know what you're bringing, and if you have a prejudice about a particular thing, you might communicate that in your teaching to others.'

'I suppose if they are coming up with [the research] questions then if they are not aware then they might only ask the questions that they think are important and not ask or wait to see what are the sort of questions from the people they're doing the research with.'

Secondly, that a degree of self-knowledge and awareness will help the clinical psychologist maintain the necessary distance and objectivity needed in various settings.

'That was what was good about my psychologist, you knew that she cared but she was very objective at the same time.'

'If the psychologist doesn't feel very clear about who they are really in that situation, there is something about being able to remain, it's a bit like the therapy thing . . . remaining objective.'

And thirdly, overarchingly, that personal development would help develop and maintain professional standards and ethical behaviour.

'When you're overseeing things, you've got so many things to think about [and if] you don't know how to handle stress, you're not going to be able to help anyone, are you?'

'I suppose it [personal development] might affect how you treat people within the group you are teaching.'

Summary

What can we conclude.? Service users and carers seem clear on a number of points. They want to meet clinical psychologists who offer warmth, respect, care, the ability to listen, a non-judgemental attitude, an absence of prejudice and assumptions, comprehensible dialogue and an understanding of power. They also want clinical psychologists to be emotionally strong enough to bear and contain pain and distress and to demonstrate a professional objectivity and professional standards of behaviour. However, what is not clear is whether this is seen or can be construed by service users and carers as linked to the need to engage in ongoing personal development. Whilst this may make intrinsic sense to professionals, does it do so to the people with whom we work? There is a need to engage in further dialogue and research in this area.

A Contribution from Tracey Holley

My own personal development and self-awareness was vital to me in my own recovery. I have been lucky enough to have had an excellent therapeutic relationship with my cognitive behavioural psychologist and have realized that if a practitioner has little or no emotional intelligence and insight themselves they will not be able to help others with theirs.

Sheila has mentioned the holistic view of well-being, involving warmth, humanity and relationship, and, to me, these are the very elements required for a truly therapeutic interaction between one human being and another – that is, the practitioner and their fellow human being, the service user. If you are not comfortable with basic interpersonal skills such as warmth and the unreserved sharing of one's humanity you had better find a career with computers or the like.

The depression I was experiencing arose from negative automatic thinking and rumination of the worst kind. I was drowning in the destructive tidal currents of negative thoughts, feelings and emotions. My head was full of this black, putrid water – there was no room for anything else – it was all I knew. Until, that is, I met my therapist, who was emotionally strong enough to pull me out of those treacherous waters and encouraged me to begin to fight against this tide of despondency and disaffirmation.

I was not an easy person to help. It was through the tenacity of this emotionally strong individual that I started to make progress. I have always thought that those practitioners involved with vulnerable people are our temporary custodians of hope, even when we think there is no hope left. They make a connection with me, Tracey, the human being, they see me, my humanity, and by so doing revalidate my existence as a person in my own right. They do not fear emotion, mine or theirs. I do not mean that an example of an effective practitioner would be one who sat down and wept with me, oh no, but one who would honour my desperate emotions with genuine empathy whilst at the same time gently pointing out for me what they truly are.

Psychologists deal with the mind. If they are not mindful of themselves and are unfamiliar with their own emotional landscapes how on earth can they help someone try to understand theirs? It would be like the blind leading the blind.

Cognitive therapy techniques can be taught to nurses, social workers and other professionals, but unless these individuals already possess emotional self-awareness and mindfulness there will be no therapy, no therapeutic element. We might just as well do our CBT sitting in front of a computer screen. It is the two-way interaction between human beings plus the emotional strength of the practitioner which acts as the spoonful of sugar that helps the medicine go down!

They are not dragged down by my dominating sense of negativity; neither are they embarrassed by my sense of self-shame and self-hatred. They do not sweep it under the carpet out of sight as something too uncomfortable for us both to deal with; they hold it up for examination, so that I can see it for what it really is – for example, just a feeling and not a fact.

The emotionally capable practitioner is not afraid to reveal their own humanity within their professional role. The sense of the emotional presence of my therapist was vital to my engaging with the whole traumatic and emotionally uplifting process that is cognitive behaviour therapy.

This sense of shared humanness came in the form of how she interacted with me on a face-to-face level. It also came from her ability to judge when she could appropriately self-disclose things to me. She had realized that I saw her as the successful professional and could not see how she could possibly relate to what I was going through, and that she represented everything that I was not and what I wished to be. She revealed things about herself I would never have believed possible in one I thought so 'together' and competent.

Mental distress is all about thoughts, feelings and emotions, often very powerful ones. Trying to describe the indescribable that is the chaos and despair of mental illness is almost impossible in clinical terms. To communicate from one emotional landscape to another requires a fluency in (in Goleman's terms), the language of the heart, of the gut, which, I think, is more a stream of consciousness than a precisely articulated translation.

When I was trying to make sense of what was happening to me when I was battling anxiety and clinical depression I came across a book called *Emotional Intelligence* by Daniel Goleman. This book reaffirmed much of what I had found out through my interactions between emotionally unintelligent as well as emotionally capable professionals. The latter knew the importance of humanity within professionalism. Throughout the whole of my four years with mental health services I came across only two emotionally capable fellow human beings who just happened to be practitioners. Without my therapist and my key worker, I would be without a doubt about six feet under by now.

I still feel their emotional presence even now, now that I am well into my journey of recovery and self-discovery. When times are emotionally hard I think back on what their reaction would be, and I remember the faith they had in my potential. I feel I belong in the same club as them now – a club that only people who are their own best friend rather than their own worst enemy can join: a club for those who have met their compassionate selves, those who understand what it is to be human: our shared humanness.

REFERENCES

Goleman, D. (1995). *Emotional Intelligence*. New York, Bantam.

Goodbody, L. (2003). 'On the Edges of Uncertain Worlds: People Who Use Services, Clinical Psychologists, and Training'. *Clinical Psychology*, 21 (January).

Goodbody, L., Hayward, M., Holttum, S. and Riddell, B. (2007). 'Integrating Service User and Carer Involvement into Clinical Psychology Training. Higher Education Academy Psychology Network'. Accessed online at: http://www.psychology.heacademy.ac.uk

Repper, J. and Breeze, J. (2007). 'User and Carer Involvement in the Training and Education of Health Professionals: A Literature Review'. *International Journal of Nursing Studies*, 44: 511–19.

Ritchie, J. and Spencer, L. (1994). 'Qualitative Data Analysis for Applied Policy Research'. In A. Bryam and R. Burgess (eds.), *Analysing Qualitative Data*. London: Routledge.

Chapter 6

Power and Identity
Considerations for Personal and Professional Development

Sarah Davidson and Nimisha Patel

Introduction

The consideration of power in clinical psychology was largely absent until the 1990s, when the development of critical, feminist and anti-racist writings has increasingly influenced theories, clinical practice, research and training in clinical psychology. Similarly, whilst psychology has a long history of writings on identity (for example, Erikson 1968), the concepts of power and identity have only come together much more recently. In this chapter we hope to elaborate upon the ways in which power is inextricably linked and central to the development of our personal and professional identities. We begin by introducing ourselves to provide a context for understanding our views on power and identity. We then outline our key assumptions with regards to power and identity and go on to illustrate how power and identity have influenced our own personal and professional identities by using excerpts of a conversation between us. We conclude with noting our responsibilities to develop awareness in this area through conversations with others better placed to help us. Throughout the chapter we show why we believe that it is an imperative, not a choice, to attend to power, not just for our own personal and professional development, but for our ability to work with those whose lives are replete with examples of how power defines, shapes and limits one's experiences, opportunities and well-being. The sharing of our journeys, partially illustrated in this chapter, is not intended to be a self-indulgent, intellectual muse but an attempt to share with readers our thoughts on how power and identity have been crucial to our personal and professional development, and to our professional activities.

Who are We?

We are two clinical psychologists who work on the Clinical Psychology Doctoral Programme at the University of East London. One of us identifies as a Black woman, Indian, a migrant to the UK, working clinically with survivors of torture, in a human rights organization (NP). The other identifies as a White, British woman, who works with children and families, including young people who believe they are in the wrong gender (SD).

How we describe ourselves already reveals which aspects of our identity we have privileged in sharing here and which we may have subjugated, intentionally or otherwise. Our areas of work are not mere coincidences, but, as will become apparent in this chapter, a telling punctuation in our ongoing journey of personal and professional development.

Assumptions of Power and Identity

Our understanding of power and identity, and their relevance to personal development, stems from a number of key assumptions. They reveal our own influences – personal histories and experiences, theoretical, professional, political and epistemological.

1   We consider identity not only in terms of fixed properties or characteristics of people (such as our biological sex and colour) but as characteristics which are understood, socially constructed and shaped by the way people are described and positioned in language and by social practices and social institutions (such as class, religion, culture and professional grouping). For example, our gender as women is meaningful in the way 'woman' is talked about in language (in both our mother tongues) and the values attached to being 'a woman' within our own, differing, cultural contexts. It is these values, or being devalued, that can become internalized, such that we come to own and experience them as apparently fixed, objectively knowable facts about who we are. In the context of Britain, whilst we share many experiences as women, the opportunities, disadvantage and oppression which we encounter present themselves differently to us, partly determined by class, 'race' and other factors – which in turn also shape how we define ourselves in language, who we 'are' as women, and how we behave and act.

2   Power infuses language and meaning, influencing peoples' choices and actions (Foucault 1980), such as how people (including health professionals) think about themselves and others. Mary Boyle notes that Foucault's production of power may not only oppress people but also *produce* them (her italics):

> it does so by creating desires (for example, the desire to be thin) and personal attributes such as locus of control, self-esteem, attitudes or personality. Bio-power also creates, rather than discovers, particular groups of people – the homosexual, the frigid woman, the agoraphobic, the alcoholic, the border-line personality, the child with attention deficit disorder – and at the same time mandates particular ways of 'managing' them. (1997: 8–9)

Identity is not only produced by, but is also the effect of power. For example, the concept of identity is not neutral nor a distinct entity, nor a collection of attributes owned by a person, but rather is non-neutral and relational. It is non-neutral in that the use of words or descriptors in language to describe aspects of identity is not a value-free, neutral activity, but an exercise of power. Here, power is understood not as visible, fixed or as possessed but as obscure, pervasive, productive and internalized. For example, the way 'White' is often not mentioned, or talked about in describing psychologists, trainees or clients (in contrast to the more liberal use of descriptors such as 'Black/Asian/BME') is related to the dominant group in society, and in psychology professions, being, and talking, White. The dominant group need not be made visible, or make visible their whiteness because this is the colour they are taken to be. The process of defining the 'other', but not the invisible norm against which the other is judged, is an exercise of power. The process of 'othering' enables the split to be maintained between White and other. Simultaneously, this process defines and constructs the 'other' as either of less value, worthless, deviant and even dangerous and hence to be feared, suppressed, controlled, oppressed; or as exotic, unusual and idealized. Thus, White is implicitly seen as being of more value and as normal because of its dominance. We therefore understand identity as being meaningful and continuously formed in relation to and in relationships with others (see Shotter and Gergen 1989).

Further, were certain identities such as 'Whiteness' or 'being White' to be exposed or 'unpacked', as McIntosh (1998) suggests in her paper entitled 'White Privilege: Unpacking the Invisible Knapsack', an uncomfortable awareness of one's privileges and entitlements associated with being White would result, and theoretically, this would demand a radical shift in the use of language and social practices. This is not to imply that exposing the use and manipulation of language, identifying absent or subjugated discourses and 'talking differently' would help eradicate structural and social inequalities, such as racism or sexism, but that it may enable a change in social practices, and in the way people are defined and define themselves. To understand identity it is essential to understand power and its operations in language and its consequences.

3   Identity is also shaped by the social and material realities of people's lives. Power is evident not only in the Foucauldian sense, but also in the materialist sense. Social and material inequalities, disadvantage and privilege, all shape the opportunities or lack of these that people have. They shape our experiences, our well-being (for example, Rogers and Pilgrim 2003; Williams 1999; Patel and Fatimilehin 1999) and the way in which we define ourselves or are defined by others, for example, in the social identities we adopt or are ascribed to because of membership of cultural or ethnic groups (Tajfel 1981).

Experiences of social disadvantage or privilege also shape choices of how we define our identities. For example, defining oneself as White or as Black is a political act. The choice and act of defining oneself as Black, more controversial in the USA since the 1960s and since the early 2000s in the UK, came out of a political movement in which many people embraced the descriptor in order to be identified as a member of, and in alliance with, groups of people who are oppressed as a result of their colour. Oppression can include institutional and individual racism, historical and current. This is not to obscure or diminish the very important differences within groups and between people identifying themselves as Black, and differences in our experiences – but significant, particularly for the purpose of this chapter, is noting the use of such an identity descriptor as a political act of solidarity in a movement against continued structural racism. In this way language becomes a political tool to construct one's identity, whilst at the same time being an act of resistance and rejection of constructions of 'Black' in dominant discourses.

4   Practising as clinical psychologists, we are in positions of influence through the way we talk about people, the way we work with people and the actions that we take, or do not take. The extent or potential of our influence is not restricted to our direct work with colleagues, clients and

communities, but it is evident in the way we position ourselves and our profession in relation to others, such as through supervising others (for example, other health professionals); in our training efforts (for example, joint training with user trainers, or absence of such partnerships); in our research activities (for instance, either 'doing to', 'doing with' or 'doing for' others); and in consultation activities (for example, to colleagues in statutory and non-statutory sectors, to government – where we may position ourselves as knowledgeable experts who should be heard, and whose views and 'evidence' should be privileged, more than others'). The processes by which we collude with existing power relations and inequalities and the strategies we use to justify our ways of talking, theorizing and our activities serve to maintain our power base and our professional identities. In this way we can not only convince ourselves that we are effective agents of change, but we can collude, perhaps inadvertently, to maintain the status quo. The people we work with can continue to be understood in certain ways (for example, 'mad', 'bad', 'dangerous', 'untreatable', 'difficult', 'confused', etc.), which can hinder their life opportunities and their well-being.

5   Jan Hughes discusses in Chapter 3 how, in order to fulfil our ethical and professional obligations and to be effective in our professional roles, we need to be aware of the discourses (such as the language we use and stories we tell about ourselves and our experiences) that we draw on, our values, vocabulary and behaviours and the impact of these. Our most important premise is that personal and professional development is crucial to enabling ethical practice and that it is via continual commitment and efforts to address power and related experiences and consequences that such awareness is developed.

Personal and Professional Identity: A Conversation

In the following we share our own experiences of trying, or sometimes being forced, to address power in our personal and professional identity development and how this has led to our growing awareness, which has influenced the work we do, the way we work and our vision for psychology. We consider different time frames over the course of our relationship to psychology to date, through excerpts of conversations about our experiences.

Choosing psychology as a profession

SD: How did you come to choose psychology?

NP: Coincidence, if you believe in that, I don't . . . but to be frank I always carried this thing my dad used to say to us – 'Whatever you do [as a job] make sure it is about health and make sure that you don't forget the poor people, use your education to help those who can't buy health.'

SD: What did he mean by that?

NP: Well, it's more telling if I simply say that my paternal grandfather died through lack of access to timely healthcare, in India. Location, money, material and physical conditions would have made a difference. My father espoused strong socialist values, and both parents and my extended family were very religious. For me that culminated in a powerful sense of duty and obligation, a painful awareness of social injustice and a belief that whatever work I did would be my attempts to contribute to social justice. Naively I thought I could do that easily through psychology!

Experiences of being a trainee clinical psychologist

SD: So how was clinical psychology training for you?

NP: Both wonderful and a shock, stimulating and deeply alienating. You know, perhaps like many others, who knows, I always felt out of place, like I was granted a privilege which deep down I believed I couldn't do justice to, or deserve.

SD: Where does that come from?

NP: Lots of things – from my family, I believed that my education was not as important or worthy as males in my family, that I had wasted the opportunity of a 'serious' and 'proper' career by choosing a 'soft' option like psychology. It also came from something a teacher in my sixth form college said to me – he told me I would not get into university, and certainly that I should not attempt to do psychology because I couldn't string a proper sentence together in English and my English in essays was very poor. He was right, at that time. I had been in the English education system and speaking English only at school, for about seven years at that point – but looking back, he wrote me off – it was the first time I consciously thought that if I wanted to do psychology I had to learn to be like, and talk like, and write like my White, mainly middle-class peers, I had to prove my worth and ability, 'despite' my apparent inadequacies.

SD: And training?

NP: Well, every lecture was a constant reminder that the theories espoused, the therapies taught etc. did not include me, or people like me, or my family; there was no synergy and few meeting points between what I was being taught and my own upbringing, world beliefs, religious and spiritual beliefs, nothing that accounted for, acknowledged, childhood and adult experiences of racism, witnessing gang violence (White youth against Asian youth etc.), and nothing on social injustices and effects on people and their well-being. Worse, was that I felt so desperately lonely and alone, so alienated, so confused, so utterly overwhelmed. I did what makes sense I guess – I split things off, I abandoned (though not totally) my religious practices, I became increasingly distanced from my Black school friends, my family . . . everything and everyone who made me, who reflected me and who validated my identity, my history, my heritage and me. That all changed, rapidly, immediately, within weeks of ending training.

SD: Why or how did that come about?

NP: I had two experiences in my last week on my last placement. One was being verbally abused, spat at, kicked at and all that by a group of White youths whilst I was out getting a sandwich for lunch – nothing unusual, I had experienced worse in school days, but in my clothes, donning my 'professional identity', I believed myself to be invisible as a Black woman, and, more so, immune from racism – because I was 'a health professional' now, in the in-group, legitimate and supposedly a respected member of society [laughs]. But I was just me, you know, still Indian, still with a brown skin, still an outsider and all that. I went back to placement, said nothing to anyone, what could you say? who to? and who would understand? Around the same time, I had offered to do a one-off assessment for my team – the man, upon seeing me in the reception area, looked disgustedly at me – refused to see me and muttered a few racist names . . . I stupidly invited him to at least come to my room so that we could talk and discuss options. He followed, but proceeded to hurl insult after insult, called me names, told me I smelt like a Paki, that I couldn't speak English, he didn't understand me . . . it went on, he left, still verbally insulting me. In reception, the team manager overheard and reassured him, in front of me, that he would be sent another appointment with another therapist. This is a decision that he defended in a team meeting, supported by others in the team, as 'ensuring client choice'. My supervisor was superb in supporting me, but to be honest, I just had a wake-up call, I woke up, and thought 'just finish the training, get out of there and do what you have to do'. This transformed, just at the right time, what I believed I wanted to and could do – what kind of psychologist I wanted to be, what kind of psychology I wanted to practise, and to what end.

Experiences of being a clinical psychologist

NP: Which parts of your identities have become salient within clinical psychology?

SD: I can connect to some of what you describe in your experiences of training. Although in the (visible) majority of being a White female I was also very much aware of the differences between me and many of my peers. For shorthand, I guess in many ways clinical psychologists are assumed to be people who have very homogenous experiences and backgrounds. One is not usually required to have personal therapy in order to qualify or demonstrate any particular reflection about one's own life. This provides a subtle message that clinical psychologists are very different from the clients they work with, and that there exists a significant space between each of them. The pathologizing language of much psychological theory only adds to this concept, with its limited emphasis on the context, such as social inequalities, for example. I remember being in a difficult place pre-training, and being advised by my supervisor that it would be hypocritical to remain in the difficult relationship that I was in and to train as a clinical psychologist. The message was that in order to practise clinically, one needed to be, and remain, untouched by some difficult life experiences.

NP: What were the implications of this for you?

SD: Like you, I think I invested heavily in my professional identity; I minimalized any differences (mostly invisible) that existed between me and my colleagues and participated in focussing on the job in hand. I felt very challenged, however, by the pain of the work. I was in a neonatal and paediatric service where there was a lot of grief, death and sadness. I worked at supporting the staff (who I identified with in part, as a nurse before) and the parents and families. But I struggled to know where to take the pain. One supervisor at that time recommended talking to my mother, since this is where she found her support. I struggled with this, given long-term difficulties between me and my mother, and felt further at odds with the backgrounds and assumptions made by those with whom I worked.

NP: So what helped, if anything?

SD: I found personal therapy very useful. Initially this was a good place to reflect on my earlier, difficult experiences and to connect these to how

I experienced the world then. It became a place where I could consider different parts of myself, different identities in relation to others. How I related to those with more and less obvious power than I, such as clients and supervisors, but also how I had more power than I sometimes thought, through the access to resoures I had now, such as education and finances. I considered too, how I had less power in relation to some I worked with, some of whom were incredibly privileged in terms of class, finances and political clout, so could be quite intimidating to work with, and who I at times felt more difficult to connect with than those with less. I could consider the risks of over identifying with some of my clients, whose early experiences reminded me of my own, and ponder the advantages of some of the resources I had developed, in the form of a greater friendship network, colleagues and awareness. I had interesting conversations with other colleagues who felt at times overwhelmed by the pain of the work. We noticed how others benefitted from partners, for example, and how, as single people, we did not have this advantageous buffer. We also noticed how psychological texts say little about acknowledging the pain of clinical work. By noticing our own and one another's responses and needs, providing one another with additional support and space to reflect, we could be more sensitive and responsive to others.

Experiences of supervision

SD: What about you, what resources have you found useful?

NP: The supervisor I have had most recently (for a few years now) is brilliant – just the right person for me at this stage in my development and career.

SD: What makes her the 'right' person for you right now?

NP: You know, all my supervisors, including post-qualification, have been White, some men, some women. I chose her with a specific shopping list in my head – she had everything I felt I needed. She is not a psychologist, but an analyst and psychiatrist, Black, a woman, as I said, and just phenomenal!! She and I negotiated a contract at the outset, and to my utter joy and relief, it was made explicit by both of us that personal and professional interface would be an ongoing theme underpinning supervision. It was with her, for the first time, that I have really felt safe, really free to really explore aspects of my identity and how this relates to how I think, talk, work and relate to clients and colleagues. Being Black, being Indian, being Hindu and a woman, what that meant in terms of how I thought about and approached, say sexuality in my clinical work, or the conflictual understandings and feelings I had about the idea of suicide, and death. My political convictions were always on the table, open to scrutiny, exploration and challenge – always linked back to how I conceptualize clients' distress, therapy and activism – in effect, how I work as a clinical psychologist. Increasingly in my career how I work bears less and less resembalnce to how I was trained – and is closer and closer to who I am – all of me, all aspects of my identity, all bits joining up, not fragmented, split, suppressed, hacked off, suspended. I also became a mother not long after I had started supervision with her – it was a phenomenal transformation for me, being pregnant and talking with mothers who had been separated from their children in fleeing conflict, persecution and political rape, for example. I had been working with survivors of torture for a while, but it was being pregnant, dealing with the idea that I was carrying life, that I would be a mother, and at the same time having to hear and help explore horrific experiences that many of my clients had lived through, which I simply could not allow myself to really connect to, really hear – I can't tell you how deeply that rocked my world. I felt guilty, torn between my political commitment to and through my work and my own immediate emotional and health needs. I felt hugely ambivalent about my work at that time, and sometimes about my pregnancy, and I questioned my ability, or capacity, to be a mother, or a 'good' mother. Everyone told me my priorities would change – what if they didn't, would that make me a crap mother? Supervision, and later personal therapy were both absolutely crucial, and invaluable to navigating this terrain.

Being trainers

NP: Now that we are trainers, how are identity and power salient for you?

SD: I think much about my training experience, of the assumption of privilege and of the smallness of the space to speak about and try to keep in mind individual differences. I co-convene the teaching on children and families and know that trainees may not have had supportive families, or have the choice to have a family (have children), or feel able to share what their experiences have been. I know that there are all sorts of assumptions in psychological theory, practice and policy and I try and attend, where I can, to the implications of this and be sensitive to differences. I say 'where I can' because I don't think it is possible to maintain a level of awareness that spots the many assumptions and prejudices that exist. I know that I may not always be aware of certain omissions and commissions, and hope to keep open to these by inviting feedback and through ongoing conversations with others. This partly relates to my own experiences and identities which make me more likely to attend to some differences than others; thus, as a heterosexual woman I may be more sensitive to sexism than I am to homophobia; so I have conversations with gay colleagues and friends about how I can attend to heterocentrisim which is so evident in child and family work particularly. Although I enjoy teaching and working with trainees, it is not always an easy place to be. Llewelyn, Cushway and Vetere (2007) elegantly summarize some of the many pulls that trainers experience in their positions of power as gatekeepers to the profession but also in being found wanting, not good enough to meet the increasing and conflicting demands required of the many stakeholders, and of not being recognized for the hard work that is undertaken for trainees' benefits. One particularly significant piece of learning came from an article by three trainees I worked with in their final year of training. Adetimole, Afuape and Vara (2005) were Black trainees who wrote of the impact of racism on their experience of training. Although I knew it would be published, upon reading it I felt overwhelmed by a mixture of hurt and frustration that my attempts to acknowledge their Blackness hadn't been recognized; of guilt and shame at not being able to have prevented their difficult experiences and pain and of my own contributions to their experience of racism; and then of profound respect that they could be so candid about their experiences and so balanced in their insights and recommendations. I went through a process described by Atkinson, Morton and Sue (1989), which, following a phase of defensiveness and immersion prompted by reading the article, included a phase of introspection where I reviewed the implications of my own Whiteness and was able to reflect more openly about where I had been colour blind or awkward in my acknowledgement of racial differences and the vocubulary I used. It took quite some time of talking to others and considered reflection before my sense of shame dissipated. I don't think that such a process ends but more that it continues like a cycle, constantly requiring further consideration and reminders of how those of us in powerful majorities can fall into lazy thinking or 'othering' – noting only exceptions to the usual (white) models or identities; waiting for those in the less powerful minority groups to speak out, rather than doing this ourselves.

Our Responsibilities

It has been through conversations such as this that we have become increasingly aware of the contexts within which we operate, the identities on which we draw and the power that the various combinations of these can afford or deny (to us and others). As professionals working with people presenting with distress and difficulties, we believe we have a responsibility to consider the contexts we ourselves are acting within, the language and discourses we are privileging and their impacts. We have referred to developing insight and awareness, which we consider not as attributes that we have or have not but as ways of thinking and talking that connect to our previous experiences and focus our attention on the information before us (or inattention where we have gaps in our awareness).

Burnham and Harris (2002) use the acronym SOCIAL GRRAACCES (Burnham, 1993) to remind us of nine different contexts (gender, race, religion, age, ability, class, culture, ethnicity and sexuality) relating to identity and culture. They recommend that consideration of these contexts, in addition to our professional cultures, through exploration with our colleagues and our clients should be part of all our work, not left as an adjunct when the 'usual' ways of relating become problematic or seem inadequate.

However, raising awareness about issues and contexts that we have less familiarity with is challenging. By definition, the language we have to engage with less familiar contexts will be less well developed than for those more frequently encountered. Burnham and Harris (2002) recommend clinicians use a 'clumsy rather than clever' approach and embrace curiosity to make the initial steps of widening the lens of understanding, to which we would add as requisite that we all take risks. Risk taking can mean thinking and talking differently, entering unfamilar terrains, finding our way – which also require time, motivation, courage and commitment. If, rather than making the time and effort to think more widely and to look at ourselves, we do not face these hazards, we risk problematizing or blaming others who are different from us for their differences.

That said, looking at ourselves can be uncomfortable. As psychologists focussed on theory, evidence and research, we may intellectualize when faced with the discomfort of our own limited vocabulary, reference points or understanding. Retreating into more familiar and dominant discourses (for instance, those driven by diagnosis) may minimize our fear of uncertainty, but do so at the expense of our being able to understand and communicate with others constructively, which can also stunt professional development through the lack of curiosity and creativity that results from such intellectualizing. Our ability to take on others' perspectives and challenge our own assumptions also depends on our own capacities to tolerate high levels of anxiety, which might otherwise increase the likelihood of splitting, particularly in the absence of a secure attachment with another who can facilitate reflection and understanding. In professional practice, we have the need for others: to force or help us to reflect, to consider the impact of our values, beliefs, behaviours and vocabularies, to give us feedback and to provide us with opportunities to explore the discourses we draw upon and the assumptions underlying our actions. Such people need to be those whom we can trust but who will also challenge us. People who may be dissimilar to us, such as those with different histories, experiences, priorities, professional backgrounds, belief systems and, importantly, different experiences of disadvantage and privilege are all essential to our personal and professional development. They may be our managers, supervisors, colleagues, mentors, therapists, clients, trainees, friends or family. In meeting our personal and professional development responsibilities it is our duty to meaningfully engage with and learn from and with others, with honesty, genuine interest, commitment and humility.

REFERENCES

Adetimole, A., Afuape, T. and Vara, R. (2005). 'The Impact of Racism on the Experience of Training on a Clinical Psychology Course: Reflections from Three Black Trainees'. *Clinical Psychology*, 48: 11–15.

Atkinson, D., Morton, G. and Sue, D. (eds.) (1989). *Counselling American Minorities: A Cross Cultural Perspective*. Dubuque, IO: W.C. Brown.

Boyle, M. (1997). *Re-Thinking Abortion: Psychology, Gender, Power and the Law*. London: Routledge.

Burnham, J. (1993). 'Systemic Supervision: The Evolution of Reflexivity in the Context of the Supervisory Relationship'. *Human Systems*, 4 (3, 4): 349–81 (special issue).

Burnham, J. and Harris, Q. (2002). 'Cultural Issues in Supervision'. In D. Campbell and B. Mason, *Perspectives on Supervision*. London: Karnac.

Erikson, E. (1968). *Identity: Youth and Crisis*. New York: Norton.

Foucault, M. (1980). *Power/Knowledge: Selected Interviews and Other Writings 1972–1977*, ed. C. Gorden. Hemel Hempstead: Harvester Wheatsheaf.

Llewelyn, S., Cushway, D. and Vetere, A. (2007). 'Why a Trainer's Lot Is Not a Happy One (A Happy One . . .)'. *Clinical Psychology Forum*, 175: 24–7.

McIntosh, P. (1998). 'White Privilege: Unpacking the Invisible Knapsack'. In M. McGoldrick (ed.), *Re-Visioning Family Therapy*. New York: The Guildford Press.

Patel, N. and Fatimilehin, I. (1999). 'Racism and Mental Health.' In C. Newnes, G. Holmes and C. Dunn (eds.), *This is Madness: A Critical Look at Psychiatry and the Future of Mental Health Services*. Ross-on-Wye: PCCS.

Rogers, A. and Pilgrim, D. (2003). *Mental Health and Inequality*. Basingstoke: Palgrave Macmillan.

Shotter, J. and Gergen, K. (1989). *Texts of Identity*. London: Sage.

Tajfel, H. (1981). *Human Groups and Social Categories*. Cambridge: Cambridge University Press.

Williams, J. (1999). 'Social Inequalities and Mental Health'. In C. Newnes, G. Holmes and C. Dunn (eds.), *This is Madness: A Critical Look at Psychiatry and the Future of Mental Health Services*. Ross-on-Wye: PCCS.

Chapter 7

Supervision and Personal Development
Joyce Scaife

Introduction

In my experience, supervision can play an invaluable role in facilitating the achievement of personal growth at work through the establishment and maintenance of a good working relationship which supports self-reflection and review. The participants in supervision need to feel confident and trusting enough in the relationship to disclose issues about themselves in the work, and to manage the feelings of vulnerability that this may entail.

The Importance of the Supervisory Alliance

The centrality of the quality of the supervisory relationship to supervisory outcomes was emphasized in Ellis and Ladany's (1997) review of studies of supervision. In a study by Beinart (2004), specific qualities of the relationship contributing to effectiveness were rapport and the experience of support. Where there is a poor alliance, supervisees have been found to 'hide' aspects of their work from their supervisors (Ladany, Hill, Corbett and Nutt 1996). Most nondisclosures to supervisors were discussed with someone else, typically a peer.

Kent and McAuley (1995) surveyed second- and third-year trainee clinical psychologists about ethical dilemmas that they had faced during training. The tendency to take feedback about personal issues as criticism is illustrated by the following quotation from one of the 85 respondents. 'I was told that I was very "sensitive" which I took to be a criticism and this soured our relationship for a while and I felt my legitimate stance had not been understood. She pathologized me, suggesting that I was making a huge fuss about nothing and my "strong views" about violence towards children were getting in the way.'

In a qualitative study (Worthen and McNeill 1996) which employed in-depth interviews of eight experienced therapists, effective supervisors were characterized by an empathic attitude, a non-judgemental stance towards the supervisee, conveying a sense of validation or affirmation, and being encouraging of exploration and experiment. These qualities are illustrated in the following comments from one of the participants:

> And what was so great, was that my supervisor was really affirming of and validating of my ability to speak clearly. I felt very much understood by her and I felt also like she appreciated those abilities that I had taken pride in in the past and which I had felt, I just hadn't felt were being recognized at all, at any level. (Stoltenberg, McNeill and Delworth 1998: 113)

General characteristics of relationships set up for the purposes of teaching and learning

Salzberger-Wittenberg (1983: 12) argues that an adult entering a new relationship with a teacher is inevitably anxious and that feelings associated with earlier relationships with authority figures are evoked: 'Any new relationship tends to arouse hope and dread, and these exist side by side in our minds. The less we know about the new person the freer we are to invest him with extremes of good and bad qualities.' Beginners in particular may be tempted to grasp at technique as the armour that will protect them from imagined public humiliation. Supervisors of budding new initiates to the profession have an important role in helping supervisees to understand that learning technique is a means to an end, rather than the end itself. It could be argued that the supervisor attempting to help a supervisee to address issues of personal development begins the task at a disadvantage because of the implicit anxiety entailed in a relationship configured by the roles of supervisee and supervisor.

The essential basis for a functional working alliance

A good beginning, effected through a sound contracting process, can establish the foundation for the development of trust, which in turn allows for the possibility of openness and risk taking. Contracting is best considered as a process that occurs over a number of sessions and from time to time for the duration of the supervisory relationship. Sensitivity to the needs and preferences of the supervisee aids the contracting process. Page and Wosket (2001) cite the contrasting examples of a counsellor attending an initial contracting session with a written list of preferences because she had previously experienced supervision as straying outside acceptable boundaries, and an inexperienced trainee plunging straight into a presentation of her case material.

The term 'psychological contract' has been defined as 'the perceptions of the two parties, employee and employer, of what their mutual obligations are towards each other' (Guest and Conway 2002). These obligations will often be informal and imprecise: they may be inferred from actions or from what has happened in the past, and may be believed by the employee to be part of the relationship with the employer. Early conversations laying out the territory in which negotiation is permitted address the psychological aspects of the contract. Talking about topics such as ground rules, the approach to supervision that each party prefers and abhors, topics or approaches likely to evoke defensive responses, what each person holds dear and the like, gives the message that these are appropriate topics for conversation in which it might be expected that people will have different views.

Effective contracting ensures a good beginning but is not enough to guarantee a stable and effective working alliance. The development of trust is an ongoing and evolving process. Successfully managing difficult feedback and its potential for creating a rupture in the relationship can be an invaluable experience for the supervisee, and can create a stable sense of trust and hopefulness in the relationship such that openness and assessment can go hand in hand. In general, a respectful attitude towards the supervisee and to other colleagues can go a long way towards the creation and maintenance of a climate of trust in supervision.

The Challenge of Encouraging Personal Development through Supervision – The Potential for Role Conflict

Purpose of supervision

The primary purpose of supervision has been identified by Inskipp and Proctor (1988) as the requirement to fulfil formative, normative and restorative functions. Within the 'normative' and 'formative' categories, the supervisor carries out the important role of assessment. In training supervision, the supervisor holds the key to the learner's entry to the profession, but, in any supervisory arrangement, the evaluative role of the supervisor and the normative function are ever present, invariably holding some sway in the dynamics of the supervisory relationship and presenting a particular challenge when the focus of the supervision is on personal development.

Supervisors, as well as supervisees, frequently develop personally through their supervision work; this can be a valuable by-product, even though it is not an express purpose of the role relationship.

Challenging personal development

When the personal qualities that supervisees bring to their work are the focus of supervision, the potential for misunderstandings, affront and hurt feelings is at its greatest and the supervisor's role as personal developer presents particular challenges. In carrying out the formative and normative functions, the approaches available to the supervisor include the use of feedback and constructive challenge. It is relatively straightforward to provide challenges for technical skills or theoretical knowledge, but to raise issues that are intended to be, or are construed as personal is much more risky, with greater potential for damage to the relationship.

Bernard and Goodyear (1998) advocate a state of playfulness as a favourable condition for supervision in which the encounter might be regarded as an 'interlude from real life' in which it can be safe to entertain feelings of confusion and question even the most sacrosanct professional ideas (Sanville 1989: 161). They argue that the process should encourage the development of a perspective in which supervisees ask themselves, 'How can I make the most of this supervision time?' rather than 'How can I avoid criticism?'

Opportunities for Personal Development in Supervision

Supervision can both aid identification of issues for personal development, that is, draw attention to clues, and focus on issues of which supervisees are already aware, thereby working at different stages of Prochaska and Di Clemente's (1983) cycle of change (discussed in Chapter 3). The restorative function of supervision often takes centre stage in relation to personal development, with a focus on the feelings of the supervisee. Supervision can provide a safe space in which to 'let off steam' and then move on to derive meaning from these feelings, and to devise strategies with which to address them. Within the General Supervision Framework of Scaife (1993) the supervisory focus would move from 'feelings and personal qualities' to 'knowledge, thinking and planning' and potentially to 'actions and events'.

Specific enquiry into feelings, underlying values and beliefs

Supervisors may vary in the extent to which they regard personal qualities and feelings as an appropriate focus of supervision, and this is often influenced by the model/s of therapy in which the supervisor works. That theoretical orientation towards therapy is related to a supervisor's manifest behaviour, roles and attitudes has long been established in research findings (Friedlander and Ward 1983; Miars, Tracey, Ray, Cornfeld, O'Farrell and Gelso 1983; Goodyear, Abadie and Efros 1984). Training in psychoanalysis, for example, requires that personal development work be undertaken in a personal analysis which takes place outside supervision (Dewald 1997). In contemporary psychodynamic approaches the counter-transference, the way in which a therapist feels as an indicator of the patient's state of mind (Frawley O'Dea and Sarnat 2001; Hinshelwood 1994), is a legitimate focus of supervision. Parallel process (Doehrman 1976; Williams 1997; Raichelson, Herron, Primavera and Ramirez 1997), the way in which the enactments in the therapy are replicated in the supervision and vice versa, is also regarded as informing the work.

In cognitive behavioural approaches it is argued that the major goal of supervision is to bring about a philosophical change in the supervisee such that CBT comes to be regarded as the basic approach for changing client's cognitions, emotions and behaviour. Rosenbaum and Ronen (1998) argue that CBT is 'not only a profession but also a philosophy of life; a way of living. You cannot ask your clients (or your supervisees) to practise this approach while you do not live according to its principles.'

Becoming aware of a different perspective

In my experience, personal development can occur as a result of increased awareness of an attitudinal or value position, leading to a conscious decision to make changes. It can also occur serendipitously when a new perspective on the self is revealed by a particularly meaningful interaction. The following example is taken from the novel *Human Traces* by Sebastian Faulks. Jacques, one of the main characters, who hails from a humble social background, has been studying medicine and has little confidence in his academic capabilities. He attends the final viva to defend his thesis and is convinced that he is to fail. The assessment committee, in contrast to this expectation, are full of praise for his work and all stand at the end of the viva to shake his hand and congratulate him. Later, he reflects on this:

> His own life sometimes seemed to him to have that quality of being made up of a series of separate phases, barely understood at the time, for all that they formed part of an unwinding whole. The moment of his appearance before the examiners to defend his thesis had marked the dramatic end of one such section. He had prepared very little for the interview – dangerously little, when he came to think of it. It was as though he could not bring himself to imagine it in advance because too much depended on it; yet he could not have foreseen what really resulted, which was not just the ending of the student years or the acquisition of a licence to practise, but the sense that he had become someone else: for a moment in the churchy upstairs room where the test took place, he had seen himself from the outside, as the examiners saw him, and he no longer felt provisional or disqualified, but filled with power and confidence. If they believed in this strange Dr Rebière, then why should he not do so too? And then, why not send the fellow out to do his life-work for him – this awe-inspiring doctor whose work of 'first-rate scholarship' had brought his superiors – no, his equals – to their feet? (Faulks 2005: 243)

Particularly in pre-registration training, the supervisor may be seen as occupying a similar position of power to that of the examining committee in the above extract. Many of the difficulties that occur in supervision can be attributed to a lack of confidence (in either or both parties), and the presentation by the supervisor of a different and more positive perspective on the supervisee's work has the potential for helping supervisees to create a different sense of themselves in the work.

Personal reactions to clients in the work of a clinical psychologist

The whole spectrum of feelings experienced towards people outside work can occur just as readily towards clients. These can include feeling elated, angry, useless, sexually aroused, confused, depressed, amused, disgusted and the like. Such emotions can be very difficult to handle since feelings of warmth and empathy are espoused. A task of supervision is to bring the transactions or 'enactments' between clients and therapists that generate these feelings into conscious awareness in order to use them in the service of the work (Falender and Shafranske 2004: 84).

Mollon (1989) gives examples of how clients' behaviour towards novice therapists can generate feelings of inadequacy that interact with the more general feelings of incompetence associated with early stages of professional development. In one case example, the client had requested the assistance of a psychologist as she reported having found previous encounters with the medical profession unhelpful to her long-standing anxiety state. Initially, the therapist felt hopeful and attributed the client's dissatisfaction with previous attempts to help to inappropriate medical interventions. As sessions progressed, the client conveyed a feeling that the psychologist should do something other than listen and talk, and the client's stance in sessions was passive – the psychologist felt that she herself was expected to identify topics. The client frequently questioned whether the work was going to be of help to her, thereby dismissing by implication the activity in which the therapist was currently engaged as having the potential to be of help. Whilst the client's behaviour was not overtly hostile, it was experienced by the supervisee as a sustained attack on her state of mind and her professional identity.

Supervision enabled the novice therapist to obtain a different perspective on the work and to make meaning of the interaction with the client which provided information about the client's other and earlier relationships. This allowed the focus of the work to move to the current interaction between client and therapist and to the nature of the relationship between the client and her parents. Mollon argues that a task of supervision is to bring the supervisee's anxiety and mental pain into the discourse so that feelings of incompetence and disillusionment regarding the capacity of psychotherapy to be of help can be seen as meaningful material that informs the work. This pertains throughout professional careers.

Mollon (1989) described the negative emotional experiences of people learning to be therapists as 'narcissistic insults'. Typically these are experienced as shameful, the responses to which may be reticence and concealment. The restorative function of supervision legitimizes such experiences. Hahn (2001) argued that supervisors should be alert to supervisee reactions to feelings of shame which were categorized as 'withdrawal', 'avoidance', 'attack on the self' and 'attack on others'. The supervisor's roles were identified as the provision of support, facilitation of understanding and enabling the supervisee to disclose shameful feelings and learn by using them to inform the work. Failure to reveal these feelings can lead clients and therapists into liaisons that may prove a danger to both.

Personal reactions to colleagues and contexts in the role of clinical psychologist

Not only may clients evoke a range of feelings in workers, but so too do the behaviours and actions of colleagues. Clues to reactions to specific colleagues are provided by the adjectives used to describe them. 'Personality disordered', 'arrogant', 'insensitive' and so on suggest a negative reaction. The attribution of such labels tends to block ways to improving the working relationship. Supervision can provide a space in which a benevolent formulation of a colleague's behaviour can be constructed and a more tolerant attitude fostered.

A not infrequent example of actions within an organization which can lead to hurt feelings is when an asset previously enjoyed by a supervisee is threatened with removal. The loss of an office, secretarial support, etc., can engender a sense of not being valued by colleagues and/or the organization. In supervision it is possible to identify self-destructive reaction patterns to such actions, and consciously to experiment with different responsive strategies. A supervisee may already be aware of the tendency to react to such situations with overt hostility, passivity or subversion. Experimentation with different responses may lead to personal development relevant not only in the work context but in the supervisee's wider life settings.

Issues brought to awareness through encountering a different value base

Values and beliefs underlie many aspects of human thought and behaviour. Some of these we are able to articulate, others we are unaware of until we come up against a different value base that causes us to question or reinforce our own. Often these differences become more apparent to us when we are functioning within a different culture: either in a different country, social grouping or work culture. In the following example, the presence of a live supervision group provided an opportunity to discuss value positions regarding physical punishment in the parental role.

A family was being interviewed in which the mother for the most part carried out the active parenting of two teenage children. The father had been diagnosed as suffering from PTSD and tended to take a very passive role in the family. The family attended the interview together and the eldest child was playing music into his headphones. The mother asked him to participate in the session, and when he failed to respond the father rose from his chair, took the headphones out of his son's ears and slapped him across the face. The therapist asked what it was like for the mother when the father tried to help in disciplining the children. The mother explained that when he did try to help, typically he 'went over the top'. The therapist had appeared to construe the father's actions within a positive frame. After the session, one of the trainees in the supervision group raised the issue of physical abuse and described her shocked reaction to the father's behaviour. This provoked a discussion of the different beliefs held by members of the group about physical chastisement and the potential for damage in this and other non-physical forms of parental behaviour management. Members of the group also reflected together on how their value position with regard to this issue had developed, and there was a sense of surprise that the beliefs and experiences within the group could be so diverse.

Such occasions are invaluable in helping to raise awareness of personal value bases and in providing the opportunity to consolidate existing beliefs or to make revisions and keep a more open mind about family patterns and the usefulness or otherwise of typical interaction sequences. Group supervision that brings together workers from different professions, levels of experience and work settings is likely to provide many opportunities for such learning whilst also providing a challenge to the leader in maintaining good group manners. It is also possible for this process to take place in dyads, particularly where there are differences in age, ethnicity, gender, faith, sexuality and professional background.

Being drawn into actions that run counter to intentions

Attention can be drawn to issues that would benefit from personal development when workers find themselves acting in ways that run counter to their intentions. Some examples would include giving a client a cigarette when the institution in which one works prohibits smoking, running over planned session time, offering reassurance and advice when having planned to take the position of enquirer, and giving a client a home telephone number. Although these kinds of behaviours might be appropriate under specific circumstances they may provoke varying levels of concern. Feelings of discomfort or 'stuck-ness' are often indicators of areas in which personal development would be beneficial. Daniels and Feltham (2004: 182) argue that 'in every personal development endeavour there is some notion of difficulty, defence mechanism, resistance, stuckness and so on'. Whilst I do not agree with this assertion, I think that these feelings are often useful indicators or clues.

Supervisees would do well to bring these feelings to supervision as a way of keeping both themselves and their clients safe. The climate of supervision needs to be such that the supervisee expects the supervisor to treat these revelations as information that will be useful to the work with the client and to the personal development of the supervisee.

Finding oneself drawn back to value positions from which development had taken place (relapse)

The relapse phase noted in Prochaska and Di Clemente's (1983) model is one that can be particularly disheartening to encounter. It is as well to anticipate the possibility of earlier value positions being elicited by contexts in which those positions are represented. For example, I was brought up in a context in which homosexuality was viewed as pathological and was regarded as an appropriate subject of treatment interventions. Having, I thought, left this position behind much earlier in my career, I suddenly found myself asking a question within a family meeting that implied I continued to hold my earlier view. This had been elicited in response to the views being expressed by the parents in relation to the sexuality of their child. I reacted with feelings of shame, and tried to redirect the conversation along the lines of my revised views. It is important to acknowledge such feelings and to recognize them as a prompt for further development along a path of changing personal values and beliefs.

Conflicting values in multicultural contexts

Sometimes supervisors are faced with difficult decisions where conflicting values and beliefs pertain. For example, supervisees may refuse to work with clients whose sexual orientation is not accepted within their faith. Within the professional culture of clinical psychology is this acceptable? There are no clear answers to this dilemma; it would seem appropriate for the issue to be one in which ongoing personal review would be beneficial.

Might a supervisee refuse to work with someone identified as a paedophile? An ethical position based on equity suggests that access to psychological services should be available to all and that it would be helpful for a supervisee with such a view to work on developing an understanding of how people find themselves in such positions, the more so since in such cases the need for intervention is particularly acute.

How Supervisors Might Intervene to Facilitate Personal Development

Whatever the framework in which supervision is conducted, a range of opportunities can be provided and taken through which personal development may be facilitated. It is helpful to create conditions in the supervisory relationship which address issues of both care and control. These are the conditions in which supervisees can feel safe enough to explore personal, and possibly difficult, issues.

Constructive challenge

'Challenge' is an invitation or undertaking to test one's capabilities to the full. Particularly early on in their careers, supervisees tend to have difficulty in identifying their own strengths as they are unclear about what they are trying to learn. The supervisor can help by noticing these and inviting the supervisee to use them more widely and in different contexts. For example, the supervisor might have noticed (or the supervisee may have described) the supervisee feeling so overwhelmed with sadness as a client described the loss of her father that he or she was unable to speak. The supervisor might challenge the strength of deep empathy, and together they might consider how to manage it, including possibly allowing a period of quietness during the therapy session. The purpose of constructive challenge is to generate new perspectives at a cognitive level and to create options for action. The challenge is to the current way of seeing or doing things.

The benefit of challenging strengths rather than weaknesses is the context of a positive frame which better supports non-cosmetic change and development. The risk of challenging weaknesses is that of prompting defensiveness, possibly leading to confrontation, argument and a hindrance to learning. A fuller description of the process of constructive challenge can be found in Scaife (2001).

Reflective writing

Reflection and review can be aided by the use of a learning log or reflective diary in which ideas about the work and any implications for practice can be noted. The process of writing down feelings, thoughts, uncertainties and tentative understandings in a learning log can help in making connections between ideas and feelings that have emerged in different settings and at different times. Reflective journals have been adopted as a means to aid learning in the context of education and counselling training since the mid-1990s (Woodward 1998; Daniels and Feltham 2004: 181) and have more recently found their way into the training of medical students (Niemi 1997), general practitioners (Snadden, Thomas, Griffin and Hudson 1996) and nurses (Button and Davies 1996).

Daniels and Feltham (2004) described a small-scale study of counselling trainees who completed a confidential journal as part of the personal development requirement of their course. They reported that although trainees were initially sceptical about the value of the process, the majority found great benefit as illustrated by the following comments:

'Writing enables me to articulate in a non-vocal way material that I wouldn't dare express in any other way.'

'Seeing them [my feelings] on paper also helps me to understand them.'

'I just write about how I feel and about significant events in a reflective and creative way.'

Private journals allow supervisees the freedom to express themselves in whatever manner they choose. The results of the individual personal reflective process may be brought to supervision, the supervisee having already undertaken a first stage of the supervision process. Bolton, Allan and Drucquer (2004) liken the silent reflective process in which writers are communicating solely with themselves to the internal supervisor described by Patrick Casement (1988; 1990). Further information on this approach to personal development can be found in Bolton, Howlett, Lago and Wright (2004) and Bolton (2001).

Purpose-made exercises

Purposely designed exercises can be used both to explore current underlying values and beliefs, and to investigate life histories and their influence on practice. Alert supervisors may notice elements of their supervisees' values and beliefs in the language they use to describe their work. What people say about their clients may be conveying at least as much about the speaker as about the subject. One option for exploring this is to audio-tape a supervision session with a view to reviewing it specifically to identify the values and beliefs of both supervisor and supervisee. An example of this is given in Scaife (2001: 43).

Life histories may be examined using genograms and lifelines. Underlying beliefs about the therapeutic process can be explored through the identification and investigation of a personal problem, an exercise which in the initial stage is privately conducted. Having identified a problem, supervisees then reflect upon the questions that they would prefer to be asked in exploration of the problem. It would be possible to choose the kinds of questions or to adopt an approach such as free association prescribed by a particular model of therapy or to think of questions at random. The task in supervision is to consider what the selected questions or approach reveal about the expectations of the supervisee about how therapy is conducted. The problem itself need not be disclosed. Through the exercise supervisees learn about the kind of approach that they believe they would find useful for themselves, their own orientation to how helping is carried out and some idea of the potential impact of such methods on clients (Scaife 2001). Judy Hildebrand (1998) gives further examples of exercises designed to promote personal development that may be conducted in groups.

Research Findings

There is a very large body of research findings on supervision in healthcare settings, most typically derived from studies carried out within the professions of psychotherapy and counselling. The relationship between supervision and personal development has been subject to little empirical scrutiny, although there is some evidence supporting a link.

Positive experiences, including facilitation of personal development, are evidenced in the following quotations from Wulf and Nelson:

> He had a pretty profound impact on my clinical style, helping me to become more practical, maybe more results-oriented, less theoretical in my thinking, and less kind of ethereal and pedantic in my thinking – being more of a human being.

> It was just a wonderful experience that really kick-started me in a lot of ways in family work. And so that's had a long-term impact. And in the context of feeling kind of beat up by a couple of these other supervisors, it was a really good experience in constructive feedback. They had good things to say about my work, and bad things to say about my work . . . I was able to really take in the constructive criticism and use it. (Wulf and Nelson 2000)

This is convergent with the finding that *non-confirming* supervision experiences are so potent that the memory of them remains affectively charged, even years later (Skovholt and Ronnestad 1992).

Falender and Shafranske (2004: 92) argue that personal influences accompany every technical intervention and facet of training, and that interventions are 'guided by science and yet are influenced by our humanity'. They also pointed out that supervisors, not only supervisees, are influenced by counter-transference reactions and cited the results of a study by Ladany, Constantine, Miller, Erickson and Muse-Burke (2000: 106–8) which identified supervisor counter-transference responses as arising from 'the intern's personal style', 'the supervisor's unresolved personal issues', 'interactions between the intern and the supervisory environment', 'problematic client–intern interactions', 'intern–supervisor interactions' and 'interactions between the supervisor and the supervisory environment'. They concluded that clinicians who are unwilling to explore issues of personal development may be regarded as unsuited to the work.

In the nursing profession there have been attempts to research the impact of supervision on personal development, particularly in terms of preventing burn out and encouraging creativity (Berg and Hallberg 1999). On the basis of a large-scale exploratory study which included interviews with a sub-set of participants, White, Butterworth, Bishop, Carson, Jeacock and Clements reported that supervisees welcomed the development of their confidence and self-esteem, the support they derived from peers and the sense of 'actually taking responsibility' for their own practice which resulted from supervision. Interviewees variously claimed that clinical supervision had made them more honest, relaxed, enthusiastic and less competitive. For some, clinical supervision had helped them to 'cope with the fear of being seen not to cope'. (White et al. 1998)

Using a descriptive qualitative design, Arvidsson, Lofgren and Bridlund (2000) analysed interviews of 10 nurses following their experience of two years of group supervision. One of their descriptive categories was 'a feeling of personal development'. They found that the participants in the study were more likely to be able to identify issues of personal development in the second year of supervision than in the first year. They concluded that as a result of supervision 'the nurses gained increased trust in their own abilities, feelings and work performance. They became more courageous, dared more and worked independently to a greater extent.'

Using Proctor's framework concerning the restorative, normative and formative purposes of supervision, Bowles and Young (1999) used semi-structured interviews to explore the benefits of supervision. Amongst the impacts of clinical supervision reported by nurses were improved self-confidence, greater awareness of their own behaviour and increased self-awareness. Positive influences of clinical supervision on self-awareness and self-value were similarly reported by Bégat, Severinsson and Berggren (1997).

It is only since 2004 that British Psychological Society accreditation criteria have included personal development as a core learning objective in clinical psychology training. Exploration of the link between supervision and personal development is a fertile area for exploration. Methodologies by which the link is addressed will be an important consideration since supervision research has often suffered through being reliant on measures of trainee satisfaction (Holloway and Neufeldt 1995; Goodyear and Bernard 1998). Goodyear and Bernard use an analogy to emphasize how this limits the findings of such studies: 'imagine asking a number of people leaving a donut shop whether they were satisfied with their donuts and would be willing to return to this particular shop. Most would probably give affirming answers to both of these questions. Their answers, though, are of no use at all to someone interested in ascertaining the nutritional value of those donuts.' Using operational definitions of the concept of personal development, research needs creatively to address changes during training that can be linked to the 'nutritional value' of supervisory interventions.

REFERENCES

Arvidsson, B., Löfgren, H. and Fridlund, B. (2000). 'Psychiatric Nurses' Conceptions of How Group Supervision in Nursing Care Influences their Professional Competence'. *Journal of Nursing Management*, 8: 175–85.

Bégat, I. B. E., Severinsson, E. I. and Berggren, I. B. (1997). 'Implementation of Clinical Supervision in a Medical Department: Nurses' Views of the Effects'. *Journal of Clinical Nursing*, 6: 389–94.

Beinart, H. (2004). 'Models of Supervision and the Supervisory Relationship and Their Evidence Base'. In I. Fleming and L. Steen (eds.), *Supervision and Clinical Psychology*. Hove: Brunner-Routledge.

Berg, A. and Hallberg, I. R. (1999). 'Effects of Systematic Clinical Supervision on Psychiatric Nurses' Sense of Coherence, Creativity, Work-Related Strain, Job Satisfaction and View of the Effects from Clinical Supervision: A Pre-Post Test Design'. *Journal of Psychiatric and Mental Health Nursing*, 6: 371–81.

Bernard, J. M. and Goodyear, R. K. (1998). *Fundamentals of Clinical Supervision*. Needham Heights, MA: Allyn and Bacon.

Bolton, G. (2001). *Reflective Practice, Writing and Personal Development*. London: Paul Chapman.

Bolton, G., Allan, H. and Drucquer, H. (2004). 'Black and Blue: Writing For Reflective Practice'. In G. Bolton, S. Howlett, C. Lago and J. K. Wright (eds.) (2004), *Writing Cures: An Introductory Handbook of Writing in Counselling and Therapy*. Hove: Brunner-Routledge.

Bolton, G., Howlett, S., Lago, C. and Wright, J. K. (2004). *Writing Cures: An Introductory Handbook of Writing in Counselling and Therapy*. Hove: Brunner-Routledge.

Bowles, N. and Young, C. (1999). 'An Evaluative Study of Clinical Supervision Based on Proctor's Three Function Interactive Model'. *Journal of Advanced Nursing*, 30: 958–64.

Button, D. and Davies, S. (1996). 'Experiences of Encouraging Student-Centred Learning Within a Wellness-Oriented Curriculum'. *Nurse Education Today*, 16: 407–12.

Casement, P. (1988). *On Learning from the Patient*. London: Routledge.

Casement, P. (1990). *Further Learning from the Patient*. London: Routledge.

Daniels, J. and Feltham, C. (2004). 'Reflective and Therapeutic Writing In Counsellor Training'. In G. Bolton, S. Howlett, C. Lago and J. K. Wright, *Writing*

Cures: An Introductory Handbook of Writing in Counselling and Therapy. Hove: Brunner-Routledge.

Dewald, P. A. (1997). 'The Process of Supervision in Psychoanalysis'. In C. E. Watkins Jr (ed.), *Handbook of Psychotherapy Supervision.* New York: John Wiley and Sons.

Doehrman, M. J. G. (1976). 'Parallel Processes in Supervision and Psychotherapy'. *Bulletin of the Menninger Clinic*, 40: 9–104.

Ellis, M. V. and Ladany, N. (1997). 'Inferences Concerning Supervisees and Clients in Clinical Supervision: An Integrative Review'. In C. E. Watkins, Jr (ed.), *Handbook of Psychotherapy Supervision.* New York: Wiley.

Falender, C. A. and Shafranske, E. P. (2004). *Clinical Supervision: A Competency-Based Approach.* Washington, DC: American Psychological Association.

Faulks, S. (2005). *Human Traces.* London: Hutchinson.

Frawley O'Dea, M. G. and Sarnat, J. E. (2001). *The Supervisory Relationship: A Contemporary Psychodynamic Approach.* New York: Guilford Press.

Friedlander, M. L. and Ward, L. G. (1983). 'Dimensions of Supervisory Style'. Cited in R. K Goodyear, P. D. Abadie and F. Efros (1984), 'Supervisory Theory into Practice: Differential Perceptions of Supervision by Ekstein, Ellis, Polster and Rogers'. *Journal of Counseling Psychology*, 31: 228–37.

Goodyear, R. K., Abadie, P. D. and Efros, F. (1984). 'Supervisory Theory into Practice: Differential Perceptions of Supervision by Ekstein, Ellis, Polster and Rogers'. *Journal of Counseling Psychology*, 31: 228–37.

Goodyear, R. K. and Bernard, J. M. (1998). 'Clinical Supervision: Lessons from the Literature'. *Counselor Education and Supervision*, 38: 6–22.

Guest, D. E. and Conway, N. (2002). 'Pressure at Work and the Psychological Contract'. London: CIPD. Retrieved 8 April 2006 from: http://www.cipd.co.uk/subjects/empreltns/psycntrct/psycontr.htm

Hahn, W. K (2001). 'The Experience of Shame in Supervision'. *Psychotherapy*, 38: 272–82.

Hildebrand, J. (1998). *Bridging the Gap: A Training Module in Personal and Professional Development.* London: Karnac Books.

Hinshelwood, R. D. (1994). *A Dictionary of Kleinian Thought.* London: Free Association Books.

Holloway, E. L. and Neufeldt, S. A. (1995). 'Supervision: Its Contributions to Treatment Efficacy'. *Journal of Consulting and Clinical Psychology*, 63: 207–13.

Inskipp, F. and Proctor, B. (1988). *Skills For Supervising and Being Supervised.* Twickenham, Middlesex: Cascade Publications.

Kent, G. and McAuley, D. (1995). 'Ethical Difficulties Faced by Trainee Clinical Psychologists'. *Clinical Psychology Forum*, 80, 26–30.

Ladany, N., Hill, C. E., Corbett, M. M. and Nutt, E. A. (1996). 'Nature, Extent and Importance of What Psychotherapy Trainees Do Not Disclose to Their Supervisors'. *Journal of Counseling Psychology*, 43: 10–24.

Ladany, N., Constantine, M. G., Miller, K., Erickson, C. D. and Muse-Burke, J. L. (2000). 'Supervisor Countertransference: A Qualitative Investigation into Its Identification and Description'. *Journal of Counseling Psychology*, 47: 102–15.

Miars, R. D., Tracey, T. J., Ray, P. B., Cornfeld, J. L., O'Farrell, M. and Gelso, C. J. (1983). 'Variation in Supervision Process across Trainee Experience Levels'. *Journal of Counseling Psychology*, 30: 403–12.

Mollon, P. (1989). 'Anxiety, Supervision and a Space for Thinking: Some Narcissistic Perils for Clinical Psychologists in Learning Psychotherapy'. *British Journal of Medical Psychology*, 62: 113–22.

Niemi, P. M. (1997). 'Medical Students' Professional Identity: Self-Reflection during The Preclinical Years'. *Medical Education*, 31: 408–15.

Olk, M. and Friedlander, M. L. (1992). 'Trainees' Experiences of Role Conflict and Role Ambiguity in Supervisory Relationships'. *Journal of Counseling Psychology*, 39: 389–97.

Page, S. and Wosket, V. (2001). *Supervising the Counsellor: A Cyclical Model*. London: Routledge.

Prochaska, J. O. and Di Clemente, C. (1983). 'Stages and Processes of Self-Change in Smoking: Towards an Integrative Model of Change'. *Journal of Consulting & Clinical Psychology*, 5: 390–5.

Raichelson, S. H., Herron, W. G., Primavera, L. H. and Ramirez, S. M. (1997). 'Incidence and Effects of Parallel Process in Psychotherapy Supervision'. *Clinical Supervisor*, 15: 37–48.

Rosenbaum, M. and Ronen, T. (1998). 'Clinical Supervision from the Standpoint of Cognitive-Behaviour Therapy'. *Psychotherapy*, 35: 220–30.

Salzberger-Wittenberg, I. (1983). 'Part 1: Beginnings'. In I. Salzberger-Wittenberg, G. Henry and E. Osborne (eds.), *The Emotional Experience of Teaching and Learning*. London: Routledge and Kegan Paul.

Sanville, J. (1989). 'The Play in Supervision'. *Smith College Studies in Social Work*, 59: 157–9.

Scaife, J. M. (1993). 'Application of a General Supervision Framework: Creating a Context of Cooperation'. *Educational and Child Psychology*, 10 (2): 61–72.

Scaife, J. M. (2001). *Supervision in the Mental Health Professions*. London: Brunner-Routledge.

Skovholt, T. M. and Ronnestad, M. H. (1992). *The Evolving Professional Self: Stages and Themes in Therapist and Counselor Development*. Chichester, England: Wiley and Sons.

Snadden, D., Thomas, M. L., Griffin, E. M. and Hudson, H. (1996). 'Portfolio-Based Learning and General Practice Vocational Training'. *Medical Education*, 30: 148–52.

Stoltenberg, C. D., McNeill, B. and Delworth, U. (1998). *IDM Supervision: An Integrated Developmental Model for Supervising Counselors and Therapists*. San Francisco: Jossey-Bass.

White E., Butterworth T., Bishop V., Carson J., Jeacock J. and Clements A. (1998). 'Clinical Supervision: Insider Reports of a Private World'. *Journal of Advanced Nursing*, 28: 185–92.

Williams, A. B. (1997). 'On Parallel Process in Social Work Supervision'. *Clinical Social Work Journal*, 25: 425–35.

Woodward, H. (1998). 'Reflective Journals and Portfolios: Learning through Assessment'. *Assessment and Evaluation in Higher Education*, 23: 415–23.

Worthen, V. and McNeill, B. W. (1996). 'A Phenomenological Investigation of "Good" Supervision Events'. *Journal of Counseling Psychology*, 43: 25–34.

Wulf, J. and Nelson, M. L. (2000). 'Experienced Psychologists' Recollection of Internship Supervision and Its Contributions to Their Development'. *The Clinical Supervisor*, 19: 123–45.

Chapter 8

Therapy and Personal Development

Caroline Rake

Introduction

A variety of psychotherapeutic approaches emphasize the importance of personal therapy for training and practising therapists. An experience of personal therapy is considered to aid the personal development of the therapist in the *client* role, as it is considered to do for any individual who embarks on a course of therapy (Buckley, Karasu and Charles 1981). In addition, it is suggested that the experience of personal therapy enhances professional development and is a fundamental component of therapeutic practice (Strupp 1955). For clinical psychologists, personal therapy has not typically been a requirement for training or practice, and this may be because of an alignment with the *scientist-practitioner* model in which importance is given to evidence-based practice. Clinical psychologists do not necessarily practise psychotherapy or psychological therapy as such, as the profession covers a broad range of specialties and working roles. However, clinical psychologists are working with people and do have a therapeutic role of some form, whether this be seeing individuals for psychotherapy or whether it be advising other professionals on the treatment of people in their care. I would argue that personal therapy, as part of the process of personal development, has a significant role to play in clinical psychology training and subsequent professional development. Moreover, I believe that personal development is closely interlinked with professional development. In this chapter I will give an overview on the impact of personal therapy on personal and professional development, including a review of the research literature and a summary of the findings from a qualitative research study that I conducted.

The Background

There is a long history of therapists being required to undergo personal therapy as part of their training. (For the purpose of this chapter I will often use the generic term 'therapist' to refer to a range of psychotherapy professions, and I will use the term 'therapy' for a wide range of psycho-therapeutic approaches.) In psychoanalytic circles it is largely accepted that the work of the therapist is supported and enhanced by the experience of personal therapy, a view that derives from the early development of psychoanalysis (Freud 1964a; 1964b). Personal analysis or therapy is seen as an essential component of training to be a psychoanalyst or psychoanalytic psychotherapist (Clark 1986; Strupp 1955; Fromm-Reichmann 1950). As Freud comments, 'where and how is the poor wretch to acquire the ideal qualifications which he will need in his profession? The answer is in an analysis of himself' (Freud 1964b: 246). In addition, the interpersonal nature of the therapeutic relationship means that 'any attempt at intensive psychotherapy is fraught with danger, hence unacceptable, where not preceded by the future psychiatrist's personal analysis' (Fromm-Reichmann 1950: 42). Other models of therapy also stipulate that personal therapy is a necessary part of training. For instance, counselling psychology views personal development and personal therapy as essential aspects of training, with 40 hours of personal therapy being a minimum requirement (Williams, Coyle and Lyons 1999).

In clinical psychology, for which training involves learning about the practice of different theoretical approaches, personal therapy is not a requirement, although it will not be discouraged (Garfield and Kurtz 1976; Norcross 2005; Norcross, Dryden and DeMichele 1992). The influence of behavioural and latterly CBT approaches is significant here as these approaches have often had considerable emphasis in the training of clinical psychologists. Previously, behavioural and CBT approaches have opposed the idea of personal therapy being needed for its trainees; however, more recently CBT would seem more appreciative of the idea, and several European countries now insist on obligatory personal therapy as part of the psychotherapy accreditation process, and this includes CBT (Laireiter and Willutzki 2005). Given that therapists of different therapeutic orientations will seek personal therapy as part of training requirements, for other professional reasons or for personal reasons, and given that personal therapy involves considerable cost in terms of money, time and emotional upheaval, then we need to consider what the benefits in terms of professional and personal development are.

Literature Review

Survey studies have identified the prevalence of personal therapy amongst mental health professionals including psychotherapists (Norcross and Guy 2005; Orlinsky, Ronnestad, Willutzki, Wiseman, Botermans and the SPR Collaborative Research Network 2005). Norcross and Guy (2005), in their review of studies in the USA, found a prevalence of around 75 per cent of respondents having at least one experience of personal therapy. An ongoing international study using the Development of Psychotherapists Common Core Questionnaire (DPCCQ) has gathered information on various facets of therapeutic practice from over 5,000 therapists and found that 79 per cent of respondents have had at least one experience of personal therapy (Orlinsky, Ronnestad, Willutzki, Wiseman, Botermans and the SPR Collaborative Research Network 2005).

In research looking at therapists' experiences of personal therapy, therapists have generally reported that their experiences have been helpful and that they have experienced improvements in various aspects of their lives (Buckley, Karasu and Charles 1981; Macran and Shapiro 1998; Norcross, Strausser-Kirtland and Missar 1988; Orlinsky, Norcross, Ronnestad and Wiseman 2005). In one study, a questionnaire given to psychotherapists asked about their experiences of their own long-term psychotherapy (Buckley, Karasu and Charles 1981). The 71 respondents reported wide-ranging positive benefits, including improvements in self-esteem, relationships and work functioning. These improvements were significantly correlated to "non-specific factors" (Frank 1971), such as the empathy and warmth shown by the therapist. However, symptom relief and character change were significantly correlated to specific technical aspects such as interpretation and insight. The authors concluded that specific technical aspects are important for change but only in the context of a positive therapeutic relationship, adding that this finding is relevant for clients in general.

Personal therapy is often considered to be a crucial aspect of practising as a therapist. Norcross, Strausser-Kirtland and Missar (1988: 36) argue that 'the goal of the psychotherapist's personal treatment is to alter the nature of subsequent therapeutic work in ways that enhance its effectiveness'. These authors suggest that there has been a 'taboo' against investigating the area of the therapist's own treatment. They are critical of the limited information available, arguing that it has often been derived from anecdotal accounts or poorly controlled surveys. In their study of psychiatrists, social workers and psychologists, a comprehensive questionnaire identified that 71 per cent of 710 respondents reported at least one episode of personal therapy. Over 90 per cent of respondents reported positive outcomes, including improvements in symptomatology and insight. Further, experiencing the effectiveness of psychotherapy and the possibility for behavioural change were identified as important lasting influences.

Overall, surveys of therapists indicate that personal therapy also has a positive influence on professional development (Buckley, Karasu and Charles 1981; Norcross 2005; Norcross Strausser-Kirtland and Missar 1988; Orlinsky, Botermans and Ronnestad 2001). In a recent study of 4,000 therapists from 15 countries, more than 75 per cent claimed that the experience of personal therapy had a strongly positive impact on professional development, whilst less than 2 per cent reported any negative effects. Personal therapy was repeatedly ranked as one of the top three sources of positive impact on professional development along with direct clinical experience and supervision. The authors of the study note that, with the exception of cognitive-behavioural therapists, personal therapy was ranked much higher than academic or educational experiences (Orlinsky, Botermans and Ronnestad 2001). In a review of studies investigating how the therapist's therapy may enhance therapeutic practice, Macran and Shapiro (1998) identify several common themes:

- it can help the therapist to manage the stressful aspects of clinical work and hopefully ensures the good mental health that is so important in this role;
- the therapist's self-awareness of personal difficulties can be heightened so that these do not impair the therapy process;
- in personal therapy, the therapist gets the opportunity to have an experience of being a client, which should thereby encourage empathic responsiveness;
- witnessing another therapist at work allows the therapist as client to learn about therapeutic techniques and experience a model of therapist behaviour;
- finally, a helpful experience of personal therapy can develop a sense of confidence in the therapy process.

Therefore, personal therapy appears to be helpful for therapists in terms of personal and professional development.

It would be hoped that the benefits of personal therapy would subsequently influence therapeutic effectiveness and outcome for patients, and that this would be demonstrated in research studies. However, reviews of studies indicate that little evidence is available to indicate that personal therapy improves the therapist's performance in relation to patient outcome (Clark 1986; Greenberg and Staller 1981; Macaskill 1988; Macran and Shapiro 1998). For instance, in one review of eight studies investigating whether personal therapy improves the effectiveness of the therapist, only two studies suggested a positive link between personal therapy and therapeutic efficacy, four studies found no link, and two indicated that the impact was negative (Greenberg and Staller 1981). The limited research looking at the impact of personal therapy on the therapist's effectiveness would appear to be inconclusive. From their review of studies, Macran and Shapiro (1998) conclude that there are many methodological problems that need to be rectified before the impact of personal therapy can be clarified in research. This concurs with the view that there are too many confounding factors to control for, to enable an assessment of the impact on client outcome (Orlinsky, Norcross, Ronnestad and Wiseman 2005).

Macran and Shapiro (1998) suggest that research should investigate the process of how personal therapy might have an impact on client outcome. They suggest that the research question should be *how* personal therapy has an impact rather than *whether* it has an impact. In a subsequent qualitative study, researchers looked at how the experience of personal therapy impacted on the therapist's therapeutic work with clients. This study involved interviewing seven experienced therapists from differing therapeutic orientations who had all experienced varying amounts of personal therapy. From the results of this study (Macran, Smith and Stiles 1999: 422), the authors identified three general themes:

1 'Orienting to the therapist: humanity, power, boundaries': participants became aware of the significant impact of their own 'personal presence';
2 'Orienting to the client: trust, respect, patience': they were able to stand back and allow the client 'space' to work on issues in therapy;
3 'Listening with the third ear': they felt it facilitated therapeutic involvement at a 'deeper or more unconscious level'.

According to these authors, the comments of participants indicated that experiences in personal therapy were translated into the tools of their own practice as therapists.

In a similar qualitative study, five psychoanalytically oriented psycho-therapists were interviewed about their experiences of personal therapy and the impact on professional and personal development (Wiseman and Shefler 2001). Interview transcripts were analysed and relevant themes were identified. These themes were grouped into the following six domains:

1 *importance of therapy for therapists: past and current attitudes;*
2 *impacts of personal therapy on the professional self: identity;*
3 *impacts of personal therapy on one's being in the session: process;*
4 *the therapist as patient: experiences in past and current personal therapy;*
5 *the therapist as patient: self in relation to the personal therapist;*
6 *mutual and unique influences of didactic learning, supervision and personal therapy.*

(Wiseman and Shefler 2001: 133)

The authors of this study concluded that personal therapy is of high importance for the personal and professional development of psychotherapists, and that personal and professional development are often intertwined (Wiseman and Shefler 2001).

Similar qualitative studies have looked at the perceived impact of personal therapy on professional development and practice. These studies have reported that participants felt that the experience of personal therapy led to an enhanced self-awareness and to socialization into the professional role. Further, the research studies all identified a close link between personal and professional development in terms of the influence of personal therapy (Bellows 2007; Grimmer and Tribe 2001; Murphy 2005).

Personal Therapy: The Impact on Therapeutic Practice - A Research Study

A qualitative research study was carried out to further develop the understanding of how personal therapy influences the therapist's therapeutic practice (Rake 2005). Using in-depth, semi-structured interviews to obtain the views of practising therapists, participants were asked about their experiences of personal therapy, what had been helpful or unhelpful, and how this had influenced therapeutic work with patients. A qualitative approach was thought to be the most appropriate way to develop a detailed understanding of the impact of personal therapy on personal and professional development.

The participants in the study were all practising therapists from a variety of professional backgrounds (including psychologists, psychotherapists and counsellors). In the group of eight participants (six female and two male) there was a range of experience, as a qualified therapist, from three to 19 years (with a mean of 10.62 years). With regard to theoretical orientation, as opposed to professional title, three described themselves as Psychodynamic or Psychoanalytic, three as Gestalt, one as Humanistic and one as Systemic. All had experienced more than one episode of personal therapy ranging from six months to 10 years in length, including four participants who were in ongoing therapy at the time of interview. The majority of the therapy episodes were comprised of once weekly sessions, but five of the therapy episodes had more frequent sessions and three of the episodes took place less frequently than once a week.

The analysis of the interview data followed the principles of *Interpretative Phenomenological Analysis (IPA)* (Smith 1995; Smith, Jarman and Osborn 1999; Smith and Osborn 2003). Pertinent themes were identified in each of the interview transcripts, themes were then clustered according to related references or meanings, and ultimately grouped into *master* themes relevant for the entire research data.

Findings and implications

Although the purpose of the study was to investigate how therapists perceive their experiences of personal therapy to influence their professional development and therapeutic practice, participants emphasized the personal impact of therapy experiences and how these were inextricably linked with the professional impact. The identified master themes, namely *learning, impact* and *negative aspects*, will now be explained and explored, with reference to quotations from the participants.

Learning
The *learning* master theme included the themes of *learning experience* and *experience being a patient*. The first of these themes incorporates the participant's experience of personal therapy as an 'educational' experience,

something that may be associated with training in psychotherapy or counselling, or may be a learning experience in its own right.

> I think in analytic therapy, that your training therapy or analysis . . . is com-
> pletely crucial. You identify with your therapist, you parrot them, and you
> take difficulties that you're having with particular patients and within your
> training situation . . . I think you learn directly about technique, about what
> is helpful and what isn't. (Participant 8)

Participants emphasized the importance of personal therapy as a means of
learning about becoming a therapist or becoming a better therapist. The
learning experience theme referred to learning about technique and theory,
and about having a therapist on whom to model oneself. Participants
valued this learning aspect of the therapy experience and reported it as a
huge aid to theoretical and technical understanding of therapeutic models,
a finding that supports the suggestion in the literature that personal therapy
is an important prerequisite or adjunct to training as a means of learning
a theoretical model and giving the therapist confidence in a given therapeutic approach (Clark 1986; Freud 1964a; 1964b; Fromm-Reichmann
1950; Grimmer and Tribe 2001; Macran and Shapiro 1998; Williams,
Coyle and Lyons 1999).

The second theme, *experience being a patient*, reflected the importance
of the experiential aspect of personal therapy as a learning experience in
itself. Participants referred to a very personal, individual and often highly
emotional experience as being informative for their work as therapists. The
powerful impact and knowledge of what it is like to be a patient/client and
the significance of the therapist were factors that were highlighted.

> I think the general experience of being a client has had a very significant
> impact on me. Just in knowing . . . what it feels like to sit in the other chair,
> and how hugely important the therapist and the therapy can be. And it's
> easy if you're doing it all day every day to perhaps forget that. I think to have
> a different degree of respect and care for clients, and to perhaps challenge
> the fact that I would think I couldn't be that important, to challenge that.
> (Participant 3)

In the current study, participants attested to the immense value of the
experience of being a patient and how this could not be learned about from
academic teaching. The experience of the therapeutic process, as opposed

to theoretical learning about the process, was described as having a potent influence on understanding the client's experience and how to manage this in a given therapy setting. Additionally, in the current study, participants cited the significance of the figure of the therapist or transference reactions as an issue that aided personal and professional understanding. The experience of working through personal issues was identified as important, and appeared to give participants the confidence as therapists to recognize and work with similar issues in clients. These findings appear to reflect suggestions in the previous research literature that the experience of personal therapy is a positive influence, enhances empathic understanding and aids personal development in a way that contributes to clinical practice (Buckley, Karasu and Charles 1981; Macran and Shapiro 1998; Murphy 2005; Norcross 2005; Norcross, Strausser-Kirtland and Missar 1988; Orlinsky, Botermans and Ronnestad 2001; Orlinsky, Norcross, Ronnestad and Wiseman 2005).

The impact

The *impact* as a master theme concerned the impact of personal therapy experiences on the participant and included the three themes *helpful aspects*, *emotional reaction* and *personal/professional impact*. The first theme, *helpful aspects*, reflected participants' views on what particular elements of the therapy experience they had found to be personally helpful. Included here were qualities of the therapist, such as their containing stance, and what the therapist did, such as listening or making interpretations.

> The helpful aspect about H is that you feel as if you could explode a bomb behind her and she would cope, so H doesn't panic. I think more important than anything in therapy is that your therapist gives the feeling that they don't panic, and that they listen. (Participant 1)

All participants commented on how their experiences of personal therapy had a positive and powerful impact on them personally as well as professionally. The *helpful aspects* theme included participants' reports of what had been experienced as personally beneficial. Here, specific comments were made about the quality of the therapeutic relationship and also the 'ordinary' human contact with the therapist. Further, participants identified the helpfulness of the therapist's comments or interpretations. This theme reflects earlier findings about the general benefits of personal therapy, and, specifically, that the 'emotional tone' of a therapeutic situation as well as specific technical aspects, such as interpretation, are significantly related to beneficial personal change (Buckley, Karasu and Charles 1981; Norcross 2005; Norcross, Strausser-Kirtland and Missar 1988; Orlinsky, Botermans and Ronnestad 2001).

The second of the themes, *emotional reaction*, referred to the strong reactions of participants to the therapy experience. This incorporated the powerful feelings that arose in relation to the therapist or in response to the therapy process itself, and also to the strength of feeling associated with the recalling of traumatic events or the exploration of internal conflicts.

> What I'm not afraid of, as a therapist, is when somebody dissolves into tears and is going through a very dark place. And I absolutely believe that comes from the position of having gone through several dark places myself and sort of come out, not just around issues of X . . . and that was obviously one of the issues that I brought to therapy and that was a very dark time in which I felt like I went to some very dark and mucky places . . . (Participant 6)

Participants reflected on the powerful emotive impact of the experience of personal therapy and the *emotional reaction* theme incorporated these essentially personal responses. This was considered a valuable part of the therapy experience as it allowed an appreciation of what was bearable, thus contributing to personal development and subsequently to therapeutic practice, as there was an enhanced ability to tolerate strong emotional reactions from clients. In terms of previous studies regarding the therapist's therapy, I am unaware of any that have explored the emotional impact in detail, or that have identified the importance of this experiential aspect in terms of learning what can be tolerated emotionally.

The third theme, *personal/professional impact*, indicated what participants saw as the resultant effects of therapy on themselves both in terms of personal development and in terms of the effects on professional life and practice.

> That's the big one that always stands out . . . just that I know myself much better. I know what I struggle with, I know what I'm more comfortable with, and I know how I've changed and grown. I've got my own personal experiences, although uncomfortable and difficult, it has made a huge difference to my life and my relationships in a very good way. So when I sit with someone in the room it makes an enormous difference . . . I think there's something about being more grounded, knowing myself, being more sorted than I was, more able to sit with people when they are in distress, and know

my own limits. If there's something going on in my life, or there's certain clients I shouldn't be working with, or if I need to take time out, I know that better, because I am not as cut off. (Participant 4)

Within the *personal/professional impact* theme it was found that personal and professional development were closely interlinked and difficult to separate out. That is, it was difficult to disentangle the personal from the professional impact of personal therapy experiences. Further, participants spoke of the importance of knowing one's self, of not disowning aspects of the self, of appreciating limitations and, consequently, being a more available presence as a therapist. Previous studies in this area have found personal and professional development to be interrelated and have identified self-awareness as a common theme (Grimmer and Tribe 2001; Macran and Shapiro 1998; Norcross, Strausser-Kirtland and Missar 1988; Wiseman and Shefler 2001).

Negative aspects

The third master theme, *negative aspects*, elucidated the elements of the personal therapy experience that were found to be detrimental, consisting of the themes *unhelpful experiences* and *training therapy*. The first theme, *unhelpful experiences*, incorporated participants' comments about what was adverse about their experience of therapy. These unhelpful aspects might be concerned with the therapist's comments or interpretations, and also the detrimental impact of the therapeutic process on the individual participant.

> Even now I think, stuck in my mind sometimes, is if he made a sharp comment . . . maybe it was a bit challenging or it might have come a bit too early or something. But all these years, it's like twenty years ago, the odd sharp comment I remember. (Participant 2)

Incorporated in the *unhelpful experiences* theme were aspects of the therapist's manner, therapeutic stance or communication. Latterly, these experiences were considered to be helpful in that participants reputedly endeavoured not to replicate such seemingly unhelpful aspects in their own practice as therapists – a finding matched in a previous qualitative study (Grimmer and Tribe 2001). In addition, participants reported on the destabilizing aspects of personal therapy, although such an impact was not seen to persist over time. Other studies report similar findings (Buckley, Karasu and Charles 1981; Garfield and Bergin 1971; Greenberg and Staller 1981; Macaskill 1988).

The second theme, *training therapy*, refers to personal therapy that takes place simultaneously with a therapy training course, often as a course requirement. Participants valued this therapy experience but specifically identified the detrimental aspects, such as the potentially destabilizing impact and preoccupying nature of it.

> When you're in training therapy, it's hugely difficult and perturbing ... I became quite interested in the effect on one's significant others ... it can impact on relationships and it can make you so self-absorbed. It can act as a huge sort of energizer and source of support, but it can also just preoccupy you when you're doing it. (Participant 8)

The theme of *training therapy* falls within the *negative aspects* domain, which may appear at odds with the participants' reports that personal therapy is seen as a positive and crucial experience for personal and professional development. All participants had an experience of therapy as a training requirement, and all but two spoke of the negative facets of this. The disturbing impact of the training therapy in combination with the obligatory nature of the experience was cited, although viewed as an inescapable, and perhaps necessary, feature of the training process. These findings compare with a previous study where participants reported concerns about the constraining nature of obligatory training therapy (Williams, Coyle and Lyons 1999).

To conclude

The themes that were identified in this study appear to coincide with findings and themes in previous studies, as reported earlier. Also, in this study there was considerable consensus across the group of participants with regard to themes, despite differences in therapeutic experience, orientation, training and age. However, as a qualitative study with a small sample of participants, interpretation of the findings and generalization to larger groups of therapists can only be tentative.

Future research on the impact of personal therapy could involve a larger sample of therapists recruited from diverse sources, with the involvement of a larger research team. The large ongoing international study looking at therapists and their personal therapy (Orlinsky, Ronnestad, Willutzki,

Wiseman, Botermans and the SPR Collaborative Research Network 2005) is a good model for achieving a wide-ranging longitudinal perspective with the use of a specially devised questionnaire (DPCCQ). However, the use of a questionnaire may fail to derive the in-depth information that can be produced in qualitative interviews. Further qualitative research could investigate the identified themes in more detail (e.g. *emotional reaction*) and could follow up participants to assess the long-term impact.

Further Thoughts

As a clinical psychologist should you consider personal therapy as part of the process of personal development? Studies indicate that therapists have found personal therapy to be a beneficial experience in the same way that clients receiving therapy do. It is considered to be a personally valuable experience, and this personal significance is often seen as interlinking with professional development and practice. However, there is a personal cost in that therapy can be experienced as unsettling and can have an impact on relationships with others. Also, it requires commitment, effort, time, and a financial outlay. Despite the apparent hardships of the personal therapy experience many therapists claim that it is an experience that is crucial for practice as a therapist. Many training courses stipulate that personal therapy is an obligatory requirement, but this position has never been adopted for clinical psychology training. If personal development is considered to be an important part of the training process then is it appropriate to introduce a requirement that trainees undergo personal therapy? If not an obligatory requirement, then how can trainees or qualified clinical psychologists make the decision to enter into therapy as part of their personal development?

I imagine a variety of reactions to the suggestion that personal therapy might be a good adjunct to clinical psychology training. Some would probably argue that personal or emotional difficulties might necessitate some form of personal therapy, but otherwise academic teaching, research and clinical supervision are sufficient to support professional practice. If, as a clinical psychologist treating a client, you enter into some form of therapeutic relationship, then you as a person and what you say or do is going to have an impact on that client. It could be argued that clinical supervision and academic learning would hopefully engender some self-reflection, self-awareness and appreciation of that impact, but may not be sufficient to lead to a more developed self-understanding and awareness of one's impact as a therapist. The study outlined in this chapter, and previous research, indicates how an enhanced self-awareness through personal therapy can lead to a better awareness of the impact as a therapist. Here, I am talking about a self-awareness that is not just at an intellectual level but also at an emotional level. This is where the experiential aspects of personal therapy come into play, as reflected in a knowledge of oneself, of what is emotionally tolerable, of what it is like to be a therapy client and awareness of the powerful effect that the therapy situation and the therapist might have. There is much to learn about the experience of receiving therapy both in terms of learning about the therapy process and gaining an enhanced self-knowledge. Working as a clinical psychologist (or training as a clinical psychologist), whilst rewarding and challenging, comes with demands that can be personally stressful and there is a need to recognize this. Personal therapy as a form of self-care can offer emotional support and containment, and the internalization of this experience, including the relationship with the therapist, can leave a sustaining impact that endures over time.

ACKNOWLEDGEMENTS

I am grateful to all the participants who gave their time to take part in the study. Also, I would like to thank Graham Paley for his advice and support as research supervisor.

REFERENCES

Bellows, K. F. (2007). 'Psychotherapists' Personal Psychotherapy and Its Perceived Influence on Clinical Practice'. *Bulletin of the Menninger Clinic*, 71(3): 204–26.

Buckley, T., Karasu, T. B. and Charles, E. (1981). 'Psychotherapists View Their Personal Therapy'. *Psychotherapy: Theory, Research and Practice*, 18(3): 299–305.

Clark, M. (1986). 'Personal Therapy: A Review of Empirical Research'. *Professional Psychology: Research and Practice*, 17: 541–3.

Frank, J. D. (1971). 'Therapeutic Factors in Psychotherapy'. *American Journal of Psychotherapy*, 25: 350–61.

Freud, S. (1964a) [1910]. 'The Future Prospects of Psychoanalytic Therapy'. In J. Strachey (ed.), *Complete Psychological Works of Sigmund Freud*. London: Hogarth Press.

Freud, S. (1964b) [1937]. 'Analysis Terminable and Interminable'. In J. Strachey (ed.), *Complete Psychological Works of Sigmund Freud*. London: Hogarth Press.

Fromm-Reichmann, F. (1950). *Principles of Intensive Psychotherapy*. Chicago: University of Chicago Press.

Garfield, S. L. and Bergin, A. E. (1971). 'Personal Therapy, Outcome and Some Therapist Variables'. *Psychotherapy*, 8: 251–3.

Garfield, S. L. and Kurtz, R. M. (1976). 'Personal Therapy for the Psychotherapist: Some Findings and Issues'. *Psychotherapy*, 13: 188–92.

Greenberg, R. P. and Staller, J. (1981). 'Personal Therapy for Therapists'. *American Journal of Psychiatry*, 138: 1467–71.

Grimmer, A. and Tribe, R. (2001). 'Counselling Psychologists' Perceptions of the Impact of Mandatory Personal Therapy on Professional Development – An Exploratory Study'. *Counselling Psychology Quarterly*, 14: 287–301.

Laireiter, A.-R. and Willutzki, U. (2005). 'Personal Therapy in Cognitive-Behavioural Therapy: Tradition and Current Practice'. In J. D. Geller, J. C. Norcross and D. E. Orlinsky. *The Psychotherapist's Own Psychotherapy*. New York: Oxford University Press.

Macaskill, N. D. (1988). 'Personal Therapy in the Training of the Psychotherapist: Is it Effective?' *British Journal of Psychotherapy*, 43: 219–26.

Macran, S. and Shapiro, D. A. (1998). 'The Role of Personal Therapy for Therapists: A Review'. *British Journal of Medical Psychology*, 71(1): 13–25.

Macran S., Smith J. A. and Stiles W. B. (1999). 'How Does Personal Therapy Affect Therapists' Practice?' *Journal of Counselling Psychology*, 46(4): 419–31.

Murphy, D. (2005). 'A Qualitative Study into the Experience of Mandatory Personal Therapy during Training'. *Counselling and Psychotherapy Research*, 5(1): 27–32.

Norcross, J. C., (2005). 'The Psychotherapist's Own Psychotherapy: Educating and Developing Psychologists'. *American Psychologist*, 60(8): 840–50.

Norcross, J. C., Dryden, W. and DeMichele, J. T. (1992). 'British Clinical Psychologists and Personal Therapy: III: What's Good for the Goose?' *Clinical Psychology Forum*, 44: 29–33.

Norcross, J. C. and Guy, J. D. (2005). 'The Prevalence and Parameters of Personal Therapy in the United States'. In J. D. Geller, J. C. Norcross and D.E. Orlinsky, *The Psychotherapist's Own Psychotherapy*. New York: Oxford University Press.

Norcross, J., Strausser-Kirtland, D. and Missar, C. (1988). 'The Processes and Outcomes of Psychotherapists' Personal Treatment Experiences'. *Psychotherapy*, 25: 36–43.

Orlinsky, D. E., Botermans, J.-F. and Ronnestad, M. H. (2001). 'Towards an Empirically Grounded Model of Psychotherapy Training: Four Thousand Therapists Rate Influences on Their Development'. *Australian Psychologist*, 36(2): 139–48.

Orlinsky, D. E., Norcross, J. C., Ronnestad, M. H. and Wiseman, H. (2005). 'Outcomes and Impacts of the Psychotherapist's Own Psychotherapy: A Research Review'. In J. D. Geller, J. C. Norcross and D. E. Orlinsky, *The Psychotherapist's Own Psychotherapy*. New York: Oxford University Press.

Orlinsky, D. E., Ronnestad, M. H., Willutzki, U., Wiseman, H., Botermans, J.-F. and the SPR Collaborative Research Network (2005). 'The Prevalence and Parameters of Personal Therapy in Europe and Elsewhere'. In J. D. Geller, J. C. Norcross, and D. E. Orlinsky, *The Psychotherapist's Own Psychotherapy*. New York: Oxford University Press.

Rake, C. J. (2005). 'Personal Therapy for Psychotherapists: The Impact on Therapeutic Practice'. Unpublished Masters Dissertation. University of Leeds.

Smith, J. A. (1995). 'Semi-Structured Interviewing and Qualitative Analysis'. In J. A. Smith, R. Harre and L. Van Langenhove (eds.) (1995), *Rethinking Methods in Psychology*. London: Sage Publications.

Smith, J. A., Jarman, M. and Osborn, M. (1999). 'Doing Interpretative Phenomenological Analysis'. In M. Murray and K. Chamberlain (eds.), *Qualitative Health Psychology: Theories and Methods*. London: Sage Publications.

Smith, J. A. and Osborn, M. (2003). 'Interpretative Phenomenological Analysis'. In J. A. Smith (ed.), *Qualitative Psychology: A Practical Guide to Methods*. London: Sage Publications.

Strupp, H. (1955). 'The Effect of the Psychotherapist's Personal Analysis upon his Techniques'. *Journal of Consulting Psychology*, 19: 197–204.

Williams, F., Coyle, A. and Lyons, E. (1999). 'How Counselling Psychologists View Their Personal Therapy'. *British Journal of Medical Psychology*, 72: 545–55.

Willig, C. (2001). *Introducing Qualitative Research in Psychology*. London: Open University Press.

Wiseman, H. and Shefler, G. (2001). 'Experienced Psychoanalytically Oriented Therapists' Narrative Accounts of Their Personal Therapy: Impacts on Professional and Personal Development'. *Psychotherapy*, 38(2): 129–41.

Chapter 9

Personal Development in a Group Setting

Fiona Smith, Sheila Youngson and Garry Brownbridge

Introduction - Sheila Youngson

This chapter is in three parts. The first and major part has been written by Fiona Smith. She reviews the literature on the rationale and efficacy of personal development in a group context, and offers some personal reflections from her own experiences. The second part comprises writing from two experienced qualified clinical psychologists reflecting on their personal development and learning within group contexts since qualifying. The third part concludes with some thoughts about the potentially contrasting viewpoints.

Part One - Fiona Smith

Overview and introduction

Mearns (1997a: 168) reports these reactions to a personal development group, all recorded after the same meeting.

'one hour of interminable boredom'
'the most alive human relating I have ever experienced'
'excruciatingly slow and turgid'
'like being in a group of scared mice'
'unbelievably exciting'
'terrifying'
'incredibly safe'
'really challenging'
'too cosy'

This clearly illustrates the question at the heart of this field of research: why do people respond so differently to experiences in groups? How can the quotations above be describing the same situation? Crucially, what are the implications for personal development and clinical practice? Like many compelling areas of research, this subject matter is fascinating but difficult to delineate and define. Although individuals have a wide, various and continuous experience of being in groups (Douglas 1995), beginning to talk and think about this central human experience is often challenging.

Although any person could use groups for personal development, the available literature is largely confined to the experiences of trainee counsellors. The absence of work relating to non-trainees, or to clinical psychologists is striking. This perhaps forms an important clue as to what such groups are felt to be for, and for whom.

As part of the work discussed in this chapter I have included reflections of my own group experiences as a clinical psychology trainee. Before embarking on this (quite daunting) task it felt important to think about the process and 'where I am coming from' in terms of my previous experiences. Groups are so central to the human experience that asking people to describe them sometimes feels like asking a fish to describe water. As the experience is universal, elemental and all-encompassing it can be very difficult to stand back from it and think reflectively. For example, I am writing this from my point of view as a member of several different groups: women, graduates, those in 'caring professions', those training to be clinical psychologists, and so on. My membership of these groups is something I think more or less about at different times and often I am not aware of it (for example, my membership of the majority white British culture). But all of these groups may influence how I respond to new group contexts.

I am also, in effect, commenting on the functioning and aims of one training group (counselling psychology) from the point of view of another (clinical psychology). This may be influenced by a number of factors, including social comparison, questioning the rationale of my own training, curiosity and stereotypes about the training of others.

Personal development groups

Interest in personal development in a group context began in the 1950s as part of early research into therapists' behaviour and attitudes (for example, Rogers 1957) and continued with the formation of encounter, 'T' and sensitivity groups (described in the review by Payne (1999)). Modern counsellor training courses typically include small groups of around eight to 12 members known as 'awareness', 'personal development', 'experiential' or 'reflective' groups. Whilst different terminology is used to describe these small groups they share the goal of increasing self-awareness and promoting personal development (for example, Irving and Williams 1996; Johns 1996; Payne 1999). Personal development groups are usually facilitated, have an open agenda, are confidential and are usually, but not always (see, for instance, many counselling courses), separate from assessment procedures (Payne 1999).

What are the advantages of personal development in groups, as opposed to other methods? Although researchers and theorists have considered many different aspects of the experience, the overarching and central issue is that such groups form an opportunity to explore social, interpersonal aspects of the self (Douglas 1995; Foulkes 1990; Raskin 1986; Thompson 1999). Commentators have suggested that such groups 'form a bridge' between intra-psychic work and the interpersonal sense we make of ourselves in relation to others (for example, Lyons 1997). A number of authors have argued that personal development groups offer the potential for learning and growth not available in other contexts. Lyons (1997) pinpoints a number of specific personal development areas which may be benefited by group work, such as process awareness, the ability to give useful feedback, immediacy and learning to tolerate difference. Payne (1999) suggests that such groups make a valuable contribution to personal development by increasing insight and self-awareness, encouraging enquiry into behavioural style and improving interpersonal communication. Perhaps the clearest rationale for this sort of work is given by Hazel Johns who notes that 'interpersonal exchanges are as vital in our development as intrapersonal exploration' (1996: 111).

When discussing different methods of personal development Mearns (1997b) rates each in terms of the opportunities they provided for raising issues, working on issues and experimenting with the developing self. He notes that personal development groups are potent places for raising issues and provide a good place for experimentation, but may involve limited opportunity for working on issues (compared to, for example, personal therapy). He observes that it can be extremely therapeutic to take part in a group where 'it is permissible to articulate feelings of inadequacy, incompetence, helplessness and shame in the knowledge that such feelings will be respected and understood, and will not be taken as signs of weakness or professional uselessness' (Mearns 1997b: 26).

However, Mearns acknowledges that such groups may not be easy to find. He notes that groups can become another setting for helpers to 'indulge in a subtle competitiveness' where feelings of incompetence are avoided or masked. Thus, an important issue is how individuals can find (or help to create) a group in which it is possible to be vulnerable and to experiment safely.

Evaluation of research evidence

Before exploring the available research evidence it is interesting to ask what methodologies could be applied to this atypical area. How can you empirically investigate personal development? As it is by its nature subjective, how can it be objectively evaluated by another person? How is it possible to determine what constitutes genuine, meaningful personal growth? Is it sufficient to simply ask the person involved? Donati and Watts (1999) note the tension between 'academic' values of assessment and open scrutiny and 'person-centred' values of individual subjectivity and confidentiality. (See Chapter 10 for further elaboration of these ideas.)

The inherent difficulty of investigating this area is compounded by the fact that there is very little available research. As mentioned previously, the literature is almost completely confined to trainee counsellors. This work is typically comment on and reaction to existing practices rather than innovative research studies. Surprisingly, given the subject matter, there is a dearth of qualitative work. The available research has been divided into research carried out by those running groups (including reviews of current practice and some quantitative assessment) and 'service-user' research which directly involves feedback from group participants. It seemed useful to compare and contrast the different perspectives of those running and taking part in personal development groups.

Research exploring early personal development groups in the 1970s reported largely positive findings. For example, in an influential review Smith (1975) suggests that participants experienced sustained benefits in personal development, although the research methodology and groups themselves differed from modern approaches. However, as early as 1979 Hartman discussed concern regarding negative effects or 'casualties' of group work. In this review Hartman notes that the number of negative reactions reported typically involved a minority of participants (less than 10 per cent of the group). He also notes that there were philosophical and ideological issues in relation to defining 'damage' or 'harm' in a group context. For example, much as in personal therapy, even very distressing initial feelings may lead to longer-term positive growth and development.

As noted in reviews of this field (for example, Payne 1999), there was an almost 20-year gap between this early research and later work. Although a number of other positive results have been reported (for example, Izzard and Wheeler 1995; Small and Manthei 1988) methodological difficulties remain an issue. For example, Izzard and Wheeler (1995) assess whether self-awareness was influenced by participation in personal development groups. They assessed 'self-awareness' by measuring the level of self-disclosure by participants, assuming that a greater level of disclosure was linked to greater awareness. This study illustrates the difficulty of measuring personal development outcomes. Is self-disclosure equivalent to self-awareness? If not, how else could self-awareness have been assessed?

Some recent work has questioned the positive effects of personal development groups. For example, researchers have drawn attention to the possibility of ineffective training, negative effects or harm for some trainees (Donati and Watts 1999; Irving and Williams 1996) as well as the ethical dilemmas involved in mandatory groups. In an influential review Payne concludes that the research evidence 'appears to indicate that personal development (whether in group work or personal therapy) may not be the panacea for leading to improved counsellor/therapist practice' (1999: 64).

Similarly, Donati and Watts (1999) suggest that the personal development experiences of trainees in groups were not 'inevitably beneficial'. Irving and Williams (1996) carry the argument a stage further and suggest that the case for personal development groups as a central part of training had not been made.

Whilst these comments reflect the paucity of the research evidence, they perhaps misrepresent the aims of personal development groups. Most authors supporting such groups would not suggest that it is 'inevitably beneficial' for all those taking part, or that it is a panacea for improved clinical practice. Rather it is seen as an important arena for the discovery of both strengths and needs which may go on to influence professional activities.

The recent critiques may have arisen partly due to a lack of clarity about what personal development groups seek to achieve, This was particularly stressed by Irving and Williams who suggest that trainers and trainees are often 'unclear about what they are doing and why they are doing it' (1996:

137). The authors note that without a clear statement of aims it is not possible to ascertain whether objectives are being met. The issue of transferable skills has also been highlighted, with authors such as Jenkins commenting: 'The danger within the experiential tradition is that self-awareness can come to be valued in itself, almost independently of its translation into observable increased counsellor effectiveness and measurable benefit to the client' (1995: 205). This interesting comment serves to illustrate the different criteria by which personal development work might be judged: is self-awareness an end in itself or is 'measurable benefit' for clinical practice essential?

Personal development groups have been defended by a number of researchers and commentators. For example, Lyons argues that there remained a strong case for group work in counsellor training. In a specific response to the earlier article by Irving and Williams (1996) she suggests that the previous authors had not recognized what personal development groups could achieve and had described inappropriately run groups 'when trainers are not properly equipped to facilitate groups either theoretically or experientially' (Lyons 1997: 211).

The role of the facilitator is a perennial and central issue within the literature. Debates surrounding this question include whether personal development groups should be facilitated, and if so, how and by whom this should be done. The perceived role of facilitation is tied closely to theoretical orientation. Psychoanalytic and dynamic group models emphasize the importance of the transference relationship between group members and authority figures, such as facilitators or leaders (for example, Agazarian and Peters 1981; Douglas 1995). In contrast, person-centred group models emphasize the application of the core conditions, empathic understanding, congruent relating and unconditional positive regard (Macmillan and Lago 1996; Raskin 1986).

Although theoretical orientation influences the perceived role of the facilitator, there is some agreement as to what are the important roles within a personal development group in a learning context. For example, the creation of a safe learning space, being alert to destructive group processes and the modelling of appropriate interpersonal skills (for example, Johns 1996). There is perhaps more debate as to who carries out such roles, specifically whether or not the person is also a member of core staff if the group takes place in a learning environment. Some authors have suggested that there is a boundary issue if the facilitator also serves an assessment role (for example, Dryden 1994). Others suggest it is 'dangerous to divest personal development to the periphery' (Lyons 1997: 117) and such work should be undertaken by core staff. This debate reflects the boundary issues involved in engaging in personal development work whilst in a training environment (revisited in later sections).

'Service user' research

Although this is potentially the most useful source of information about the process, few researchers have asked group members in a non-directive, open-ended way about their experiences. In an early study of this type, Aveline (1986) describes members' perceptions of a personal development group for health professionals. A number of themes were identified, including the opportunity for intimate dialogue, the idea of the 'helpless helper' and the experience of giving, as opposed to receiving, care. Although many members valued sharing their experiences, Aveline notes that they reported fears in relation to self-disclosure (particularly the possible effects on their career) and worried about the relationship between the facilitator and other organizations within the NHS.

In a similar study, Macmillan and Lago (1996) asked 139 members of large groups to describe their experience of facilitation. Unfortunately, only 11 questionnaires were returned, making generalizing from the findings problematic. However, some experiences of facilitation by the group leader were described (for example, making integrative comments, responding to individual's emotional states) and of members facilitating each other (making supportive statements, for instance). The authors note that "a look, a touch or even another's attentive silence were experienced as facilitative" (Macmillan and Lago 1996: 602).

Hall, Hall, Biddulph, Duffy, Harris and Hay (1997) viewed the work of Irving and Williams (1996) as a challenge to review the efficacy and safety of small group work. The authors therefore asked participants about their experiences of a 10-week mandatory Rogerian group occurring as part of counsellor training. Table 9.1 describes those interpersonal skills participants felt were enhanced by taking part in the groups. The authors did not report the total number of participants, but the responses to individual questions were relatively large, involving between 50 and 150 people.

Participants were also asked whether they believed their experience of taking part in the small groups had been damaging in any way; 97.8 per cent (89 participants) believed it had not been damaging in the long term. These figures were slightly different for damage in the *short* term, with 12.4

Table 9.1 Counselling skills described as enhanced by participation in Rogerian small group, in order of frequency

Skill/Area	Cited by percentage of participants
Handling silence	77
Self-disclosure	73
Giving and receiving feedback	73
Listening	69
Challenging	58
Accepting sensitive self-disclosure	57
Expressing negative feelings	57
Empathy	56
Expressing positive feelings	56
Recognizing incongruence in self	53

per cent (11 participants) believing the group had caused them transient difficulties. However, these short-term effects were not necessarily felt to be a bad thing, as one group member noted, 'This was stinging and raw but essential for my personal growth at the time. I don't find the word "damaging" appropriate for how I felt – to me it hints at destruction and that was not so – I think it was constructive pain and hurt' (Hall, Hall, Biddulph, Duffy, Harris and Hay 1997: 183–4).

Participants were also asked 'Would you perceive others as a casualty of the group?' A total of 45.3 per cent (39 participants) said yes. This finding forms an interesting indication that group members may be more likely to perceive adverse effects in others.

In the most extensive investigation of this type Helen Payne (2001) explored perceptions of a dance-movement therapy (DMT) experiential group. This confidential and closed group was conducted weekly over the two years of the DMT course. There were seven participants in total, contributing a total of six semi-structured interviews each over the duration of the course. Phenomenological analysis of the data revealed a major theme of 'safety', particularly in relation to confidentiality and boundaries of the group. As one participant noted, 'It can't be totally a therapy group because it is something that is within college . . . it's more like a course module . . . I feel my ease with it is limited partly because it is in some way part of the course' (Payne 2001: 276).

Participants talked about interactions between the experiential group and the wider training cohort. Some trainees articulated concern that expressing feelings towards others within the group might affect future relationships. The interrelationship between the experiential group and the rest of the course became particularly salient when a rift occurring between group members socially (when on holiday together) surfaced within the experiential group. Participants commented, 'It has taught me that group issues can come up if people in the group have a relationship outside the group' and 'The location of the DMT group on a course presents danger and . . . fear . . . a holding back . . . fear of the group breaking apart . . . it feels unprotected' (Payne 2001: 281, 282).

Lennie (2007) conducted focus groups with 88 trainee counsellors at different stages of their training. Qualitative analyses revealed that a combination of three factors was felt to contribute to self-awareness: intrapersonal (for example, courage), interpersonal (for example, group cohesion) and environmental (for example, personality of the facilitator). This distinction echoes that proposed in the model describing engagement in personal development groups (discussed in the following section).

It is important to be cautious in generalizing findings from 'service user' research as it is possible that group members who felt more positively about the experience were more likely to participate in studies. However, research to date has provided valuable information about the experience of personal development groups from the participants' perspective. This work has revealed interesting differences in emphasis; for example, increased concern about boundaries, especially the relationship between the group and the wider working environment (training cohort or work colleagues).

Factors influencing engagement in personal development groups

What might influence individual response to personal development in a group context? Although the available evidence is limited, it is possible to hypothesize that three different types of factors might influence engagement:

1   *Factors relating to the individual*
    preferred learning style;
    'personality' and interpersonal style;
    family background.

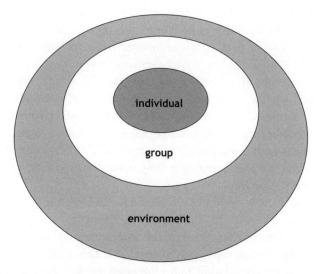

Figure 9.1   Possible factors relating to engagement in personal development groups

2   *Factors relating to the group itself*
     how clear its purpose and aims are;
     how it is facilitated.
3   *Factors relating to the environment in which the group takes place*
     interrelationship with peer group;
     perceived or actual appraisal of personal development;
     wider environmental context.

These different levels can be visualized as circles (Figure 9.1).

It is hypothesized that engagement in groups is a product of the combined influence of all three factors. (This maps on to the realms of personal development discussed in Chapter 3.)

'Individual' factors influencing engagement may include preferred learning style, personality and past experiences. Some of the existential dilemmas described by Johns (1996) may also be relevant, such as the need for intimacy as opposed to autonomy. Some people may feel they can meet their needs for intimacy without compromising autonomy, others may find that their need for autonomy overrides their need to share experiences with others. Family background is also likely to be significant (for example,

Agazarian and Peters 1981; Thompson 1999). As Payne notes, 'Early experiences with parents, siblings and peers are more easily brought out in a group. Hence the dynamics can mirror those in members' families' (2001: 286).

The nature of the individual's family may interact with that of the group: for example, whether openness is valued more than independence, how emotion is expressed and the strategies used for dealing with conflict. A combination of intrapersonal factors is likely to influence engagement; for example, those with a less emotionally expressive family background and a greater need for autonomy may find it harder to engage in personal development in this way.

As well as factors within the individual, the way the group itself is structured is likely to be influential in terms of engagement. The research literature has emphasized the importance of agreed aims and appropriate facilitation (although exactly what this entails is a debate in itself). It can be hypothesized that groups established with clear ground rules and appropriate facilitation are likely to increase engagement. Members may also stand to gain most from participating in such groups.

The impact of the wider social environment on personal development groups is a relatively ignored area within the research literature. Most of those taking part in personal development groups have pre-existing relationships with each other, as work colleagues, as friends and often as part of a training cohort. This can lead to a 'group within a group' dynamic, reflected in the service user research (Aveline 1986; Payne 2001). How does taking part in a personal development group influence pre-existing relationships? Equally, how might pre-existing relationships and group dynamics influence the personal development group?

Lyons (1997) suggests that personal development groups may offer trainees the chance to explore relationships with one another in a 'safe space' where potentially difficult group processes could be contained and held. She makes the interesting observation that 'victimising, scapegoating, rescuing and so on go on incessantly in groups whether a space is allocated for group work or not' (Lyons 1997: 212).

A more negative hypothesis might be to speculate that victimizing, scapegoating and rescuing that would not have otherwise occurred (or come to the surface) may be potentiated by the personal development group. Whether or not this is ultimately beneficial for individuals within the group is a complex issue. However, it is likely some trainees may be reluctant to jeopardize group cohesion by taking risks with their relation-ships with one another, however valuable this may be for their eventual personal development.

The trainee cohort is also likely to have its own group dynamics (norms, rules, roles, power distribution and possibly leaders), which may be more or less congruent with the aims of the personal development group. Engagement may be more likely when the interpersonal style of the trainee cohort 'fits' in some way with that of the reflective group, for example, being emotionally expressive and able to risk experiencing conflict.

It is also necessary to acknowledge the wider context in which personal development groups take place, particularly how the groups fit in with the philosophy of the organization or training environment. In the world of counselling, where the majority of this research has taken place, such groups are typically valued as a central part of trainee development, relating clearly to the therapeutic model of the course. However, in clinical psychol-ogy the prevailing course model (if there is a dominant model) may have ambiguous or even hostile views towards this sort of work. How do trainees value and engage in personal development groups in these circumstances? It is likely that engagement will decrease if the aims of the personal devel-opment group are significantly at variance with the wider environmental context.

Further, even in situations where there is coherent and comprehensive support for personal development groups, there is likely to be some hesitation in engagement, or some censuring of what is shared, if the par-ticipants know or believe there is an explicit or implicit assessment process.

Whilst it has not been possible to explore in depth each type of factor (individual, group, environmental) it can be seen from the material dis-cussed that all are likely to influence engagement to some degree. This model is suggested as a way of thinking about the different factors that might influence engagement. It is also important to note that engagement should be seen as a continuum, rather than a categorical distinction. It often seems from the research literature that personal development group members, especially trainees, are seen as either 'engagers' or 'non-engagers'. However, at a particular group at a particular stage of their lives an individ-ual may not engage fully, yet they may engage well with another group, or with the same group at a different time. This may be comparable to the reasons clients choose not to engage in therapy (for example, Jacobs 1993:

32–5). It is also possible that similar therapeutic methods might be used to facilitate engagement. (See also models of change as described in Chapter 3.)

Personal reflections

In order to explore how helpful these ideas are for thinking about personal development groups I have chosen to structure my own reflections in the same way. I have tried to think about how individual, group and environmental factors affected my engagement in a reflective group, as well as what I feel I have gained (and risked) by participating. My clinical psychology training course started reflective personal development groups in my second year of training. These groups were mandatory and took place following personal development workshops on a variety of issues (for example, talking about difference and diversity).

Individual factors
Ironically, one of the key things I learnt from taking part in the group is that my internal perceptions are unlikely to completely reflect my behaviour, but hopefully this imperfect record will still have value. I believe I was relatively open, interested and took an active role within the group. I tried to take some risks in what I brought to the group, and to talk about topics I found challenging. However, I was conscious of a need to be liked. I tried not to let this limit what I said but it could be difficult. I wondered if sometimes I said things in a light or jokey way because I was worried about others' discomfort. I also worried about talking too much. I could find silences quite hard to manage and sometimes felt frustrated by the lack of communication.

When wondering why I responded to the group in this way I have thought increasingly about experiences I had never previously considered as relating to 'groups'. It struck me how central our experience of the family group is and how much of what we later encounter is shaped by this. It is always extremely difficult to identify how your own family differs from others, but I believe that mine was a family in which open communication was encouraged and supported, vulnerability accepted and not criticized. I realize that this is not everybody's experience.

I feel I have benefited from thinking more about these aspects of myself, and that there are a number of issues I will consider further in my clinical work. For example, I have thought about times when I have tried to avoid conflict. A possible disadvantage of the way I have responded to the group is that I sometimes feel a bit 'out on a limb' and that I am talking too much. I am also conscious of wondering why others find the group so difficult.

Group factors

I think that the structure of the group increased my engagement. I felt that the ground rules were clear and the style of facilitation helped create a sense of a safe space. I also found it helpful that the facilitator was a member of the course staff. However, I can see the potential for confusing boundary changes. I have wondered about whether reactions to the group may have been different if it had been introduced earlier in the course. Introducing the group in year two meant that the peer group (and associated interpersonal style and dynamics) was already well-established when the reflective group began.

Environmental context

When participating in the reflective group I often thought about the 'group within a group' issue, particularly about how the dynamics of my year group influenced responses to the reflective group. I experience the interpersonal style of my year group as very warm and supportive but also quite 'stoic'. For example, we often seem to discuss difficult experiences some time after the event when people were ready to talk about them. Sometimes people seem to minimize hard things (myself included) and cope with humour to lighten situations.

I believe that the wider context in which the group took place is also significant. The messages trainees received about this sort of group work have been mixed. On the one hand, we were required to attend the mandatory groups introduced in the second year. On the other hand, we were aware that these groups had been previously discontinued by the course, presumably because of concerns about either their value or safety. I think this sort of situation is highly likely to influence engagement in the group and also the possible advantages of doing so.

In summary, I believe that my reactions were related to the nature of the group and the environmental context as well as my own interpersonal style. I think I may have behaved very differently in a different context and with different people, though I suspect I would still have found it hard to keep quiet!

Conclusions

Social-constructionist approaches encourage us to think about the multiplicity and subjectivity of human experience; the importance of not assuming that there is a single objective truth, rather that there are multiple and various 'truths' from many different perspectives, each with its own validity and importance (for example, Bruner 1990; Nightingale and Cromby 2002). This is particularly evident in people's reactions, recollections and roles within groups. It seems that much of this area relates to our beliefs about what a counsellor or psychologist 'should' be like interpersonally. This may also explain why so much work takes place in training environments. Much of the literature can be read as a debate about how counselling trainers believe counselling trainees should react to the personal development groups (that is, be open to new experience, able to take risks, reflective). As noted previously, clinical psychology courses may have a different model of what a therapist should be like, both intra- and interpersonally. It seems significant that most of the research and virtually all the debate is confined to personal development groups for trainees. If work of this kind is only undertaken prior to qualification, people will come to the not unreasonable conclusion that such groups are specifically to do with training (and thus possibly assessment and scrutiny) rather than forming an ongoing resource for self-development.

Lyons reports that trainees described personal development groups as an opportunity to learn 'to tolerate silence, conflict, extreme emotion, uncertainty and unknowing' (1997: 212). This quotation captures not only why personal development groups are important but also why they may be so threatening. This is also reflected in the issues of boundaries and safety which resurface throughout this work, particularly in group members' accounts of their experiences. Responding as a trainee myself I can see that negotiating conflict and extreme emotion are very important transferable skills for clinical work. I can also see why trainees may want to limit their exposure to these challenging areas within the relatively safe confines of the trainee cohort. The training environment is the most nurturing I have personally experienced, which makes it safer to take risks but, paradoxically, sometimes makes me feel less like doing so.

Part Two – Reflections on Experiences in Groups from Two Experienced Clinical Psychologists

Additional thoughts on personal development in groups: a post qualification, group analytic perspective –
Garry Brownbridge

Since qualifying as a clinical psychologist my continuing personal and professional development has benefited from a great many and wide-ranging group experiences. Among the most powerfully influential have been the group analytic 'experiential' groups, which I joined during a range of introductory and advanced group work courses, and the personal group analysis that I eventually undertook as part of a full training in group analysis.

The experiential groups, conducted by qualified group analysts, were not run as or intended to be *therapy* groups but were therapeutic nevertheless. They also succeeded as intended. Through an experience of being in a group analytically run group, I could see the group processes and theoretical concepts, learned about in parallel, being enacted by myself and others in the group. I could also begin to learn directly how these processes would be operating in other interpersonal and social situations, including any therapeutic situations I might contrive as a professional practitioner.

It is not appropriate to share *detail* of my personal development in these groups, but by recalling some of the main *areas* addressed I hope to convey the magnitude of learning brought about. I had powerful experiences of transference, that is, experiencing the conductor or other group members as if they were members of my family. I learned about the early role I had taken in my family and how this could relate to my professional role. I learned about the unconscious, and about splitting and projection in myself and in groups. I gained insight into different parts of myself, seen in my reactions to the conductor or to other group members or mirrored in the interactions between others. I was involved in face-to-face, but contained, conflicts around race, culture and gender. Overall, I observed the tremendous potential of groups for personal development and therapy and as a clinical and organizational intervention approach.

These benefits are also the reason I went on to undertake the full group analytic training. I attended the Institute of Group Analysis block weekend training in Manchester – 10 weekends per year, Friday to Sunday inclusive, for four years. An integral part of the training is the personal group analysis acquired during the 'Small Groups' of the blocks – five, one-and-a-half hour meetings each weekend. I now appreciate the emphasis that psychotherapy trainings place on personal therapy. Perhaps my most important learning from the Small Group was to experience my self as a *patient*. (I deliberately use the word 'patient' here, with its connotations of pathology; 'client' or 'service user' might miss some of the point.) I had to learn about, acknowledge and accept, and/or do something about, my own psychopathologies. Even more important to the future therapist was my increased empathy for *my patients* and for patients in general. I have experienced being in the patient position. I know what it is like to discover an uncomfortable truth about myself – by having it repeatedly and assertively pointed out by a group of admired others. I know what it is like to feel sudden powerful personal and interpersonal insight. As a patient I know how the therapist or group can impact on me and as a therapist I know how the group and I can impact on the patient.

In the group analytic training my personal therapy, clinical practice and theoretical understanding were inseparably combined. Like the clinical psychology training that preceded it, but much more explicitly so, it *was* personal and professional development.

From this perspective, if we are to consider the theory of group analysis as applied to trainee therapists and their 'experiential groups' or 'small groups', then any and all of it applies. It applies to us just as it applies to our would-be service users. For a very readable and engaging introductory text I would recommend Behr and Hearst's (2006) *Group-Analytic Psychotherapy: A Meeting of Minds*. Alternatively, in my own paper 'The Group in the Individual' (Brownbridge 2003), I have also tried to introduce the basic tenets of group analysis including Foulkes's concepts of: the dynamic group matrix and the foundation group matrix; the basic interrelatedness of people; the false dichotomy between individual and group processes or internal and external psychic phenomenon; and the mental paradigm shift necessary to fully appreciate the group, in a society which has become too individually orientated (Foulkes 1990).

Reflections on my being in groups – Sheila Youngson

What have been the pivotal forces in my own personal development, during the time I have been a qualified clinical psychologist? Two stand out. Firstly, personal therapy on a one-to-one weekly basis over a three- to four-year period, with a psychodynamically oriented psychotherapist. And, secondly, all the many experiential groups in which I have been a participant, and occasionally a facilitator, within the person-centred tradition. My reflections here are to do with the latter.

I have been in largely unstructured, nondirective person-centred groups that have varied hugely from each other in a number of ways. Some examples: I have been in a group of 14, completing a diploma course in supervision, that met weekly or fortnightly for three hours at a time over a year, plus two weekends. I have been in a group of 30 that met intensively (12 hours per day) over one weekend. I have been in a group of 150 at a conference where we spent five hours in each of four days in community group time. Last summer I was in a two-day encounter group with 80 others speaking in excess of 12 different languages. I am in a personal development group with five others who meet for two hours every month. In comparison to many groups of clinical psychologists, I have been surrounded, in these contexts, by significant differences in terms of age, gender, ethnicity, religion, culture, dis/ability, sexuality, class, race and first language.

In these contexts I have learnt an enormous amount about myself. I have been challenged to recognize and examine my stereotypes, assumptions, prejudices and intolerances. I have seen the patterns set long ago, resurrecting themselves particularly when I feel anxious, or fearful, or misunderstood. I have been moved by others, and by their pain and resilience. I have been moved by mine. I have learnt how others experience me, and that is sometimes concerning, and sometimes warming to the soul. I have learnt, very powerfully, that I can stay with emotional tension and distress and work through mine, or mine with another, or another's, and not only survive but move to a different depth of understanding and relating.

These days, in a professional clinical and training context, I spend considerable amounts of my time (at least 50 per cent) working in groups of 5, 10, 15 or more. I can be in those groups in a variety of roles: leader, teacher, consultant, supervisor, team member, facilitator. Thus, it does seem imperative that I know how to be in groups, in all those roles, and be able, at one and the same time, to be fully present, know what are my strengths and weaknesses, and hold an overview of the processes unfolding.

Hence, for me, personal development in a group context significantly helps to maximize my learning about myself (for all the reasons outlined in Chapter 3), and it encourages and promotes the skills that are necessary and required to be able to work in a competent and efficacious manner in groups.

Part Three – Summary and Further Thoughts – Sheila Youngson

Fiona Smith has summarized the literature on personal development groups. She found it sparse, almost completely relating to trainee counsellors, and mostly asking participants to reflect on existing practice. She notes that there is little qualitative research, and this is surprising given the individual and idiosyncratic nature of personal development.

In Chapter 11, Horner, Youngson and Hughes report on a survey of clinical psychology courses. Of the 14 courses that provided information, nine had mandatory personal development groups, and three had optional groups, although these groups varied considerably in terms of size, frequency, focus and facilitation. The fact that the staff respondents named personal development groups as the most useful forum for trainees' personal development is striking.

In Chapter 12, six very recently qualified clinical psychologists reflect on their personal development during training. The positive aspects of personal development groups are mentioned, and yet overall there is a sense of ambivalence about the group experience, and an acknowledgement that not all trainees welcome this structure. Indeed, in talking with trainees over the years, it is clear that whilst some willingly engage in the process, others struggle with groups and find them hard and deeply challenging.

Finally, this chapter has included writings from two experienced clinical psychologists focussing on their experiences in groups post-qualification, group settings that were designed, at least on one level, to increase self-knowledge and awareness and develop interpersonal understanding and ability. Both writers clearly state that their experiences in these groups continue to promote their personal development in very significant ways. Further support for this view comes from informal conversations with other professionals.

What is to be made of these potentially differing views, or at least emphases? On the one hand those involved in training clinical psychologists, and experienced clinical psychologists, are strongly supporting having personal development groups as part of the learning process. On the other hand, trainees are mixed in their views – there is some support, there is ambivalence and there can be hostility. Chapter 2, in outlining the historical context of clinical psychology, demonstrates that the profession has not until quite recently placed much emphasis on personal development. Could it be the case that those embarking on clinical psychology training have little experience in reflection, in talking about self with others, and are therefore understandably anxious, and even frightened? Or is this more of a universal response when one first encounters the group experience? In talking with those involved in counsellor training, where there is much more of a tradition of personal development, comes the realization that their trainees experience a range of similar feelings and responses to personal development groups. And in reflecting on the experience of being in groups, most people do recall a time when they felt anxious, exposed, frightened, even if at the same time, interested, hopeful, excited. Thus, it is suggested that it is probably the group experience, with its heightened intensity and emotion, that is the critical factor.

A further potential explanation for the sometimes ambivalent reactions/ responses of individuals to the group experience comes from the group analytic literature. Nitsun (1996) describes the anti-group phenomena, which suggests that we all have fundamental, deeply rooted ambivalence about groups. We know about the downside of groups for us individually – less personal attention, less agreement, we have to share, listen to others. We may have had 'bad' experiences in groups in our lives, feeling bullied, ignored, overlooked, misunderstood, disliked, shamed. We know about the potential for destructiveness in groups, and from groups: war, fascism, terrorism, genocide, for example. Thus, it is not surprising that we have ambivalence. However, if these phenomena are recognized, talked about, worked through, and understood, the group can be strengthened, more integrated, more useful, and more effective.

This leads to a deeper consideration of how to prepare trainees for the group experience, and include clear aims, conversations about boundaries, knowledge about group dynamics, group ground-rules. This *is* important. Having said that, experience leads to the recognition that one can only really learn about self, and self in relation to others, in a group context, by being in a group and learning from the experience. Some safety in groups can be built in, but ultimately learning about self cannot always be comfortable and without emotional pain.

One final question: why is the group experience necessary? Fundamentally, and crucially, because clinical psychologists are spending increasing amounts of their professional lives working in groups. This can be in a variety of roles: as team member, team leader, teacher, consultant, supervisor, therapist. It is important that clinical psychologists can work effectively in all these contexts. There is a need to know how to manage process, dynamics, conflict, emotion, challenge. In order to be useful and effective there is a need to know a good deal about one's own patterns of relating and personal triggers. There is a need to know how one is perceived and how one perceives others, and to be able to receive and give feedback. Being a group participant is surely one of the most immediate ways of promoting this necessary learning.

REFERENCES

Agazarian, Y. and Peters, R. (1981). *The Visible and Invisible Group: Two Perspectives on Group Psychotherapy and Group Process*. London: Routledge and Kegan Paul.

Aveline, M. (1986). 'Personal Themes from Training Groups for Health Care Professionals'. *British Journal of Medical Psychology*, 59: 325–55.

Behr, H. and Hearst, L. (2005). *Group-Analytic Psychotherapy: A Meeting of Minds*. London: Whurr.

Brownbridge, G. (2003). 'The Group in the Individual'. *Group Analysis*, 36(1): 23–36.

Bruner, J. (1990). *Acts of Meaning*. Cambridge, MA: Harvard University Press.

Donati, M. and Watts, M. (1999). 'Personal Development in Counselling Psychology Training: The Case for Future Research'. *Counselling Psychology Review*, 15: 12–21.

Douglas, T. (1995). *Survival in Groups: The Basics of Group Membership*. Buckingham: Open University Press.

Dryden (1994). *Developing Counsellor Training*. London: Sage.

Foulkes, S. H. (1990). *Selected Papers: Psychoanalysis and Group Analysis*. London: Karnac.

Hall, E., Hall, C., Biddulph, M., Duffy, T., Harris, B. and Hay, D. (1997). 'Group Work in Counsellor Training: An Evaluation'. *Counselling Psychology Review*, 12: 179–86.

Hartman, J. J. (1979). 'Small Group Methods of Personal Change'. *Annual Review of Psychology*, 30: 453–76.

Irving, J. and Williams, D. (1996). 'The Role of Group Work in Counsellor Training'. *Counselling*, 7: 137–9.

Izzard, S. and Wheeler, S. (1995). 'The Development of Self Awareness: An Essential Aspect of Counsellor Training'. *Counselling*, 6: 227.

Jacobs, M. (1993). 'Client Resistance'. In W. Dryden (ed.), *Questions and Answers on Counselling in Action*. London: Sage.

Jenkins, P. (1995). 'Two Models of Counsellor Training: Becoming a Person or Learning To Be a Skilled Helper?' *Counselling*, 6: 203–6.

Johns, H. (1996). *Personal Development in Counsellor Training*. London: Cassell.

Lennie, C. (2007). 'The Role of Personal Development Groups in Counsellor Training: Understanding Factors Contributing to Self-Awareness in the Personal Development Group'. *British Journal of Guidance and Counselling*, 35: 115–29.

Lyons, A. (1997). 'The Role of Group Work in Counselling Training'. *Counselling*, 8: 211–15.

Macmillan, M. and Lago, C. (1996). 'The Facilitation of Large Groups: Participants' Experiences of Facilitative Moments'. In R. Hutterer, G. Pawlowsky, P. Schmid and R. Stipsits (eds.), *Client-Centred and Experiential Psychotherapy: A Paradigm in Motion*. Frankfurt: Peter Lang.

Mearns, D. (1997a). *Person-Centred Counselling Training*. London: Sage.

Mearns, D. (1997b). 'Achieving the Personal Development Dimension in Professional Counsellor Training'. *Counselling*, 8: 113–20.

Nightingale, D. J. and Cromby, J. (2002). 'Social Construction as Ontology: Exposition and Example'. *Theory and Psychology*, 12: 701–13.

Nitsun, M. (1996). *The Anti-Group: Destructive Forces in The Group and Their Creative Potential*. London and New York: Routledge.

Payne, H. (1999). 'Personal Development Groups in the Training of Counsellors and Therapists: A Review of the Research'. *The European Journal of Psychotherapy, Counselling and Health*, 2: 55–68.

Payne, H. (2001). 'Student Experiences in a Personal Development Group: The Question of Safety'. *European Journal of Psychotherapy, Counselling and Health*, 4: 267–92.

Raskin, N. J. (1986). 'Client-Centred Group Psychotherapy, Part 1: Development of Client-Centred Groups'. *Person-Centred Review*, 1: 272–90.

Rogers, C. R. (1957). 'The Necessary and Sufficient Conditions of Therapeutic Personality Change'. *Journal of Consulting Psychology*, 21: 85–103.

Small, J. J. and Manthei, R. J. (1988). 'Group Work in Counsellor Training: Research and Developments in One Programme'. *British Journal of Guidance and Counselling*, 16: 33–49.

Smith, P. B. (1975). 'Are There Adverse Effects of Sensitivity Training?' *Journal of Humanistic Psychology*, 15: 29–47.
Thompson, S. (1999). *The Group Context*. London: Jessica Kingsley Publishers.

FURTHER READING

Lago, C. and MacMillan, M. (eds.) (1999). *Experiences in Relatedness: Groupwork and the Person-Centred Approach*. Ross-on-Wye: PCCS Books.
For details of workshops and training in group analysis see www.groupanalysis. org

Chapter 10

Evaluating Personal Development in Clinical Psychology Training

Sheila Youngson with David Green

Introduction

Earlier chapters have outlined the importance of personal development in clinical psychology, proposed a model that aims to make clearer the concept of personal development and the processes involved, and explored different views of, and approaches to, personal development in various contexts. It surely follows then, that, if the centrality of personal development to professional life has been established, consideration must also be given to how personal development is encouraged, monitored, evaluated and assessed. This chapter will begin with some preliminary thoughts about potential tensions and outline a professional cultural context. David Green will then consider and explore assessment of personal development during selection of candidates for clinical training. Concerns about current assessment procedures are then discussed. This chapter will then offer, as one example *not* an exemplar, how personal development can be promoted, monitored, evaluated and assessed during postgraduate training, based on the programme at Leeds.

At the heart of the Youngson–Hughes model of the processes involved in personal development is the notion that the individual is motivated continually to examine their personal growth. However, is there an argument that this willingness and endeavour, and the expected resulting growth, should and/or could be evaluated externally? Certainly, mandatory supervision is one such 'check', assuming that personal development conversations form part of the agreed contracting, but should there be further evaluation, perhaps especially (but *not* exclusively) during training at the start of a career? Given the current climate of increasing accountability, the emphasis on following the evidence base, and statutory registration, it is clear that some manner of assessment is necessary.

A Tension between Exploration and Assessment

Immediately, a tension arises between two standpoints: that of the rigour of academic assessment and pass/fail criteria, and that of the openness to experiment, to do things differently, to face challenges, to examine mistakes. How can these be reconciled? Here, it is argued that any assessment of personal development needs to have both summative (that is, pass/fail) and formative (that is to say, feedback, constructive comment, discussion) elements. Summative elements are needed to emphasize the importance of personal development and the necessity to engage in this aspect of training, as well as to provide a gate-keeping function (for the profession) if an individual is unable (for whatever reason) to demonstrate the ability to engage in personal development in all the realms identified in Chapter 3. Formative assessment and feedback is appropriate in many instances for, at least, four reasons. Firstly, it is notoriously difficult to quantify and make judgements on what is a very individual and often internal process. Secondly, it is equally problematic to be prescriptive on what is deep enough, broad enough, or simply enough in terms of personal development. Thirdly, it is frequently quoted (for example, Boud 2007) that once personal development becomes something that will be formally assessed then individuals cease more freely and spontaneously to experiment with their personal development and become less open and honest, more resistant, less likely to take risks with personal development strategies and less communicative about difficulties and progress. Fourthly, throughout this book it is argued that much of personal development is achieved through an exploration of self in relation to others, and thus having ongoing discussions and feedback from another, genuinely concerned with one's progress and process, is surely a useful resource.

A Cultural Context

It is essential, firstly, that the culture of the workplace understands and values personal development. Looking back to Chapter 3 for a moment, it is evident that it is important to consider the impact of the community on the individual. Such a community could be groupings in a range of contexts, for example, the body of service users and carers, the clinical psychology community, the teams in which we are embedded, or the training community with all its players and stakeholders. Personal development will only be seen as important if it becomes an accepted currency in as many of these settings as possible. Service users stress the need for robustness in practitioners; clinical psychologists and their managers need to demonstrate the value they place on personal development; all the constituent members of the training community need to be transparent in the emphasis they place on their own personal development. In essence there needs to be, and be seen to be, a reflexivity, in which we do indeed 'practise what we preach'. It should then follow that individuals at all stages of their careers will accept and talk about doubts and difficulties as well as successes; stresses as well as rewards; weaknesses as well as strengths. Subsequently, the sometime fear associated with revealing one's self and being assessed or judged should diminish, and a personal development culture be established. Hopefully, this book is part of that culture shift.

David Green, Clinical Director, Doctor of Clinical Psychology Programme, University of Leeds, will next consider how personal development, and the potential for personal development, can be assessed during the selection for training process.

Assessment during Selection – David Green

In Chapter 11 Horner, Youngson and Hughes report a survey of UK clinical psychology courses investigating current practice in the promotion of personal development on their programmes. Roughly a third of the universities contacted replied, but the vast majority of those that did and were asked about selection processes (10/11) indicated that they include some form of assessment of potential for personal development in their selection procedures. So at least some clinical psychology trainers appear to believe that it is both desirable and achievable to discriminate between applicants on the grounds that some might be more self-aware or critically reflective than others. How do they justify prioritizing these particular qualities? How do they design their selection strategies?

Clinical psychology as a profession has traded heavily on its scientific credentials. The dominant discourse in the training community remains that of the scientist practitioner whose combination of high-level research skills and technical therapeutic proficiency is seen as defining the unique contribution that clinical psychologists can make to the NHS. The contemporary enthusiasm of healthcare commissioners for promoting evidence-based practice has consolidated this ideological stance. However, our profession has always spoken with an engaging variety of voices, and there is an alternative tradition which, though currently somewhat subjugated, remains influential. This discourse draws on the importance of personal factors such as the capacity to establish and maintain working relationships as opposed to procedural correctness in determining therapeutic outcome. It also displays a sensitivity towards, and advocacy of, the service user's perspective. It follows that the selection approach adopted by any clinical psychology training programme will reflect the relative importance accorded to these alternative sets of priorities within that particular community. At Leeds we try and have the best of both worlds . . .

Clinical psychology courses in the UK attract many highly capable applicants – more than 20 per place on occasions. This is a good problem to have. However, discriminating between apparently similarly qualified candidates presents a considerable conceptual and logistic challenge. Ideally, we would like to choose individuals who will be able successfully to complete the training programme in a straightforward manner, but how do we assess that *potential* ability, and what are the constituent parts of that ability? Selection for training is a high-risk investment in potential. There is no 'playing safe' option. Since the early 1990s, the academic status of our professional qualification in the UK has been a doctoral degree. Unsurprisingly, therefore, courses closely examine the scholastic record of all applicants. Since 2007, applicants have been obliged to provide a certified academic transcript providing details of all marks awarded during their undergraduate careers. This facility seems to provide a wealth of 'hallmarked' evidence that programmes can use to discriminate between candidates on an academic track record basis. Quite a seductive option. I find myself reminded of a classic music hall sketch in which a person is scrambling around at the foot of a lamp post. A passing policeman asks him what he's up to:

'I'm looking for my wallet, Officer.'
'Where did you drop it?'
'Over there.' (The person points 10 yards off into the darkness.)

'Then why on earth are you looking here?' demands the exasperated PC. 'Because the light's better,' is the polite repost.

Not exactly a rib-tickler but I hope it makes a basic point. As selectors we too may miss out if we unnecessarily restrict the range of our investigations. We may, for example, fail to focus on those qualities that matter most to the consumers of clinical psychology services.

For the last three years I have conducted consultations with a number of user groups to try and develop a sense of the characteristics that they value most highly in clinical psychologists. The method we have adopted is termed 'the nominal group approach' (Delbecq and Van de Ven 1971) which is a highly structured system of questioning that aims to give equal weight to the opinions of all consultees. So everyone in the group (usually 5–8 people) is invited to consider privately 'which three things' we should be attending to when selecting trainee clinical psychologists. The group facilitators then write down all these suggestions on flip charts, taking care to understand and appreciate each contribution, without critical challenge. Finally, each group member votes on which of the ideas generated he or she considers to be the most important (in a fashion oddly reminiscent of the Eurovision Song Contest).

We have organized nominal group consultations with members of a range of client groups – people with learning disabilities; older adults; individuals in forensic settings; adolescents; and users of adult mental health services. Although there have been some concerns that were of especial importance to particular subgroups (for example, issues of confidentiality for those involved in the legal system), it has proved easy to identify a number of recurrent themes. We were advised to select skilled communicators who listened attentively and expressed themselves in a comprehensible fashion. The importance of ethical and respectful attitudes towards those seeking therapeutic help was understandably emphasized. But there was also a strong thread of opinion that linked with the major concerns of this book. We should look out for those who 'are able to admit their mistakes', who are 'not easily shocked', who can demonstrate flexibility in their approach and are 'not always thinking they know best'. In essence the message was to value self-awareness in relation to others – not an inner directed self-absorption, but a capacity to reflect honestly on the key relationships in our lives.

Our interviews at Leeds are based on the principle of behavioural interviewing, whereby we ask applicants to consider and describe a specific past individual experience and then to respond to a range of predetermined 'probe' questions. In this way we hope to maintain adequate consistency of practice across interviewing panels whilst opening up possibilities for personal reflection. An example of applying this format to the recommendations arising from our consultations with users of clinical psychology services follows:

Can you think of a time when you had a very strong negative reaction to a client or colleague?
Can you describe the situation please?
Can you recall how you felt?
What sense did you make of your reaction?
What did you do?
With the benefit of hindsight would you have done anything differently?
Do you think you learned anything from this experience?

These sorts of questions are not easy to anticipate. They force candidates to think on their feet and are generally experienced as challenging but pertinent. The range and quality of answers that applicants produce certainly allow our selection panels to do their job – to select some interviewees over others. Whether those choices ultimately result in the training of a better clinical psychology workforce is a moot point. The research on the validity of interviews in job selection suggests we should be wary of overstating our powers of prediction. However, I think it is reasonable to say that when a training programme chooses to pose questions about personal development in their selection process, they are nailing their professional colours to the mast to some extent. They are flaunting something of their value system. Perhaps the most reliable selection effect that then follows is that aspiring clinical psychology trainees who recognize the importance of personal development in their professional training will apply to courses that promise to meet that expectation.

Evaluating Personal Development in Clinical Psychology Training

In reviewing the (sparse) literature on assessment of personal development (for example, Wheeler 2002), reading the questionnaire responses from clinical psychology training courses (see Chapter 11) and talking to counselling, psychotherapy and clinical and counselling psychology trainers, it is clear that all are struggling to find a meaningful, fair and useful way to assess personal development. A typical response is 'Well, for the moment, we're trying it this way.' Counselling courses frequently put most emphasis on their personal development groups, and may require a report on individuals from the group facilitator, as well as self- and peer-assessment of performance within the group. Other courses promote the use of personal development journals that may be open to scrutiny and assessment; others again ask for written self-appraisals, reflective practice portfolios, self and other structured assessments. Based on a variety of criteria these may be marked summatively, or not.

However, overall, it is probably true to say that there is a general dissatisfaction with current assessment procedures. This results from a number of factors. Some have been detailed above, and can be summarized here by the question 'how can one individual (or several key staff members) make accurate judgements about the depth, breadth and quality of another's personal development?' Such judgements can be open to bias and prejudice, and may not take into, or not be able to take into account the context of that individual's life. Further, self-appraisals and reflective journals are a very individual and internal process, and, as has been noted, the changing context of professional practice requires clinical psychologists to think and work on a more collective than individual basis, and on a more multidisciplinary platform. (This is supportive of the notion of personal development in a group setting – see Chapter 9.) Also, there is sometimes a pessimistic view of even attempting assessment of personal development when the organization within which the course is embedded neither understands nor wishes to take into account what it regards as a nebulous concept, and would certainly not support a 'failure' on this dimension alone, if all academic components had been passed. And, finally, for some there is a more ideological problem, whereby assessment of personal development is seen as antithetical to the notion of multiple routes and strategies, flexibility, and the richness and complexity of individual and interpersonal experiences.

Experiences at Leeds

Here I return to a more personal manner of writing, and talk about and present the current personal development strand on the Leeds clinical psychology doctoral programme, for which I have professional responsibility. I offer this purely as one example. It is, and always will be, a work in progress and process, and sometimes transition, particularly when contexts change. It has been shaped and formed through multiple conversations with various stakeholders, through experience and feedback, through critical comment, through ongoing debate and discussion. It is overseen and reviewed on a regular basis by a subcommittee of the programme management committee (the Personal and Professional Issues Sub-committee – see Chapter 2).

We wanted a personal development strand that had a clear ethos and fulfilled a number of criteria, including the British Psychological Society' Clinical Psychology Accreditation Criteria for Training Courses. The ethos centres around the perceived centrality of personal development to the profession, to individual psychologists and to the work, for all the reasons outlined in Chapter 3. The ethos also embraces the adult learner model, in which programme participants have individual responsibility for directing their learning within a supportive structure. Finally, the ethos holds that there are multiple and individual and idiosyncratic routes to personal growth and development; it is a rich and complex business and not always comfortable. However, having said that, the time spent in training is the place to begin, or continue experimenting with personal development, in what we hope is a safe and supportive environment.

We choose to have a combination of summative and formative assessments. The summative assessments are one essay completed in the second year of training, and part of each of the five clinical placement assessments. The essay demonstrates the ability to write in a reflective way about a particular aspect of professional practice, and the personal/professional interface. In the assessment of clinical skill development on placement, there are 10 learning outcomes, and one of these relates specifically to personal and professional development, and in particular emphasizes the development of personal development strategies. Thus, here the trainee has to demonstrate personal development in applied practice. All other assessments are formative. Our belief is that personal development is very much about self, and self in relation to others, and we wanted a significant part of our assessments to be about ongoing and developing *conversations* between people, and not solely about presentation followed by judgements from the other.

What follows is the introduction to the Personal and Professional Development (PPD) programme as written in our Programme Specification.

Then the learning outcomes, and associated elements, for the whole PPD programme are listed. Finally, the Personal Development strand is described in detail including the assessment procedures. (The full document is on the Programme's website.)

Personal and Professional Development – A Core Theme

One of the fundamental skills in clinical psychology is the ability to make relationships with others. This needs to be done when in a variety of roles and in a number of contexts. Roles can include: therapist, supervisor, supervisee, consultant, teacher, trainer, researcher, peer, manager, team member, team leader, and so on. Contexts can include: individual or group therapy, supervisory dyads, team working, multi-disciplinary team meetings, management meetings, informal contacts, and a host of other settings.

The ability to make, maintain, and nurture this range of relationships is a significant skill. In order to help trainees develop this skill, and understand the roles and contexts involved, the Personal and Professional Development Programme (PPD) has evolved.

The Programme recognizes that individuals who embark on clinical psychology training bring with them their life experiences to date. These experiences will have shaped the individual, to some degree, in terms of opinions, attitudes, beliefs, expectations, prejudices, patterns of interaction, etc. Individuals bring their own selves to training, where they will meet new experiences and challenges, and develop further, both emotionally and psychologically. One of the key issues in forging and understanding human relationships is a clear knowledge of what one is bringing to that relationship and how one is affecting that relationship. Therefore, it is crucial in training, and beyond, that individuals make a commitment to developing self-knowledge and self-awareness, in order to make and maintain relationships of quality. So that, by the end of training, trainees will be able to demonstrate that they can be empathic, genuine and sincere in their relationships with others, have integrity, resilience, show respect for others, acknowledge their own strengths and weaknesses and seek out constructive criticism, employ skills competently, be fair, possess wisdom and courage.

The PPD Programme is a major theme with two strands: personal and professional. The major theme that combines personal development with professional development recognizes that the two are inextricably linked. The two strands recognize that, to some extent the two can be separately conceptualized, whilst acknowledging that the two are closely interwoven.

Personal and Professional Development – Learning Outcomes

The thematic learning outcomes for this theme are grouped. They are to enable the trainee to:

Power and socio-political context issues

1.1   understand the importance and relevance of issues to do with power and social inequalities, on both a personal and professional level
1.2   work effectively with difference and diversity

Associated elements: the trainee should be able to:

a)   recognise and understand the effects of power imbalances, and how they can be minimised
b)   critique a range of theoretical models and related practices for the ways in which power imbalances and social inequalities are maintained and reproduced
c)   understand the roots of oppression and its role in the aetiology of psychological disturbance, and the consequential need to develop anti-oppressive practices
d)   recognise and work with difference and diversity, and commit to developing cultural (in the broadest sense, including e.g. issues to do with class, age, race, religion, culture, gender, dis/ability, ethnicity, sexuality) competency in all aspects of professional life.
e)   apply knowledge and understanding in all these areas in an increasingly sophisticated manner, and in increasingly complex situations

Personal development

2.1   Show an active continuous commitment to develop self-knowledge and self-awareness

Associated elements: the trainee should be able to:

a)   experiment with a variety of personal development strategies, and explore new ways of interacting with others
b)   engage with the personal and professional development curriculum and goals, maintaining an open attitude
c)   adopt strategies to manage the emotional and physical impact of the work, and seek out help when required
d)   invite critical comment and respond in a constructive manner

Professional attitudes and behaviour

3.1 show a consistently open attitude towards all aspects of learning and development

3.2 fullfil the employer's expectations regarding professional behaviour, including active engagement in all supervisory arrangements

3.3 demonstrate an ethical framework for all aspects of work, including a working knowledge of relevant practice guidelines, policies and legislation

3.4 work collaboratively and constructively with other professionals, colleagues and users of services

3.5 behave respectfully to others at all times

3.6 prepare for professional employment, having clear aims and objectives for continued professional development

Associated elements: the trainee should be able to:

a) demonstrate a continuing openness and keenness to learn, to seek knowledge and develop new skills

b) demonstrate active participation in all supervisory relationships and arrangements, including negotiation, preparation, utilisation and recording of sessions

c) manage own learning needs and develop strategies for meeting them

d) demonstrate reliability, conscientiousness, and an ability to meet deadlines

e) apply expertise in judging the consequences, for self and others, of maintaining / relaxing boundaries in all professional relationships

f) approach conflict situations with thoughtfulness, and from a constructive stance

g) consistently consider ethical issues and apply these considerations in complex clinical contexts

h) actively consider attempts to gain informed consent

i) understand and put into practice the boundaries and limitations of confidentiality

j) demonstrate knowledge of professional practice guidelines

k) understand the importance and have knowledge of relevant local and national policies, procedures, guidelines and legislation, and their relevance to professional practice

l) work collaboratively and constructively with other psychologists, other professionals, and users of services, respecting diverse viewpoints

m) show a respectful and valuing attitude to all others

n) demonstrate knowledge and understanding of employment practices and related issues
o) demonstrate appropriate preparation for job interviews
p) demonstrate a purposeful plan for continued professional development

Professional autonomy and professional limits

4.1 Manage a workload, including multi-tasking, and show a clear recognition of the limits of individual competence.

Associated elements: the trainee should be able to:

a) negotiate for and manage an appropriate case and workload at different stages of training, and prioritise the caseload effectively
b) recognise the extent and limitations of personal and professional competence and seek out timely and appropriate consultation and assistance when required
c) develop the ability to multi-task

Strand 1: Personal development

(Strand 2 is Professional Development – see course website for the full document)

The Personal development strand of the PPD Programme runs across all three years of training. Trainees are required to make an active continuous commitment to developing their self-knowledge and self-awareness (Learning Outcome 2.1) through a variety of routes. Some can be self-determined, some are part of the Programme curriculum. Overall, each trainee is required to demonstrate (as we saw in Chapter 3, but worth repeating here):

1 A preparedness and willingness to become more and more aware of self;
2 A preparedness and willingness to understand self;
3 A preparedness and willingness to explore and experiment with self, i.e. to risk doing things differently, face fears, invite challenge, examine one's character and personality, learn to confront, etc.

Further, trainees are given Mearns (1997) framework of four domains (again outlined in Chapter 3). This framework is reflected in the four elements of Learning Outcome 2.1:

The psychologist in clinical training will be able to

1   Demonstrate a willingness to experiment with a variety of personal development strategies, and explore new ways of interacting with others;
2   Demonstrate a willingness to engage with the personal and professional development curriculum and goals, maintaining an open attitude;
3   Demonstrate a range of adopted strategies that help to manage the emotional and physical impact of the work, and seek out help when required;
4   Show an active commitment to asking for critical comment, responding in a constructive manner.

However, the framework whilst having a focus on self, expands this concept to include the understanding and development of self in a number of roles and contexts, therefore also highlighting again the interwoven nature of personal and professional development. In actuality, the self cannot be seen or conceptualized in isolation: the practice of clinical psychology requires the communication of self in relationship with others.

A developmental perspective

It is expected that trainees will show an increased depth and breadth of recognition and understanding of themselves, and themselves in relation to others, including themselves as therapists and adult learners, over the three years of training. Personal development is thus conceptualized as a dynamic process that is encouraged by the training Programme, and is continued in post qualification practice. Also, as trainees progress through the three years of training, their conversations and practice should more and more reflect the interweaving of the personal and professional.

Thus the Strand's headings for the 3 years are:
Year 1 – Introduction to personal development
Year 2 – Continuing personal development
Year 3 – Consolidating personal development

Year 1 – Introduction to personal development

Personal development strand led
•   There is a 3 hour workshop in the Introductory block teaching that introduces trainees to the PPD theme and programme, and the two strands of personal development and professional development.

- In this workshop trainees are given their personal development journal and an explanation as to how it may be used over the three years of training.
- Of the nine x 3 hour PPD workshops in Year 1, three have the explicit focus of personal development. One explores personal development strategies, one considers self-care and the impact of the work, and one involves preparation for the personal development groups.
- In the monitoring and assessment of each placement, there are 3 meetings involving a clinical tutor (the allocated clinical tutor stays with the trainee for the 3 years of training). In each of the first two meetings (placement planning meeting, and mid-placement visit) trainees will be asked to provide a paragraph for discussion that summarizes the personal development tasks undertaken since the previous meeting, and highlights the goals and tasks to be taken forward.
- In the final placement meeting, at the end of Placements 1 and 2, trainees are required to present a Reflective Case Study, which will include personal reflections.
- At the end of Placements 1 and 2, trainees complete the circumplex of evolving clinical competencies (a 'wheel' depiction of the 10 learning outcomes for clinical skill development and their associated elements, that trainees use to appraise their satisfaction, or not, of their own development), which includes aspects of personal development. This is then discussed with their supervisor(s), and their clinical tutor in the next placement planning meeting.
- Trainees are encouraged to discuss aspects of self, when appropriate, in clinical supervision.

Learning outcomes and associated elements: 1.1, 1.2 (a), (c), (d); 2.1 (a), (b), (c), (d); 3.1, 3.3, 3.4, 3.5 (a), (b), (c), (d), (e), (f), (l), (m); 4.1 (a), (b), (c), and potentially many others.

Professional development strand led
- In the remaining six PPD workshops that have a more professional development focus, there is an embedded but usually explicit task of reflecting on one's personal reactions and responses to the content of the workshops.

Learning outcomes and associated elements: 1.1, 1.2 (a), (c), (d); 2.1 (a), (b), (c), (d); 3.1, 3.3, 3.4, 3.5 (a), (c), (g), (l), (m).

Training programme led
- The Training Programme staff are committed to the PPD theme, and hope to show this by being themselves self-reflective and engaging in ongoing personal development.
- The Training Programme staff encourage trainees to come and talk about any aspect of personal development or personal difficulty. We regard this as an integral part of our training role.
Learning outcomes and associated elements: 2.1 (a), (b), (c), (d).

Self-directed
- It is expected that trainees will understand the need for, and engage with the process of personal development. Thus they will actively pursue methods and ways of learning more about themselves, in addition to those prompted or promoted by the PPD Programme. (This is similar to trainees following up on handouts and reading lists, and directing their own academic learning.)

Learning outcomes and associated elements: 1.1 (a), (c); 2.1 (a), (b), (c), (d); 3.1, 3.4, 3.5 (a), (b), (c), (e), (f), (l), (m); 4.1 (b).

Year 2 – Continued personal development

Personal development strand led
- A monthly personal development group during term time (total of nine meetings).
- One of the nine x 2 hour PPD workshops has an explicit focus on personal development, and concerns issues of power and identity as related to self, and self in relation to others.
- Continued use of the personal development journal.
- Continued discussion of personal development gains, and aims with clinical tutor, at placement meetings (reviewing the placement plan, and mid-placement visit).
- At the end of Placements 3 and 4, the presentation of the Reflective Case Study.
- At the end of Placements 3 and 4, the completion of the circumplex and associated discussions.
- Trainees are encouraged to discuss aspects of self, where appropriate, in supervision and reflect on wider issues as well as clinical case supervision.

Learning outcomes and associated elements: 1.1, 1.2 (a), (c), (d), (e); 2.1 (a), (b), (c), (d); 3.1, 3.2, 3.3, 3.4, 3.5 (a), (b), (c), (e), (f), (g), (l), (m); 4.1 (a), (b), (c), and potentially many others.

Professional development strand led
- The eight x 2 hour remaining PPD workshops in Year 2 have the focus of working with difference and diversity, each with a particular theme, e.g. ethnicity and culture, gender, class, etc. Part of each workshop includes time (usually in the form of an experiential exercise) that requires trainees to reflect and talk about their personal experiences, and their reactions, and responses to the topic.
- Essay 3 – the essay questions concern professional practice issues, and ask for some personal reflection on the chosen topic.

Learning outcomes and associated elements: 1.1, 1.2 (a), (c), (d), (e); 2.1 (a), (b), (c), (d); 3.1, 3.3, 3.4, 3.5 (a), (c), (e), (f), (g), (l), (m); ; 4.1 (b), and potentially many others.

Training programme led
- As in Year 1.

Learning outcomes and associated elements: 2.1 (a), (b), (c), (d).

Self-directed
- As in Year 1.

Learning outcomes and associated elements: 1.1, 1.2, (a), (c), (d), (e); 2.1 (a), (b), (c), (d); 3.1, 3.2, 3.3, 3.4, 3.5 (a), (b), (c), (e), (f), (g), (l), (m); 4.1 (a), (b), (c).

Year 3 – Consolidating personal development

Personal development strand led
- A monthly personal development group held during term time (a total of nine, including a final group in the last week of training).
- Three of the eight x 2 hour PPD workshops have the focus on personal development. One reviews self-care strategies, one considers the personal/professional interface, and one looks at wider personal development strategies preparing for transition. All three have an element of looking forward to post-qualification practice.
- Continued use of the personal development journal.

- Placement 5 (elective) usually involves working with more complex psychological presentations and situations, which will challenge and promote aspects of personal development.
- At the three placement meetings involved in monitoring Placement 5, continued discussion on personal development gains and aims.
- The completion of the final circumplex.
- Trainees are encouraged to discuss aspects of self in relation to clinical work in clinical supervision.

Learning outcomes and associated elements: 1.1, 1.2 (a), (b), (c), (d) (e); 2.1 (a), (b), (c), (d); 3.1, 3.2, 3.3, 3.4, 3.5, 3.6 (a), (b), (c), (e), (f), (g), (l), (m); 4.1 (a), (b), (c), and potentially many others.

Professional development strand led
- A further workshop looks at Continued Professional Development (the BPS term) that also includes consideration of personal development.
- The remaining four workshops allow time for personal reflection on the content/issue raised.

Learning outcomes and associated elements: 2.1 (a), (b), (c), (d); 3.6 (p); 4.1 (b)

Training Programme led
- As in Year 1 and 2.

Learning outcomes and associated elements: 2.1 (a), (b), (c), (d).

Self-directed
- As in Year 1 and 2.
- At this stage of training it is expected that much personal and professional development is self-determined, self-directed, and largely integrated. It is expected that trainees will continue to utilize personal development strategies, clinical supervision, and discussions with programme staff to reflect on progress made and plan for future, post-qualification practice.

Learning outcomes and associated elements: All.

Annual appraisals

Each trainee has an annual appraisal based on the KSF (Knowledge and Skills Framework). This includes the core item – Personal and People development, which details evidence of the use of various strategies to develop self (e.g. use of supervision) and to consider one's self in relation to others (e.g. seeking out feedback from others).

Learning outcomes and associated elements: All.

Assessment of Personal Development

Summative assessments

Essay 3
Trainees chose from 3 offered titles that broadly cover personal and professional development issues. Whichever title is chosen trainees are asked to include some personal reflection.

Assessment of Placements 1–5

The clinical supervisor makes an overall assessment of the trainee on the ten learning outcomes specified in the Placement Assessment Form. This includes a Clinical Skills Learning Objective related to Personal and Professional Development:

> The psychologist in clinical training should be able to demonstrate a range of personal development strategies and professional attitudes and behaviour, including an awareness of power and socio-political issues.

It is unlikely, but not impossible for a trainee to fail a clinical placement based only on their performance on this learning objective (e.g. if a trainee was unable to see how personal issues were impeding and/or damaging inter-personal relationships, despite help and advice from supervisors and his/her clinical tutor, then a failure could be recommended.)

Formative assessments

All other assessment of personal development is formative, for the reasons given earlier in this chapter. Detailed formative feedback is given at various stages of the Training Programme.

Formal settings for formative feedback
The clinical tutor (the same person for all 3 years of training) provides formative feedback at the following meetings:

- The meeting between trainee and tutor that reviews the start of placement (placement planning meeting). Feedback here is involved as part of the discussion that follows the trainee presenting their summary paragraph of personal development gains and aims. Further feedback follows a review of the circumplex, also at this meeting, that will have been completed towards the end of each placement. Feedback in these contexts is more about reaching understanding through talking together, although the tutor may offer their understanding and appreciation of the personal work the trainee has demonstrated.

- In the event that a trainee struggles to identify or talk about personal development, the tutor will offer guidance and support. If the trainee continues to find this difficult, additional avenues for assistance will be considered. It is a requirement that each trainee demonstrates the ability to communicate the personal development undertaken/in progress.

- The meeting between trainee and tutor that form part of the mid-placement visit. Feedback, as outlined above, again follows the presentation and discussion of the trainee's summary paragraph.

- The end of placement meeting, after the presentation of the Reflective Case Study, and again through discussion. This does not occur in Year 3 when there is no Reflective Case Study (it is replaced by a more formal case presentation in a different setting). However a conversation about continued professional development (including personal development) occurs instead, to mark the approaching end of training.

It is expected that the clinical supervisor will also give formative feedback to the trainee during the supervised clinical placement, and will be asked for feedback at the mid-placement visit. This will be discussed with the trainee if this has not already occurred.

Informal settings for formative feedback
The Training Programme staff may give formative feedback in a variety of other settings, e.g. in individual meetings, and often at the request of a trainee.

Conclusions

This system of evaluating and promoting personal development on the Leeds Programme has been in operation for several years. Overall it seems to work well. It is of course dependent on there being a perceived culture that holds that personal development is a valued and respected part of training, and it is hoped this is what is perceived by most. It is also dependent on the trainee and clinical tutor, and the trainee and clinical supervisor, building relationships that feel safe enough for open, honest, thoughtful and reflective conversations to take place. I believe such conversations need to be a two-way process with mutual learning. In my conversations with trainees, I do want to offer insight from my professional and personal experiences, but also I find that each conversation helps me to think broader and deeper, and provides fresh insights. We can, and do, learn from each other.

In considering cohorts of trainees, and the individuals involved, experience has shown that some people enter training keen to develop themselves, will experiment with whatever method or strategy is suggested, and are willing to be known on many levels. Others are less sure and will think carefully about what strategy to utilize and how much of themselves they feel comfortable in sharing. Others again will struggle with this element of training, question the relevance and be reluctant to engage in any 'public' process or be known outside a professional role. In these latter two situations we hope it may be helpful to use the content of Chapter 3 to explain/explore why personal development is important, and the Youngson-Hughes model of the processes involved (Chapter 4) to illustrate how to proceed. It may also be useful to consider what barriers (Chapter 4 again) to personal development are present, which of them may be overcome and how. Finally, it will be important to consider what part we, as trainers and supervisors, are playing in this situation, and maybe our messages about personal development are unclear, mixed or conflicting.

In final conclusion, I want to state that the overarching aim in promoting, and in insisting on personal development, and in assessing competency in this area, is to help a trainee develop skills and an emotional robustness that will stand the test of time and career.

REFERENCES

Boud, D. (2007). 'Rehabilitation or Rejection? Relocating Reflection in the Context of Practice'. Paper presented at Standing Conference on University Teaching and Research on the Education of Adults. University of Leeds.

Delbecq, A, and Van de Ven, A. (1971). 'A Group Process Model for Problem Identification and Program Planning'. *Journal of Applied Behavioral Science*, 7: 466–91.

Mearns, D. (1997). *Person-Centred Counselling Training*. London: Sage.

Wheeler, S. (2002). 'Assessing Personal Development'. *Counselling*, August: 13(7): 40–1.

Chapter 11

Personal Development in Clinical Psychology Training – 'The Story So Far . . .'

Clea Horner, Sheila Youngson and Jan Hughes

Introduction

This chapter aims to examine the current status of personal development in clinical psychology training. The basis for the chapter is a survey reporting on personal development in clinical psychology training courses in the UK conducted in 2006. This builds on a previous survey covering personal and professional development conducted by Gillmer and Marckus in 2003. The current survey looks specifically at finding out what courses are doing to promote and support personal development amongst their trainees.

Gillmer and Marckus's Survey

Gillmer and Marckus (2003) published their survey in the special issue of *Clinical Psychology* on Reflective Practice in July 2003, which highlighted the growing recognition of the importance of reflective practice in clinical psychology and explored issues of how to define, teach and assess this credibly. Gillmer and Marckus's research emerged from a reflective practice workshop for clinical psychology trainers in 2001, which aimed to examine and foster personal and professional development (PPD) in clinical psychology training (Hagan 2001). According to Gillmer and Marckus, professional trainers were already aware of the difficulties encompassed in the 'familiar yet slippery concept' of reflective practice. Personal development itself creates dilemmas with which courses must contend and provide both structures for trainee support and space for uncertainty (Gillmer and Marckus 2003). This dilemma is further illustrated by Gillmer and Marckus who state: 'Personal development is central to the notion of the reflective practitioner, but remains peripheral to the real training issues, which lie in the domain of the scientist practitioner' (2003: 20).

Gillmer and Marckus's survey endeavoured to clarify more precisely how courses were actually implementing personal and professional development (PPD), looking at how courses defined and evaluated PPD in addition to what support was actually given. The findings of this survey will be compared where possible alongside those of the current survey in the discussion. Gilmer and Marckus found they found they were able to group their findings into *Type A* (the good), *Type B* (the bad) and *Type C* (the ugly). Type A courses were found to have PPD clearly defined, that it was regarded as a competency in its own right and that it occupied a clearly demarcated programme within the overall programme curriculum (n = 6/17). Type B courses did define PPD but did not have it as a core competency (n = 3/17). Finally, Type C courses did not provide a clear definition yet included aspects of PPD in their programme (n = 8/17). In this current survey attempts will be made to apply these groupings to the data.

Methodology

Design

This was a questionnaire-based survey, covering all the key components of the Gillmer and Marckus (2003) survey but with additional questions to elicit information specifically about personal development. The questionnaire was designed to gain descriptive, quantitative information about aspects amenable to such investigation, for example, numbers of courses with a definition of personal development and hours of teaching spent on personal development. However, there was also a need to gain respondents' views on personal development in particular; therefore, a number of open-ended questions were devised to elicit more qualitative responses. Given the initially small number of returned questionnaires, an attempt was made to address this and a briefer telephone interview was devised. The telephone interview was designed to provide the same type of data as the questionnaire.

Procedure

All 30 institutions that appear in the Clearing House Handbook (2006) as offering doctorate in clinical psychology courses on the UK mainland were approached and an electronic questionnaire was sent to key personnel. It was suggested that if people preferred telephone contact to complete an abbreviated version of the survey then they could do this, and one course took up this option. A number of reminders were sent to courses, which resulted in two telephone interviews being completed.

Full data sets (that is, an electronic version of the questionnaire completed in full) were received from 11 of the 30 courses; three telephone interviews were completed; one course provided partial data in the form of course documentation; and one course explained that they were not in a position to complete the survey as their course was in its infancy.

Analysis

Two levels of analysis were performed. The first level is descriptive and summarized the quantitative components of the questionnaire and interview, utilizing frequency tables and graphical representations. Along with these figures, there are some corresponding descriptive responses such as boxes depicting examples of personal development activities mentioned by respondents.

Some questions were intended to offer an opportunity for the respondents to provide fuller and richer accounts. Although the data for these questions was richer than the other data produced by the questionnaire/interview, it was still in the form of reasonably discrete answers. As such, a method of analysis that could provide a systematic way of organizing this data through grouping the findings thematically was needed. Thematic analysis was chosen as it offers an accessible and theoretically flexible approach to analysing qualitative data, providing a method for identifying, analysing and reporting patterns (themes) within data (Braun and Clarke 2006).

Table 11.1 shows an example of the thematic analysis process utilized.

Respondents

Respondents provided their professional positions and responsibility for personal development on their courses. A large number of respondents

Table 11.1   Example of thematic analysis for this study

Data extract	Initial coding	Searching for themes	Reviewing themes and final naming of themes
If a trainee's performance on the course is seen to be affected by personal issues that may be addressed through personal therapy, the course is prepared to fund this (r6)	Personal therapy	Crisis Management	Reactive
	(?)		
The ppd system also uses the wider university services and local employing trust for trainees (r10)	Use of wider structures		
Clinical tutors can always do extra placement visits if needed, learning support if needed (r5)	Extra placement Visits		

were clinical tutors or clinical directors/deputy clinical directors but others were academic tutors or programme/assistant programme directors. The areas of responsibility for personal development are shown in Table 11.2.

Survey Results

Table 11.3 compares the findings of this current survey with the findings of Gillmer and Marckus (2003). The additional findings of this survey, including the thematic analysis of the qualitative components, are presented below.

Table 11.2   Respondents' responsibility for personal development

	Frequency count
Overall joint responsibility	1
Personal Development Module leader	9
Personal academic tutor	1
Lead for Personal Development	4
As a clinical tutor	1
Through doing annual appraisals	1
Organizing trainee support systems	3
Clinical skills teaching and co-devising Independent Personal Reviews	1
Total	21 (some respondents responsible for a number of activities)

Separating personal development from professional development

As this survey had a specific focus on personal development it was necessary to ascertain whether courses conceptualize personal development and professional development separately or together. There was an equal split of courses that conceptualize these concepts together and those who see them as being separate.

There were a range of reasons given for why courses do or do not separate personal from professional development. More varied reasons are given for the former case. The most common reason given for not separating the two elements was their inextricable connection. For one respondent, to separate the two elements was seen as 'antagonistic'. For another respondent, the two concepts were not separated for reasons associated with 'tradition'. Finally, one respondent referred to using the two components interchangeably, sometimes referring to them as linked and at other times not. There was no conceptual reason behind this; rather, they saw the concepts as evolving entities that could be adapted to meet different needs and priorities.

Selection

Of the courses for which information was provided, 10 out of 11 respondents stated in regard to selection interviews that they assess aspects of

Table 11.3 Clinical training personal development programmes with comparison to Gillmer and Marckus's (2003) survey results

Personal development curriculum components	Yes	No	Salient comments
Courses providing a definition of Personal Development	10*	1*	Courses using Gillmer 2003 = 2
	9	8	Courses using Walsh and Scaife 1998 = 1
			Group of trainers definition 2001 = 1
			Most courses refer to the personal and professional skills section of the criteria for the Accreditation of Postgraduate Training Programmes in Clinical Psychology (BPS 2004)
Courses specifying Personal Development as a core competency/theme (Type A)	14	0	A core theme running through 3 years
	9	8	A central philosophy
			Overarching ethos
Specified aims	6	9	Most courses in this survey had a personal and professional development module but not a personal development module
Specified outcomes }	8	10	
Specified evaluation	7		Attempts to address how personal development was evaluated were not answered fully by respondents
Course providing group work	12	2	Balint group for case discussions
	7	10	Facilitated fortnightly throughout 3 years of training
Mandatory attendance	9	3	9 × 45-minute groups in years 2 and 3, approximately 1/month.
	5	12	Facilitated group to encourage personal reflection and development
			2 × groups/year facilitated by an independent clinician and personal development tutor
Courses providing a buddy system	14	0	
	14	3	
Personal therapy	10	4	
	3	14	
Subsidy or funding	4	10	
	3	14	

Note: (n. = 14: questionnaire only* = 11, telephone interview = 3)
Gillmer and Marckus's (2003) results are given in bold text.

Table 11.4   Developments in light of new accreditation criteria

Examples of developments

- Expanded and systematically monitored personal reflection sessions
- Access to personal therapy list
- More extensive and better structured buddy system
- Improved quality standards and guidelines for personal tutor advisor systems
- Use of study leave monies for personal therapy
- Changes to personal development group
- Learning objectives for teaching changed
- Personal development module developed
- Reflective log for trainees introduced
- Required self-reflection in some assessed work
- Explicit conversations about personal development in placement meetings with clinical tutor
- Developed Independent Personal Review System

personal development through their selection process (as reported in Chapter 10). Most courses referred to assessing candidates' ability to demonstrate self-reflection and self-awareness. One course explicitly stated that one question out of six taps into level of self-awareness. For another course 'personal qualities' was one of five selection criteria, all of which are equally weighted. Response from another course explicitly states that they did not ask any overt personal development questions in their interview; however, they did make reference to asking candidates to indicate their strengths and weaknesses, which could be interpreted as an assessment of self-awareness.

Developments in light of the 2004 accreditation criteria

A number of courses had made changes to their personal development activities as a result of the 2004 BPS accreditation criteria (Table 11.4). Of those courses that had not made any developments three had always regarded personal development as significant and had pre-existing personal development components in their course structures. The response of one course was that they had not been aware of the revised accreditation criteria and thus could not comment on any developments in light of them.

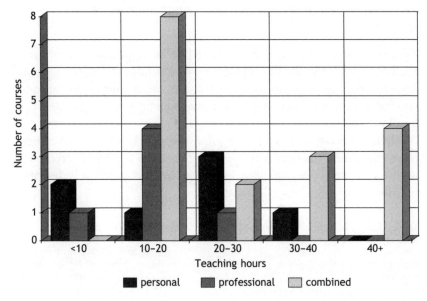

Figure 11.1   Total personal development teaching time for all years combined

Personal development modules

At this stage no course has a personal development module. A review of the course documentation makes apparent that most courses have a personal and professional development module. As such, personal development topics are included in the academic programmes, often intertwined with professional development topics to a greater or lesser extent.

Teaching time

Figure 11.1 shows that more time is spent on personal and professional development teaching combined than is spent on them as separate components. The most frequent amount of time spent on personal development teaching is between 10 and 20 hours per year. Another interesting observation is that all the charts show that personal development on its own is least implemented, with the minimum number of hours spent on this.

Personal development activities – what courses report they do

Table 11.5 presents all activities referred to by respondents with a frequency count for each. The top section of the table shows the personal development activities that are carried out by most courses. As this table illustrates, there is a range of personal development activities not delivered by all the courses.

Although personal development groups were referred to by 10 courses, when examining the data it is apparent that there is a wide variation in what constitutes a personal development group; this variation is described in Table 11.6.

Table 11.5   The range of different personal development activities described

	Mandatory	Optional	Total
Teaching	14	0	14
Set conversations with clinical tutor	11	3	14
Buddy systems	6	6	12
Personal development groups	9	3	12
Annual appraisals	11	0	11
Reflective journals	5	6	11
Case studies	8	2	10
Assessed work	9	0	9
Mentoring from a local CP	2	5	7
Personal therapy un-funded	1	5	6
Presentations	4	1	5
Access to university counselling	0	4	4
Personal therapy funded	0	2	2
Personal therapy part funded	0	2	2
12-session therapy option	0	2	2
Personal development tutorials biennially	1	0	1
Therapy network	1	0	1
Peer supervision group	1	0	1
Funded therapeutic consultations	0	1	1
Research supervision	0	1	1
Lesbian, gay and bisexual group	0	1	1
Black and ethnic minority group	0	1	1
Support scheme for trainees who are carers or parents	0	1	1
Support scheme for male trainees	0	1	1

Table 11.6 Variation in types of personal development groups offered by different courses

Psychodynamic	Unstructured and boundaried	Person centred	No single model	Reflective group × 2/year
Balint group for case discussions	Facilitated fortnightly throughout 3 years of training	9 × 45 minute groups in years 2 and 3 approximately 1/month	Facilitated group to encourage personal reflection and development	Facilitated by independent clinician and personal development tutor

'Top three' personal development activities

In this question respondents were asked to give their 'top three' personal development activities, defined as those deemed to be the most successful at promoting personal development amongst their trainees. Figure 11.2 presents the findings. This illustrates that respondents view personal development groups most consistently as their *'number one'* personal development activity. The next most popular activity is teaching. Developmental tutoring and annual appraisals have the same pattern of responses in third place.

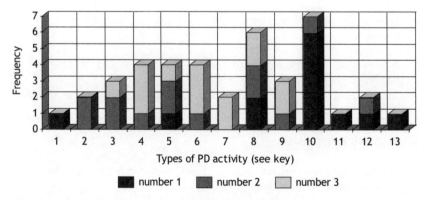

Figure 11.2   Top three personal development activities
Key: 1 academic tutorial system; 2 reflective journal; 3 mentor system; 4 development tutoring; 5 personal tutor system; 6 annual appraisals; 7 buddy system; 8 teaching; 9 assessed coursework; 10 personal development groups; 11 12-session therapy option; 12 supervision; 13 peer supervision group

Some of the reasons that respondents gave for their choices are as follows:

Personal development groups

reflective practice group, because that is all about reflecting on personal issues and how you cope with these

small, closed groups that continue for all three years allow depth in reflection, and awareness of reflexivity. These groups are generally regarded very positively by trainees. I think one main element of their success is that they do not include staff members

Teaching

because it is mandatory and all trainees are obliged to attend and address the issues and wider considerations

professional issues module - makes people reflect on themselves

Developmental tutoring

because of personal encouragement, trust and expectations that this engenders

continuity of conversations with clinical tutor where this is safe and supportive

Annual appraisals

held with the same Personal Tutor gives good opportunity to punctuate the process of personal development explicitly

Table 11.7 presents a grouped representation of respondents' 'top three' personal development activities. It is clear that respondents have emphasized those activities that are integral to the course as opposed to

Table 11.7 Grouped representations of respondents' 'top three' personal development activities

One-to-one with course staff	Other course activities	Individual and internal	External to course
Developmental review meetings	Reflective practice seminars	Reflective journal	Mentoring systems
Personal tutorial system	Buddy systems		12-session therapy option at Tavistock
Annual appraisals	Teaching		Personal therapy
Training reviews and line management system	Assessed coursework		Clinical supervision
Developmental clinical tutoring	Personal development groups		
Academic tutorial system	Peer supervision group		

individually focussed personal development activities or those personal development activities that are external to the course.

How flexibly can courses respond to trainees' requests for personal development activities?

The qualitative responses to this question have been grouped thematically, producing five themes: barriers to being flexible, reactive, assisting change, individual issues and trainees.

Within the *barriers to being flexible* theme, timetabling is referred to most. The following quotation illustrates this: 'It is difficult to respond as the timetable is set in advance and introducing something new means dropping something else and it's hard to find something to drop.'

The theme *reactive* is essentially concerned with times when there is an urgent need to address trainees' personal development, be this through personal therapy, extra placement visits or the wider structures to support and assist the course and trainee. This is exemplified by the following quotation: 'If a trainee's performance on the course is seen to be affected by personal issues that may be addressed through personal therapy, the course is prepared to fund this.'

The theme of *assisting change* refers to all aspects that enable changes to happen. The aspect most frequently referred to was feedback. Notably, courses refer to actively seeking feedback from trainees and using it to inform decisions about change. For instance: 'We routinely collect trainee feedback to inform our practices. For example, we have – from time to time – modified the length, structure, as well as content of Personal Development teaching to better suit trainee needs.'

An *individual issues* theme refers to one respondent's statement that it was easier to change factors relating to an individual as opposed to a group as a whole.

A *trainees* theme refers to trainees' own efforts at bringing about change on their courses: 'Peer supervision came from trainees who chose their own models, and each year group adapts this to their own needs.'

Barriers to encouraging personal development in clinical training

Again, the qualitative responses have been collated thematically, with the themes emerging being *trainee factors, staff factors, course-related factors* and *facilitative factors*. The main barriers seemed to cluster at the level of the individual, with both *trainee* and *staff factors* represented. Different views towards personal development appeared to be mostly from the staff perspective but trainee viewpoints also played a role. The following quotations illustrate this barrier: 'The biggest barrier is theoretical orientation where some value self-reflection more than others', 'Obtaining a consistent view across the whole team of the importance of personal aspects of development is challenging, we often each hold differing views of what is really meant by reflective practice' and 'Variation in trainee views which can make it hard to respond to feedback'.

Course-related barriers referred to resources of time, money and staffing: 'Usual restraints of time (balancing teaching days and placement days) and resources (e.g. funding for personal learning sessions)'. The demands of training were highlighted with reference made to trainees already being put under a lot of pressure by training courses. Perhaps this course was cautious of putting extra pressure on trainees, especially for activities that the course themselves were not certain would benefit them: 'Barriers imposed by multiple demands of the course on trainees, hard to ask them to do extra things: e.g. reflective log – how do you judge it is an effective way of doing Personal Development without evaluating the trainee?' Having a clear rationale was identified by one respondent who stated that: 'There needs to be a rationale for how the personal development aids professional practice for it to "count" as valid activity.'

Interestingly, some of the respondents reframed their barriers as factors that could facilitate (*facilitative factors*) personal development rather than impede it. Under this theme personal development was seen as something that needed to be integral to all aspects of a course and embedded within the curriculum to ensure that it was a meaningful activity. Another respondent referred to a staffing issue that had been a barrier to personal development and how the course had addressed this, serving to facilitate personal development in the future. A further respondent acknowledged personal development as a developmental process during which trainees need to be encouraged and supported to engage fully with it.

Finally, there were other responses that did not easily fit with the themes already described. The first was an answer framed as a question to be answered. This has been included as it highlights an interesting point for discussion regarding what courses mean by personal development and reflective practice in general: 'How do you select people who are reflective and what do we mean by that?'

The last responses were from respondents who stated that there were no barriers to doing personal development.

Ideas for the future

Figure 11.3 represents the collated responses to the question regarding courses' future promotion of personal development. One course took the position of needing to monitor the current situation before implementing other activities. Some courses clearly stated the specific activities that they were interested in implementing. Whilst describing these some respondents went further in their descriptions, stating some of the issues, barriers or attitudes that should be considered before implementing specific activities. These descriptive components are indicated in the boxes 'Issues to address', 'Staffing', and 'Attitudes towards' with arrows into the corresponding activity. Finally, three respondents did not have any current ideas

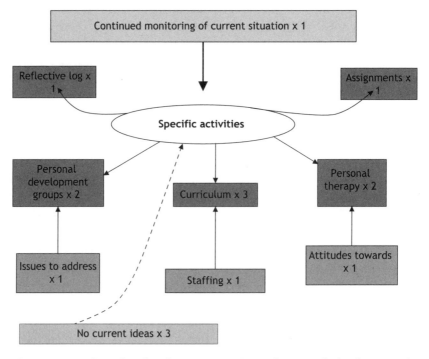

Figure 11.3 Ideas for the future promotion of personal development in training

regarding specific activities, although one of these people did say that they were looking forward to this book.

Points for Discussion

Limitations of the survey

For this current survey, 14 out of the 30 courses completed either the questionnaire (n = 11) or the telephone interview (n = 3). A further two courses responded, but one had no data and the other gave partial data in the form of course documentation. This represents a response rate of 53 per cent. This overall response rate is lower than that for Gillmer and

Marckus, who had a response rate of 71 per cent, with 17 out of 24 courses responding. The response rate for this current survey may have ramifications for the findings, such as the potential for response bias.

Definitions

The majority of respondents (n = 10) stated that they had a definition of personal development. This finding is similar to Gillmer and Marckus (n = 9), but they also had a greater number of courses that did not have a definition (n = 8) compared to this survey where only one course stated they did not a definition. The finding that most courses had a definition of personal development could indicate that responding courses have a more formulated programme of personal development, as compared to the non-respondents. This hypothesis cannot be further explored, as there is no data from those courses that did not respond. Taking a critical stance of those courses that state they have a definition, it is not always clear what that definition is and often it is a description of personal development that is presented. Similarly to Gillmer and Marckus, definitions given were centred around the development of self-awareness and the effect of the person's history and training on their professional development.

Personal and professional development

As this survey is mostly concerned with the state of personal development in clinical training it was necessary to find out whether respondents conceptualize personal development separately from professional development. Interestingly, the split was virtually equal. For those people who separated personal development from professional development it was apparent that personal development had to be identified in its own right to enable its intrinsic value to be seen. Importantly, the separation of personal development from professional development also acknowledges how trainees may meet their personal development in a range of ways and that personal development is not solely linked to the course.

Popular personal development activities

Respondents were asked to give their opinion of their 'top three' personal development activities (that is, those that were the most successful at promoting personal development for their trainees). Out of a range of responses the most frequently referred to activities were personal development groups at number one, teaching at number two and developmental tutoring and annual appraisals at number three. It is interesting to note that all these activities are carried out by most, if not all, courses. This indicates that there is some consistency between the activities constituting personal development and also some uniformity between respondents' views of which are the most successful activities at promoting personal development amongst trainees. It is apparent from Table 11.7 (which illustrates the broad range of activities referred to by respondents in their 'top three') that one-to-one meetings with course staff represent a large proportion of that considered to promote personal development. Not all courses offer all of these activities but each course has some face-to-face contact with their trainees. It would be interesting to compare courses' aims and protocols for these face-to-face meetings to further explore how they address personal development in these contexts.

Group work

Group work was carried out by most courses. In this survey the nature of personal development groups differed widely between courses, with the variation from a reflective group twice a year to a facilitated group fortnightly for the whole three years of training. Of course, such variation is not necessarily negative but what is clear is that trainees will experience these groups very differently and the depth of personal development gained from these different interpretations of personal development groups is likely to be marked. Interestingly, most of those courses with personal development groups run them on a mandatory basis; to a certain extent this could be seen as emphasizing their importance to trainees and staff, but it may also have an impact on the motivation of trainees to attend.

Support systems

A number of support systems are in evidence, with those most frequently used by courses being clinical tutors, buddy systems and personal development groups, similar to Gillmer and Marckus's findings. Other activities that were not referred to by Gillmer and Marckus but were found in this survey to be equally popular were teaching, assessed work, annual appraisals and reflective journals. Gillmer and Marckus also found that mentoring from a clinician external to the course was a popular form of support for trainees. In the current survey approximately half of the respondents referred to this. It would additionally be necessary to consider how trainees themselves view such activities as assessed work, teaching and annual appraisals as meeting their personal development needs. This highlights that there could be a potential discrepancy between courses and trainees over what they consider to promote personal development. The views of recent trainees (in training at the time of this survey) and their thoughts on personal development and what has helped them are presented in the next chapter.

Therapy

Personal therapy is clearly advocated by a number of courses, but for the majority of courses it is not funded. Only four courses fund or part fund personal therapy. Some courses have attempted to provide their trainees with a 'taste' of a therapeutic experience, be this a 12-session therapy option at the Tavistock Clinic, a therapy network in which trainees can seek out local clinicians in confidence to discuss problem-focussed issues, or a number of therapeutic consultations, again with local clinicians.

Reflective journals

Most courses referred to reflective journals, and respondents stated that trainees were encouraged to complete them. However, in general, respondents' justifications for reflective journals were vague and assessment of this activity was limited. This presents a dilemma for training courses, for if reflective journals are seen as a useful and positive way to support trainees' personal development there needs to be a way to enable trainees to integrate them into their practice and to see them as facilitative rather than burdensome. It is clear that research needs to be done to ascertain whether reflective journals do help trainees and the mechanisms by which this occurs.

Responsiveness

The thematic analysis relating to how flexibly the courses can respond to trainees' requests for personal development activities clearly highlighted the barriers to being flexible. Issues such as timetabling, time, balancing the activities of training and the demands on trainees arose. For some courses, flexibility related to being able to react to difficult situations or crisis points in the training journey. Some courses specifically referred to things that assisted change and hence enabled flexibility, such as the trainees themselves being motivated to impact on their own training experience and courses consistently gaining and responding to feedback to improve teaching and so on. Finally, some courses referred to the specific examples that, to them, illustrated their ability to be flexible, for instance, the implementation of a personal development group following a request from trainees.

Barriers

Barriers to encouraging personal development were mostly clustered around the level of the individual, for both trainee and staff. This suggests a perceived variation between staff views and trainees' views about what is meant by personal development. Reluctance and fear were themes at both the staff and trainee level, indicating that personal development may not be the easiest activity with which to engage. These findings reflect some of the familiar tensions concerning personal development, as individuals are constantly left grappling with the construct of personal development and what it means to them. Courses have a challenge to embrace these variations and to convey them in a way that enables trainees and staff to see personal development as a valid and meaningful activity. There is also a responsibility within courses to ensure both staff and trainees understand personal development. This challenge is reflected in the other themes identified, course-related barriers and facilitative factors.

The future

When asked to consider the future, most respondents gave specific examples of the personal development activities they might introduce. This demonstrates that some courses are willing to try and promote personal development further. Importantly, none of the respondents portrayed a negative view of personal development, even if they had few ideas of what to do next. This suggests a general consensus on the value of activities that promote personal development for trainees.

Conclusions

Reviewing Gillmer and Marckus's criteria for Type A courses it is apparent that most (if not all) courses that responded closely fit these criteria. This is an interesting finding compared to the 2003 survey, in which six courses fulfilled these criteria. This suggests that there have been some changes to training courses and how they promote and support personal and professional development; however this is not a surprising finding given the emphasis on personal development in the BPS accreditation criteria in 2004.

It is apparent that although there is some general movement towards more integrated personal development curricula, the position of personal development specifically is less well defined, and perhaps a lack of clarity translates to trainees as confusion about personal development more generally. Nevertheless, there appears to be a general trend of embracing personal and professional development that inevitably communicates to trainees the importance of this along their training journeys. It is important to compare the trainers' views about what they deliver and what they feel is important with the views of the trainees on the receiving end. This is the focus of the next chapter . . .

REFERENCES

Braun, V. and Clarke, V. (2006). 'Using Thematic Analysis in Psychology', *Qualitative Research in Psychology*, 3: 77–101.

British Psychological Society (2007). *Criteria for Postgraduate Courses in Clinical Psychology*. Leicester: British Psychological Society.

Gillmer, B. and Marckus, R. (2003). 'Personal Professional Development in Clinical Psychology Training: Surveying Reflective Practice'. *Clinical Psychology*, 27: 20–3.

Hagan, P. (2001). 'Fostering Personal and Professional Development in Clinical Psychology Training: Ways and Means'. Workshop presented at Group for Trainers in Clinical Psychology Conference, July 2001, Oxford.

Chapter 12

Processes in Personal Development in Training
The Trainee's Experience

Jan Hughes and Sheila Youngson (with contributions from Kevin Baker, Steven Coles, Kathryn Dykes, Simon Platts, Nick Shelley, Stephanie Sneider, Vicky Tozer)

Introduction

In Chapter 11 we examined the current status of personal development in training programmes. This is the provider's view – what programmes feel they are delivering and achieving. But what of the consumer's view? Obviously it is important to hear the experiences of trainees who have undertaken the training.

Our strategy for achieving this was to approach a number of recently qualified clinical psychologists to listen to their experiences and opinions. We felt this would provide a richness of data that would be unavailable in a survey of a large number of trainees. We also felt it was important to approach those who had qualified in September 2006. These are the cohort who had been third-year trainees when the survey reported in Chapter 11 was conducted and would have been party to the processes described. We also felt it would be helpful for individuals to have had a few months away from training and would therefore be able to reflect on their experiences.

We felt that we would like to hear the voices of at least six trainees and would like them to come from a variety of training courses. We had contact with a number of courses and were also able to approach trainees who had graduated from Leeds and Sheffield. Course staff team members were approached for the University of East London, Leicester, Surrey and Lancaster courses. They were requested to approach newly qualified clinical psychologists from their course to ask whether they would be willing to contribute to this book. They were asked to:

- reflect on their personal development during training;
- comment on how their course approached personal development;
- say what was important and worked well;
- note what did not work.

It was emphasized that this was very much about their own experiences and was not a formal academic piece. Contributors were all given a brief summary of the book along with a description of the chapters and an explanation of where this chapter would fit. They were also all given a copy of the Model of Personal Development Processes (Chapter 4). Everyone was asked to provide 500 words. They were informed that they (and the course they had attended) could remain anonymous; however, all were happy to be identified.

No changes have been made to the contributor's words, which are shown here in full.

Refection One – Simon Platts

The situations that I was exposed to during training had a variety of effects on me and provided me with an enhanced understanding of myself and others. I came into training with some strong ideas of social justice and equality, how 'normative behaviour' may constitute distress, and the disciplinary effects of power. I wanted training to develop these ideas in relation to operating as a psychologist, and my first placement fitted with this and enabled me to experience how the division between our personal and professional selves can be largely illusory. This gave me the confidence to be myself and greater freedom in how I related and interacted with others.

However, at different times after my first placement I felt I encountered the kind of disciplinary practices that I had been so aware of before training (for example, the process of being constructed as a clinical psychologist within the dominant professional discourse). This had various effects on my personal development. For example, it made me reflect on my personal values and beliefs and how these can be nurtured in environments where my perspectives were in the minority. I also experienced the discomfort and distress of being influenced in ways that were not consistent with my sense of self and identity. At these times I struggled with myself and in my work as I felt a deep sense of confusion and discord between what I wanted to be and what I felt I was expected to be. Experiencing these processes in the context of the University of East London training, with its emphasis on critical theory and the operation of social power, provided a certain sense of mindfulness, encouragement and solace. I also attempted to resolve these issues in supervision or with tutors; however, sometimes I felt silenced or unable to discuss such matters with people who were assessing me. Nevertheless, I recognized that my silence was temporary and functional to enable the placement or course to be completed. It also made me think about others in intolerable situations, and how we survive and eventually overcome difficult situations. This led on to another development point that I had partly taken for granted, which was thinking about the importance of my social networks, both within and outside the discipline. Their support enabled me to cope with and ultimately survive training, and I am grateful for the considerable time and energy people have invested in me, both prior to and during training.

Clinical training also developed me in ways that surprised me, such as how I responded to and dealt with struggle. For example, my 'psychodynamic placement' challenged me practically and ideologically, and the discourses around learning and training made me feel like I was 'failing' in some way. I am now more able to incorporate psychodynamic ideas into my thinking and practice, but this makes me appreciate how taking on different perspectives requires considerable time and effort.

Training also made me examine some 'stuck' stories about myself, for example, being constructed as 'obsessional' and 'perfectionist'. These ways of being often had positive consequences (e.g. rewards), but also carried their constraints. Consequently, the training was in some ways a liberating experience, in that I have developed ways of managing these stories about myself in a way that is useful and functional.

Reflection Two – Kathryn Dykes

My recollection of the person who arrived to begin the DClinPsy course was someone who probably looked a little like a rabbit caught in the head-lights of a rapidly approaching car! At the start, what I required was to be directed and contained. A task that I think the course, on the whole, did really well. The dilemma within my year group seemed to be enabling trainees to develop sufficiently so that this support can be withdrawn in the right way and at the right time for each trainee, handing the responsibility for development over to each individual.

There are tensions inherent in clinical training: the role of directed student versus autonomous professional in the same week; the knowledge that supporters may also be assessors; one staff team trying to meet the needs of a diverse range of trainees. I know people who struggled with these tensions more than I did. I sought support from fantastic peers when tensions were too great, and have learnt to recognize not just where support is but where *appropriate* support is and *when* it is needed.

Numerous individuals were put in place by the course structure to offer me support and it was really left to me as to how I utilized them. This allowed me to take responsibility and to learn to identify what I needed in order to be able to continue to develop, both personally and professionally, and how this shifted with the various stages of training.

I found people who I trusted, who would explore and support but also challenge my thinking about tricky situations. Reflection groups were difficult to negotiate but ultimately became an important forum and provided different perspectives and opportunities for development. These resources allowed me to publicly and privately acknowledge my shortcomings and, more difficultly, my strengths. I began to develop the capacity to consider and formulate situations that were difficult, considering the system within which I was functioning, both the course, multi-disciplinary teams and the wider NHS system, and my role and relationships within them.

By the end of training, my awareness of my responsibilities in ensuring my continued personal development was heightened. Importantly, though, I recognize that my personal and professional development have emerged alongside each other and are mutually symbiotic. My training course provided a vital structure and space within which personal and professional development was facilitated and encouraged. I now acknowledge that this is not a static process but the foundation of a career-long journey that feels vital in ensuring effective therapeutic care for the people I work with.

This blossoming internal ability to reflect has enhanced confidence, self-awareness and personal relationships. In addition, it has enabled me to contemplate working relationships and pre-empt some of the potential pitfalls of being newly qualified. I am still falling down a few holes, but at least I have learnt to make a considered plan on how I can best climb back out again. This feels like a vital piece of my armoury when working on the front line in the NHS.

Reflection Three – Kevin Baker and Steven Coles

KEVIN: I remember the video counselling simulation was the earliest opportunity for personal development when we had to look at ourselves, share this with others and then get their reflections, which we used to consider ways of changing ourselves. Course staff were important at supporting this reflection process.

STEVEN: I never originally thought about the video simulation as personal development, but I agree it was a good experience. I think the format was useful as it wasn't assessed formally, so it wasn't completely threatening – even though we were all nervous about what others would think of us.

KEVIN: It made me think that personal development is something you can't successfully do on your own because you've got to have varied input from others giving you feedback – but it needs to be done in safe way, a way that facilitates taking a risk and sharing.

STEVEN: I think it *can* be done on your own, because you can have an internal critical perspective or imagine what others might say. So in one way you're on your own but in another you're not, as you're taking another's perspective. I suppose we're talking about relationships and safety in relationships that enable some form of personal development. There is also something about seeing different events as opportunities for personal development.

KEVIN: You're right about relationships. I found the context where I developed most was in my relationships with my clinical supervisors on placements. I thought of my supervision explicitly to be about personal development.

STEVEN: I agree about supervision, it was the arena where I feel I most developed, but I suppose I didn't make this explicit. It would more come out in how much I shared about myself when discussing clinical work. Again, I could do this more with some supervisors than others – we're back to relationships again.

KEVIN: Each placement supervision was different according to specialty, the personality of the supervisor, gender, etc. All these factors had an effect on supervision. For example, I only had one supervisor who was older than me and one who was a woman.

STEVEN: Do you think, then, that these varied people *or* audiences made a difference to what you shared and your personal development?

KEVIN: Not sure if they did. For me it was the process of thinking about my supervision that was important. For example, my observation that they were all younger was a reflection I used in order to focus on my self. It wasn't a problem but rather an opportunity for me to reflect on why I was observing that difference.

STEVEN: About difference, we both had different reflective practice groups; I think you got more out of yours than mine. I don't think people felt safe or contributed much in mine or maybe they didn't see the use of that particular opportunity for personal development.

KEVIN: Yes, I think there were also differences in the way our reflective practice groups were set up – mine had an external facilitator, while yours had a member of staff co-facilitating.

STEVEN: Yes, the course staff member, not intentionally, represented or symbolized the training course which always felt more about passing and failing – maybe making the group feel less safe for some people. Again, it's about the relationship with the people you're having the personal development opportunity with.

KEVIN: Aside from reflective practice, there were also instances when I began to think about things differently in lectures or workshops as part of the teaching on the course. This didn't happen very often, but some sessions stick in my mind. It wasn't so much about the person teaching (although this was relevant), but the way in which some of the sessions were taught and the content.

STEVEN: I suppose all experiences can be seen as opportunities for personal development, but some lend themselves more easily to personal development than others. Actually, we haven't mentioned the personal development group that was offered at the beginning of the course!

KEVIN: Oh yes! I had forgotten about that. Funny that the thing which seems to offer the most direct way of doing personal development is the thing that didn't work for us. Do you remember how it was set up for us?

STEVEN: It seemed that it was all a bit unclear and some of us felt uncomfortable with it as we were a new group and felt that it was forced on us – it wasn't sold very well. I kind of wish I had attended it now. Do you think that the course cares more about the academic side rather than the personal/experiential stuff?

KEVIN: I suppose it's easy to think that, but we've talked about how some of the staff had a different focus on the course, like the clinical tutors were more focussed on the clinical work (obviously) and they seemed to be involved in the experiential side of things (like the video simulation and reflective practice groups). But maybe the power structures on the course make it easier for the academic staff to present the academic standards as more important, and I think that the university wouldn't care too much about the experiential side of things because this isn't assessed and doesn't fit into the university's world view.

STEVEN: I was thinking that the case studies could be an area where a certain amount of reflection and personal development could take place. But I didn't feel that actually happened, because you are trying to cram some theory in and thinking about what kind of mark you are going to get. But the video case study was more useful as you had to look at yourself doing clinical work – you had to look at yourself from the outside and see what others see.

KEVIN: Yes, it seems that personal development is really about reflecting on yourself to an audience and learning from it – a bit like personal therapy.

STEVEN: I don't think that clinical psychology has a big emphasis on personal therapy – I was talking to a counselling psychologist who didn't think you could actually do work with clients adequately without it.

KEVIN: When we were on the course, I didn't feel like doing anything of any depth like personal therapy as I had two babies at home. And so did you, didn't you? I remember us talking about it and that family life seemed to be a bit more important than putting yourself through personal therapy. Although now I feel definitely that I would like to have a limited number of sessions with a therapist and see how I can use it.

STEVEN: Yeah, it's another opportunity.

Reflection Four - Nick Shelley

The beginning of clinical psychology training in October 2003 marked the end for me of the seemingly endless round of moving jobs and writing application forms that had been going on since graduating two years previously. During those first few weeks on the course it felt like I had to make the shift from displaying competency and employability to an attitude of knowing little and wanting to know more, a sponge ready to absorb the words of wisdom being imparted to me. Personal development was something I had always ignored as a concept prior to starting the course. Being presented with a personal development journal, blank and ready for my reflections when starting training, I found myself challenged to stop and reflect on my own experiences.

Having never used a journal before (except a few aborted childhood attempts at writing a diary), I found I didn't know how to do it. It was easier for me to engage in external forms of personal development, such as supervision, personal development groups or end of placement reflections. During these times I found it helpful to have feedback which could guide me on whether I was 'doing it right' and there were also opportunities to observe what others were doing and learn how to do it right from them. Left on my own to write in my journal, or using any other formal method of internal reflection, I felt uncertain about how to proceed, worried that I would be doing it 'wrong'. Regular prompting from my clinical tutor finally got me to a point where I thought that I would give it a go. Looking back on those first writings now, I am aware of how quickly I went from being reflective about my own work and trying to understand more about myself to more practical considerations about planning my work.

The second-year optional personal development group on the course was, for me, a valuable source of personal and professional development. Through participation in this group I became aware of my tendency to fill silences and to jump in with solutions to problems. Over time I became more comfortable with gaps in conversation and learnt that to be listened to is of benefit even when no solution exists. These are skills that have been important in my clinical work, but have been significant in my personal life as well. Although the third-year mandatory group continued to be beneficial to me, I found it harder to explore significant issues in the bigger group, and was also aware that some were reticent about speaking out in the large group at all.

I continue to value external forms of personal development, and find that, over time, I have become increasingly reflective and less practically orientated. As I write this I feel challenged to return to my personal development journal (currently shelved). Perhaps, over time, that too will become less focussed on practical planning and more reflective. I also hope that in time I will be able to allow more of me, my personality and spirituality, to influence my personal development in a work context.

Reflection Five - Vicky Tozer

When I was asked if I would be willing to contribute some thoughts on the process of personal development to this book I was happy to agree, but when it came to sitting down and putting my thought into words I was quite daunted. However, I decided that for me it's important to consider how who we are impacts on our work, for example, how our personal experiences, beliefs, culture, etc., influence our opinions and the relationships we form with the people that we work with. The process of personal development involves developing an awareness of this and being able to question, and, if necessary, challenge ourselves.

When I think about how the course supported my process of personal development I think there were a number of systems in place that I found helpful. For me, the relationship that I developed with my supervisors on my clinical placements provided me with a context in which I could reflect on aspects of myself and how these were impacting on my work. I had the same clinical tutor throughout my three years of training and was able to develop a good relationship with her, and I think some of the conversations I had with her were extremely helpful. Another feature of the course that I think was helpful was the appraisal process, as it provided a time when you thought about the experience of training, how you were developing both personally and professionally, and your goals.

Throughout my training I have considered what it is about me as a person that has led me to the conclusions I have reached, why it is I have certain expectations, and how I have changed and developed, and I think I have become much more aware of myself in the process. However, the process of personal development is ongoing and doesn't end when you leave training. Honesty about yourself and your feelings is necessary if you are to learn about yourself and develop as a person. I think it is much easier to be honest with someone if you have been able to form a good relationship with them, and I have always thought the supervision relationship is important in the process of personal development. One of the things I value about my current supervision is the opportunity to reflect on what sort of psychologist I am and how my sense of personal identity influences my work, as well as how my work influences my sense of self. I think that during training we are provided with an almost unique opportunity to engage in that process, we are actively encouraged to reflect and consider ourselves, we are exposed to both formal and informal systems to support our development, and we have a wide range of supervision experiences. This provides us with a context in which we can reflect about ourselves and our development. Ultimately, though, it is down to us: no matter how many systems are put in place to encourage the process of personal development it will only be of benefit if we actively engage with it and take these opportunities to develop awareness of, try to understand, and sometimes challenge ourselves.

Reflection Six - Stephanie Sneider

For me, personal development during the training course was closely linked to my professional experiences and progress. Upon entering the training course I experienced a sudden increase in awareness of my own lack of professional practice and skill. This 'conscious incompetence' was unexpected and challenging. I felt at risk of losing confidence and feeling deskilled. However, with the benefit of hindsight, I think that losing some of my 'newbie arrogance' led to increased motivation to learn and to identify my own training needs. I think this change in my awareness of my (in)abilities enabled a period of personal growth.

What helped me to grasp hold and take control of worry about my abilities was an explicit recognition by course staff that clinical training, and indeed a career in a mental health discipline, can place great demands upon personal resources. In order to support and encourage our progress, the course created 'Personal development & reflection' (personal development) sessions. The training course opted to employ an experienced person-centred counsellor to facilitate bi-monthly year-group sessions.

Consideration of personal development had never been raised during my time as a psychology or research assistant, and, whilst interested, I was unsure what I could expect to gain from dedicated formal sessions. Furthermore, exploring personal development in full view of 20 plus course-mates could at times feel unsafe and nerve-racking. Nevertheless, the explicit focus upon personal development did provoke internal reflection about my progress and encouraged me to consider the impact of my training experiences as well as personal life events. To be honest, I did more personal development during the couple of hours commute to and from the sessions, and I have continued to do this whilst travelling to my current job! At these times I reflect upon the outcome of daily events and evaluate the factors involved. I consider the likely impact on my personal life and also aim to become aware of my own stress levels and consider how to manage these using supervision, case discussion, or, at home, through leisure time or with support from newly qualified peers.

At various times during my training I felt that my professional and personal development would have benefited from having a dedicated training course tutor who carried out all of the placement visits and annual reviews during the three years. These reviews are an ideal opportunity for reflection on personal and professional development. However, I found that full use of the reviews was impeded by changes in course tutor for each placement. My motivation to enter into discussions about my development at annual review time was hindered by an apparent focus upon academic progress and grades, which, whilst important, in my opinion paled by comparison to clinical experiences and development related to this.

I found that discussing my personal reflections during supervision further validated and encouraged my commitment to ongoing development. Supportive peer supervision was a great space in which to compare reflections, and whilst this was undertaken informally and voluntarily by a small group of friends from the training course, I think we would have valued a more formal approach with dedicated time for this small-group approach. Successful use of clinical supervision for this purpose varied, and was dependent on the quality of the supervisory relationship. A supervisor who was particularly interested and supportive enabled me to make the most of supervision and share my personal reflections about my progress. I will be sure to support and encourage supervision for this purpose in the future.

Emerging Themes

How did the course approach personal development and what was helpful/unhelpful?

Some contributors gave an overall sense that their course was helpful in developing personal development, for example, in its philosophy and ethos, the course 'directed and contained', 'facilitated and encouraged' personal development. It seems that the active encouragement of personal development and recognition of the demand placed on the individual by the profession were important. A theme emerged of the importance of relationships in a number of different arenas. Most importantly, this was highlighted within supervision and the development of a positive supervisory relationship was seen as pivotal to personal development. Relationships in other areas were important, for example, with course staff, and it was felt valuable to have the same clinical tutor across the three years to allow for developmental progression. Relationships within the year cohort were also important as was the use of peer supervision with colleagues. Peer supervision was felt to be important when it was not course directed.

A number of contributors identified individual course processes that had been helpful. The mechanism provided by the course that was most often quoted as being useful for personal development was supervision. A number of contributors also discussed personal development groups and had had mixed experiences within these. Where an external facilitator had been used in the groups this was seen as more positive – groups with an internal member of staff who also had an evaluative role were seen as less helpful. One course had provided video counselling simulation and this was felt to be a helpful way for students to look at themselves and develop personally. One contributor felt that the teaching they had received prompted reflection and development, and another felt that it was helpful to have had annual appraisals in which the conversation was based not just on their academic development but on their development as a whole. The use of personal development journals was another course process that was discussed, and it was felt this had helped highlight a personal development need. Overall, the conclusions from the different course processes is that it is the individual's responsibility to engage in these and that it is helpful to be challenged within a safe context. Another emerging theme was that sometimes this challenging was extremely hard but that ultimately it had been useful in developing personally.

Personal development methods outside of the course were also mentioned. Therapy was seen as a potentially valuable way of developing, although there was a recognition that consideration needed to be given to when to engage in this, given the many pressures of training. Social supports and networks and talking to peers were also felt to be important. A final method was the use of reflective space when travelling to and from placement.

An overview for trainees

Taking these six reflective pieces together, it can be seen that personal development is an individual process, and individuals approach it in a variety of ways. Some people begin training having already had some focus on personal development; for others, it is a new and somewhat scary concept. For some, it is important to talk with others both formally and informally; for others, the emphasis is more on internal reflection. For some, self-care is stressed. However, all recognize that clinical psychology training, and the process of training, throws up many challenges to self, and the perception of self. Adding to one's self-knowledge and awareness is seen as important, if not crucial, and also seen as a life-long process. Finally, all acknowledge, explicitly or implicitly, that there is a responsibility to engage in the process of personal development, and a requirement to continue to question and challenge one's self throughout a career.

How Does This Compare to the Training Course Perspective?

There is some overlap of these emerging themes with the results from the survey of courses presented in Chapter 11. Interestingly, supervision was not acknowledged within the course processes as being a valuable way of encouraging personal development, maybe because those responding were focussing on processes within the course structure. The most popular method of personal development quoted in the survey is personal development groups, although it was highlighted that how these were defined was extremely variable. The viewpoints of the trainees on groups above are mixed, and it is important to understand this variance, which is addressed in Chapter 9. The next three most popular methods in the survey are teaching, developmental tutoring and annual appraisals. These are all highlighted above as being helpful from the trainee perspective.

Realms of personal development

Fitting these findings with the four realms of personal development highlighted in Chapter 3 (self, self in relation, self in community, self in role), it is apparent that there are special emphases in training within these realms. Trainees are encouraged to use personal development methods within the realm of self, mainly through the use of reflective journals. There is much more emphasis on personal development within the realm of relationships. This is seen as being important in terms of the supervisory relationship, relationships with course staff and tutors and with their cohort and peers. Interestingly, there is less emphasis in developing personally within the individual's community. Some guidance and support about developing personally within their roles within work is given to trainees, however – for example, through teaching, through group work, through supervision and through therapy.

An overview for clinical psychology training courses

Integrating the themes that have emerged from the trainee's viewpoint and from the courses' viewpoints (in Chapter 11), it is suggested that it is important for training courses to consider their approach to personal development on different levels:

Level 1: The ethos and the culture of the course and how this is portrayed to trainees (and other stakeholders) in relation to personal development. The emphasis here is on personal development being encouraged and facilitated within a 'safe' environment.

Level 2: Developing personal development within relationships (for example, clinical, academic and personal tutor and supervisor) and being aware of the helpful nature of consistent ongoing relationships for trainees.

Level 3: Developing discrete tasks and processes (for example, groups, teaching and reflective logs to help trainees further their personal development). Using the four realms of personal development can be helpful in terms of ensuring trainees have opportunities to develop within a wide range of approaches.

If clinical psychology training courses can refine/progress on all levels, this will give trainees the best possible opportunities to develop personally within and outside their training.

Chapter 13

The Present and the Future
Sheila Youngson with Jan Hughes

Introduction

And so, the end of the book is reached. Our hope is that the reader, whether reading from cover to cover or dipping into chapters of interest, will have been provoked. Provoked to think and to feel, to reassess and to re-evaluate, to feel challenged and to feel supported. Above all, to experience and/or re-experience the necessity to engage with the process that is personal development.

There are no right and no wrong questions, and no right and no wrong answers when the development of the person is considered. There are only growing and shifting acknowledgements, understandings, searchings and debates. There is no end to the process, it is a life-long task. Perhaps another hope is that this book will have stimulated new ideas and approaches to the task.

We have deliberately chosen not to write and bring together a purely academic book. Different styles and ways of writing will hopefully make the book as accessible and intriguing as possible. Even within this final chapter, changing styles of writing are utilized, from the more academic to the more lyrical, perhaps illustrating how the personal and the professional are irrevocably intertwined, and that neither is entirely academic or lyrical!

This chapter aims to pull out some of the emerging themes, and then consider the question 'Where next?' It will end, in true personal development style, with personal reflections from the two editors on the process of bringing this book to publication.

Emerging Themes

Context

As we stated at the start of the book (see Chapter 2), we live in changeable times. Clinical psychology is being challenged on a number of fronts, and challenge can produce useful and meaningful outcomes. At an individual level, clearly contracted supervision is now mandatory for all clinical psychologists. So is continued professional development, and a yearly log must be submitted to ensure attainment of one's Practising Certificate. (Colleagues in related professions may be surprised that this has only recently happened for clinical psychologists.) We need continually to evaluate and re-evaluate the extent and limitations of our many roles, identify additional training needs, learn to do things differently, embrace new knowledge, be creative in response to circumstance and individual or setting, bear and contain psychological distress and stress, be fit for purpose, be fit to practise, know when we need support and how to access it. These are considerable professional and personal requirements.

At a professional level (New Ways of Working), we are being asked to consider and develop more clearly and specifically, the many roles taken on, on a previously *ad hoc* basis (for example, supervisor, researcher, trainer, consultant, leader). This has profound implications for pre-qualification training and post-qualification further training. As part of New Ways of Working we are tasked to respond actively to the national Improving Access to Psychological Therapies programme and all it may entail in terms of structuring and restructuring services and meeting the training needs of extant and potential levels of staff. For the profession of clinical psychology all of these developments have associated threats and opportunities.

At a national level, there is increased accountability. Statutory regulation of clinical psychologists has arrived under the Health Professions Council. National Service Frameworks and NICE Guidelines specify standards to be met and the imperative to utilize, and indeed add to, the evidence base. And, finally, on a legislative level, the Mental Capacity Act (2005), and the new Mental Health Act (2007) have implications for our practice and role.

All of this can, and should, be related to personal development. Change requires us to rethink and re-evaluate our identities and roles, to ask again of ourselves, some fundamental questions. What attracted me to the profession? What parts of the job do I like, and what parts do I endure? Why do I struggle here? How do I manage change? How do I manage conflict? Who do I want to be, in this role? If I reflect on my past, how does that inform my understanding of my struggles and my triumphs? How do I order my priorities? What are my principles, and which can be compromised? How do I manage my own stress levels?

This is a time of significant shifts – of gear, of culture, of paradigms. It is necessary therefore to pay close attention to self, self in relation to the professional tasks, self in relation to others, and self as a life-long learner.

Power and identity

Moving on from the current context, the next emerging theme is a consideration of power, and power in relation to identity. Consideration of power, its use, its consequences, its constructions, and its impact runs throughout this book.

Power shapes our lives and affects our choices, on all the levels from a world view to an individual perspective (see Chapter 6). We live in a time in which social disadvantage and privilege seem very stark in their contrast. Although that is to simplify the reality, in which at one and the same time we can experience oppression and be oppressing another. If clinical psychology is concerned with promoting understanding of how psychological health is constructed, deconstructed, formed and reformed, then it has to understand power in all its contexts and on all levels.

On a societal level, it is important to understand how social disadvantage and privilege, social exclusion and inclusion, dominant discourses and the experience of being 'the other', can all have a direct impact on how we are perceived, perceive and identify ourselves, and on how we perceive others. This in turn impacts on our psychological health. We need to be aware of how the language that we use and engage with both directs and is reactive to these constructions.

As clinical psychologists we are often in positions and situations in which we can have significant, and sometimes profound influence. We argue that we have a responsibility always to include an understanding of the context of people's lives and lived experience, our own included, in our work. We need to understand our own position in relation to privilege and disadvantage and continually seek to know more and be open to challenge.

On an organizational level, where we may be in positions of management and leadership, there is a further need to understand how power operates, and which theories of power may help decision-making in terms of how and where and when to intervene. We also need to be clear about our own ethical bases and principles, and professional integrity.

On an individual and personal level, there is an additional need to be aware of our own developing histories in relation to our experience of power. We need to strive to uncover our assumptions and prejudices, and more, seek out opportunities to have conversations with others around perceived or actual difference. And, finally, we need continually to explore our own identities, as they shift, change and develop as we live our lives.

The perspective of service users and carers

Much of what we do involves being in relationship with service users and carers, be it in direct contact, or talking about and trying to make sense of their lived experience (for example, in supervision, consultancy, research), or in working with service users and carers in developing our programmes and projects. Therefore, it is critical and crucial that we learn about the views of service users and carers in terms of the importance they do or do not place on the personal development undertaken by the people they see.

There is some consensus (see Chapter 5) about the desired personal characteristics of the therapists seen, for example, that they should demonstrate a non-judgemental attitude, be warm, friendly, really able to listen and utilize non-jargonistic language. Whilst some of these characteristics could be related to personal development, there is much more to learn, and take into account, from a service user and carer perspective, including a consideration of views in regard to the many roles clinical psychologists inhabit. Thus, there is an immediate imperative to engage with service users and carers in discussion and research around these issues.

The individual and idiosyncratic nature of personal development

We believe that this book has demonstrated that personal development is a non-negotiable imperative throughout one's career as a clinical psychologist (see Chapter 3). It is as important as developing a range of core competency skills; if not more so, as personal development underpins all that we do, enabling us to engage successfully with others with honesty and integrity and openness.

That said, there is considerable flexibility in how one approaches personal development, what strategies are used and how that will change over time. For some individuals personal development is much more of a private and largely internal process; for others it is more about learning about self in relation, through conversation in a multiplicity of contexts; for others it is both.

We hope this book has provided some meanings, some methods and a 'map' in the way of a model that may act as a guide (see Chapter 4). However, it is really up to the reader to decide what is personally useful and meaningful, what helps and what doesn't. Personal development is a very individual and idiosyncratic endeavour.

What is exciting is that there are so many methods and strategies available: supervision; personal and group therapy; personal development groups; writing; reading; talking with those who know us well; being reflective in response to music, theatre; additional training opportunities; learning from relationships with other professionals (see Chapters 7, 8, 9). The list is, in actuality, endless.

Learning about one's self is not always easy and often uncomfortable. It can be emotionally draining and emotionally challenging. We can uncover parts of ourselves that we didn't know and do not like. We can be confused and lost and lonely. We may change in ways that impact on others and our relationships with partners, family and friends. Sometimes it feels like we have scaled the mountain only to find a higher peak or even range before us.

If that sounds hard, yes it is.

It is also what we ask service users to do every time we meet with them in a therapeutic context.

And yet, and yet . . . Personal development is transformational, and that can be exhilarating. Through it we come to recognize patterns set long ago that have hindered us and constricted us and take a risk to do things differently. We see parts of us that are likeable and loveable, and embrace them. We come to understand and accept our regrets. We learn what needs to be tackled, what can be altered or changed, and what will probably endure as a neurotic trait (Sheila's talking here!). Personal development can help us to reach a place and a space where we feel able to be open and honest and non-defensive in our relationships with others, knowing that there will always be more to learn and take on board. We hope to reach a place and a space where we will actively seek out challenge and different experiences with the aim of further growth and development – to reach a place and a space where we can sit with our selves and enjoy the company.

Where Next?

The training context

It is our understanding, as clinical tutors with experience on a number of clinical psychology training courses, that most trainees commence their training with some appreciation of and enthusiasm for personal development. What they require and ask for is some guidance, structure and support from the course and from their supervisors and from the wider training community.

It is hoped that parts of this book will be helpful for all in this context. Chapter 3 offers an understanding of personal development and its importance. Chapter 4 outlines a model of the personal development process. We have used this model in workshops with trainees for several years, and it has proved useful, as well as generating debate. Chapter 10 gives a detailed account of one approach to providing a thorough personal and professional development programme, and of how it is brought into operation in a rigorous way, including learning objectives and methods of assessment. Chapters 11 and 12 indicate what is currently happening in training in terms of personal development and give trainee experience in response.

However, as we have said above, personal development is an individual and idiosyncratic process, and whilst trainees ask for structure, the structures we provide are not always welcomed or liked by all. Thus, training courses need to be inventive and flexible, as well as determined and rigorous in their approach to personal development. There is also a need to provide some sense of stability in the programme whilst being open to change, and to know that personal development is always a 'work in progress' and a life-long endeavour. No easy task!

Our experience is that it works best when trainees have a sense of ownership and influence and are involved in a co-construction of the programme and in monitoring and evaluating process and outcome. Having a committee with trainee representatives from each year that oversees the whole programme and makes suggestions as to improvement is one way towards achieving this. Another is involving trainees in teaching, for example, a third-year trainee reflecting on her or his experience of training in a self-care workshop for first-year trainees. Another is to invite trainees to conduct small- or large-scale research into aspects of the programme, for example, evaluating the outcome of personal development groups.

In summary, in a training context we need to be explicit about personal development requirements; devise a detailed personal development programme that runs throughout the three years of training; involve trainees in all aspects of programme planning, delivery and evaluation; involve service users and carers in all aspects of programme planning, delivery and evaluation; liaise closely with supervisors and external teachers/trainers and be open to all voices that suggest change and development.

The post-qualification context

As we have seen, the work that clinical psychologists undertake is hugely varied, multifaceted and multifactorial and highly complex. It also requires an advanced ability to multitask. All of this is what draws people to the profession, and makes it at the same time enthralling, fascinating, rewarding and emotionally challenging.

As a profession we talk about the need and the requirement to practise self-care and attend to our personal development. However, there is also a competing, largely unspoken culture that suggests that if you want to progress in the profession you need to work for more than the contracted hours and do parts of the work (for example, teaching preparation, research) in your own time. Thus, what frequently happens is that self-care and personal development are relegated to the bottom of the priority list. This can also happen simply in response to increasing workloads and service pressures. In Chapter 3 we have written of some of the dangers of de-prioritizing personal development.

This emphasis on personal development during training, and a potential tendency to de-emphasize it once qualified, is therefore concerning. Some personal development learning happens in the course of day-to-day activities and ongoing reflection. Some will happen during supervisory discussions. However, we argue that clinical psychologists need to have additional and designated time for further personal development throughout their careers. This could be discussed and planned for in annual appraisals with line managers and a method developed of recording learning. Individuals could choose what route to take and could be encouraged to depart from tried and tested personal development strategies, from time to time, to explore what new and different learning might occur.

We also argue, and know that this is a controversial challenge, that clinical psychologists should engage in personal therapy at some point in their careers. We regard this as a moral imperative, as well as knowing how much we can learn about the therapeutic process, and ourselves, by sitting in the other chair (see Chapter 8).

In summary, qualified clinical psychologists need to continue to plan their aims for personal development on a yearly basis; have designated time to engage with personal development; experiment with different strategies, and develop ways of recording and assessing outcome, for self and with their line managers.

The context for the profession and the national picture

As we have seen in Chapter 3, the British Psychological Society through the Division of Clinical Psychology and the Department of Health insist that we continue to address our professional and personal development throughout our careers. In most of the documentation reviewed in Chapter 3 there is little separation of the personal and the professional, and the major emphasis is on keeping up to date with, and developing, professional knowledge and skills.

We argue that it is sometimes important conceptually to separate the professional from the personal, whilst acknowledging that the two are intertwined. As we showed in Chapter 1, this can best be illustrated by asking these two questions: 'What have I learnt about myself that will have an impact on how I approach my work and my understanding of it?' (the personal dimension), and 'What have I learnt that has added to my psychological knowledge and skills?' (the professional dimension). We believe that if we do not explore the answer to the first question on a continual basis, our answer to the second may be lacking, partial and/or, incomplete, because we may be unaware of the biases, prejudices and assumptions that continue to operate in our view of who we are, our perceptions of others and our attitudes towards our work. This is underlined in Chapter 6, with its consideration of power and identity.

In looking at the Continued Professional Development log we are required to submit on an annual basis, which gives or withholds our practising certificate, it is clear that the emphasis continues to be on the acquisition of knowledge and skills. The need to develop personal qualities and personal standards is mentioned, and supervision and personal therapy are given as potential strategies, but the overriding focus is on knowledge and skill development.

We believe that there should be a requirement to have some personal development plans, aims and stated learning outcomes as part of this submission. Given that this could involve quite personal information we would not expect great detail to be provided, but the strategies utilized could be listed along with planned actions and aims for the future.

In summary, there is a need to conceptually differentiate between the personal and professional development dimensions in line with the two questions asked above and make, address and complete plans to develop in both dimensions.

The research context

There is much work to be done. We have argued that personal development is critical and crucial. There is a need for research evidence to confirm or invalidate this hypothesis, both in terms of whether personal development makes more effective practitioners and whether it produces more emotionally robust and psychologically healthy individuals. Many personal development strategies, for example supervision, personal therapy, personal development in groups have their proponents (see Chapters 7, 8 and 9), but what is the evidence beyond personal experience and anecdote?

Finally, and centrally, there is a clear need to ascertain the views of service users and carers (see Chapter 5) about the importance they place on the need for personal development in the people they entrust with their histories and their stories, and whom they hope will help with their recovery.

Service users and carers seem to have some clear views on the personal characteristics they wish clinical psychologists to have, and these could be linked to personal development. However, there is much more to uncover in terms of what constitutes an 'emotionally intelligent practitioner', as indicated in Chapter 5.

In summary, there is a need to consider how to conduct research into whether personal development results in more effective practitioners; whether personal development results in more robust and psychologically healthy practitioners; what personal development strategies work and in what way, and what the views and wishes of service users and carers are about the perceived importance of personal development in the clinical psychologists with whom they work.

Final Personal Reflections from Sheila Youngson and Jan Hughes

On writing and bringing together this book – Sheila Youngson

As my memory stick finally fills with a list of 13 chapters all saying 'final and edited', there is time to reflect on the past months, as well as book the restaurant table I promised Jan an eon ago.

A number of moments stand out:

– A forwarded email from Jan letting us know that the publisher had accepted the proposal for the book, and the mixture of excitement and doubt as to our ability that we both immediately experienced.
– The punch-the-air joy when I found on the Internet an article that purely and wonderfully answered a question that I'd wrestled with for weeks.
– A period of two to three months when I thought what I was writing was simply stating the obvious and the reviews would be lukewarm (ah, the need for other approval still remains . . .).
– An afternoon when I presented the model of personal development processes we had developed to first-year trainees and they said they understood it and it was really helpful, as well as suggesting some changes.
– A sense of building empathy bridges with third-year trainees as we all spent evenings and weekends writing and felt guilty for watching 'Wire in the Blood' on TV, pretending it was work-related.
– Being able to cite The British Sub-Aqua Club as a reference.

However, most of all I recall the times Jan and I spent together, whenever we were stuck with an idea or concept or direction. We are two very different people who approach personal development in (some) very different ways. When we get stuck, I tend to turn to an exploration of experience and Jan tends to turn to an examination of theory. This never got in the way, quite the reverse, it always resulted (after pacing up and down in my flat) with an 'a-ha' moment, where we found the way forward. We have discovered that we work together in a very complementary way, in which each viewpoint sparks the other to think further, broader and deeper and relate experience/practice to theory and theory to experience/practice.

Throughout the production of this book, I have continued to learn more about myself.

I discover that I can be a great procrastinator unless I am truly motivated and excited by an idea, and this is linked to an enduring self-doubt about my academic capabilities. I have realized how much humour means to me, and how I judge when to use it in various contexts. I note how much more intolerant I have become as I have grown older, and that saddens me. I am reminded of how much I love lyrical prose, and the power of it, and the pleasure I get from writing in that style. I find again just how important my political and ethical stance is to me, and that this sustains me, as well as bringing challenge and sometimes personal and professional grief.

Finally, working together with Jan only underlines, *for me*, how much personal development is about talking, thinking, reflecting, experiencing with another. It *is* relational.

Thanks Jan.

Personal reflection   Jan Hughes

Writing this book has been a large part of my own personal development journey in the last few years – although becoming a mum for the second time does win! From the first vague glimmer of an idea, to (eventually) persuading Sheila, to getting the publication deal, to spending hours in front of the computer trying to find that one right reference, to sitting with Sheila reading through every chapter to make the final changes . . . this has been a huge learning experience. Throughout, Sheila and I have been very aware of our differences, which will no doubt be reflected in the way we make our summaries in these final pages. At times the book has felt like a huge weight and commitment – and indeed it has been. I have learnt through the process of writing the book that I am not very good at looking after myself. This is difficult – admitting that I do not always practise what I preach. But it is never too late to change.

However, so much of the process has been positive. What stands out for me? I feel I have gained a much clearer insight into my own style of learning. I like to experience and feel first, and then think and use theory to help me reflect. Bringing together experiences, feeling, theories and reflections has helped me gain a greater insight into how, potentially, people learn and develop, and this has helped me think about how to enable people in the multiple roles I can have within work – as clinician, trainer, manager, supervisor, researcher, team member and leader. This has also helped in my roles in the other realms of personal development – as partner, friend and mother. Developing this book has helped me recognize that everyone learns and develops in so many different ways, and that they may be so different from mine. But the way to connect and learn from each other is to recognize and utilize the difference. To embrace and celebrate difference feels immensely freeing.

The experiencing and feeling aspect of this process, for me, has mainly been through conversations. I do enjoy conversations generally in every aspect of my life but some have been particularly pertinent. Sheila and I have forged a life-long friendship based on the conversations we have had and the understandings we have gained from each other through our shared commitment to the book and through supporting and caring for each other. I have also found the conversations I have had with first-year trainee clinical psychologists particularly helpful; they have shared their experiences, challenged the models and used the ideas to create their models of their own personal development – a wonderful way of seeing the book put into practice.

Index